CRIP COLONY

CRIP COLONY

*Mestizaje, US Imperialism, and the Queer
Politics of Disability in the Philippines*

Sony Coráñez Bolton

DUKE UNIVERSITY PRESS
Durham and London
2023

Designed by A. Mattson Gallagher
Typeset in Portrait Text by Westchester Publishing Services

Library of Congress Cataloging-in-Publication Data
Names: Coráñez Bolton, Sony, [date] author.
Title: Crip colony : mestizaje, US imperialism, and the queer politics
of disability in the Philippines / Sony Coráñez Bolton.
Description: Durham : Duke University Press, 2023. |
Includes bibliographical references and index.
Identifiers: LCCN 2022039532 (print)
LCCN 2022039533 (ebook)
ISBN 9781478019565 (paperback)
ISBN 9781478016922 (hardcover)
ISBN 9781478024187 (ebook)
Subjects: LCSH: Racially mixed people—Philippines. | Sociology of
disability—Political aspects. | People with disabilities in mass media. |
Queer theory. | Imperialism. | Philippines—Colonization. |
BISAC: SOCIAL SCIENCE / Ethnic Studies / Asian Studies |
HISTORY / Asia / Southeast Asia
Classification: LCC DS665 . C67 2023 (print) | LCC DS665 (ebook) |
DDC 305.8009599—dc23/eng/20221004
LC record available at https://lccn.loc.gov/2022039532
LC ebook record available at https://lccn.loc.gov/2022039533

Cover art: Julie Lluch, *Spoliarium* (detail), 2020. Cold cast
marble. Courtesy of Julie Lluch and Galerie Stephanie.

DUKE UNIVERSITY PRESS GRATEFULLY ACKNOWLEDGES
THE OFFICE OF THE PROVOST AND DEAN OF THE
FACULTY AT AMHERST COLLEGE, WHICH PROVIDED
FUNDS TOWARD THE PUBLICATION OF THIS BOOK.

For Dave

CONTENTS

ACKNOWLEDGMENTS

A book is a community. So it gives me great pleasure to highlight the communities that have buoyed me, cared for me, and challenged me as I wrote this.

This book benefited immensely from the powerful, committed, and thorough engagement of Jodi Byrd, Iyko Day, Julie Avril Minich, and Joseph Pierce; thank you for your kindness and constructive feedback on earlier versions of this manuscript. I am also grateful to the two anonymous reviewers whose feedback was incredibly generative and generous.

During my time as an undergraduate and masters student I benefited from the very kind mentorship of so many faculty members at Marquette University in Milwaukee, Wisconsin; they truly embodied the *cura personalis* that is the cornerstone of any Jesuit education. Because I was at an institution that did not have institutionalized ethnic studies at the time, I sought it out in the study of US Latin American and Latinx literature. To my mentors in what was then the Department of Foreign Languages and Literatures, I especially want to thank Eugenia Afinoguénova, Belén Castañeda, Dinorah Cortés-Vélez, Sarah Gendron, Armando González-Pérez, Todd Hernández, Jeannette Kramer, Jason Meyler, Anne Pasero, and Julia Paulk. I also wish to thank Bryan Massingale, Jodi Melamed, and Theresa Tobin, for crucial mentorship at a sensitive time of self-discovery. It was actually you, Jodi, whom I can blame for inspiring my move to American and ethnic studies. While I have never abandoned literatures in Spanish, I had no idea of the depth and splendor of Filipinx American studies, which you encouraged me to explore. If not for you, I wouldn't have had the opportunity to meet some amazing people as I pursued my doctoral work in Ann Arbor, Michigan.

At the University of Michigan, I was an enthusiastic graduate student who tended to overcomplicate things. I remember fondly the kindness and patience that so many faculty members showed me as I developed intellectually. I am especially grateful to Evelyn Alsultany, Ruth Behar, Amy Sara Carroll, María Cotera, Deirdre de la Cruz, Vince Diaz, Julie Ellison, Colin Gunckel, Sandra Gunning, Jesse Hoffnung-Garskof, Brandi Hughes, Mary Kelley, Larry LaFountain-Stokes, Emily Lawsin, Victor Román Mendoza, Susan Najita, Lisa Nakamura, Sarita See, and Magdalena Zaborowska. All of you were exceedingly generous with your time and energy. There are a few whose interactions have really stayed with me through the years whom I would like to highlight.

Jesse, you were my first point of contact with Michigan; I was so delighted to receive your call offering me admission into the department. I am also so grateful that I had the opportunity to teach with you in "History of Latina/os in the United States," a class that was really an important touchstone for me. Susan, your incredible patience and goodwill are unmatched. It was such a luxury to spend time in your office speaking about literature and postcolonial theory at length. This kindness is one I try to emulate as a professor every day. Julie, you deeply read my prospectus with extraordinary attention to detail and gave me some of my first bits of advice as one writer to another, for which I am grateful. Colin, you supported my weird notion that I could be a Latinx studies graduate student; you and Amy supported my application into the graduate certificate program with a lot of passion and generosity. Amy, you were instrumental in getting my first journal article published; it is inconceivable to me now the amount of time and endurance you displayed reading my winding prose line by line. The ways that you phrased things, always with an eye to aesthetics and literary value (even in academic writing), continues to be inspirational to me even if I can't always execute it like you do. Ruth, you taught me what it is to be a vulnerable and exposed writer; any moments of daring in this manuscript I can trace back to your class "Ethnographic Writing and Film." Brandi, you taught me to go for what I want and to not be ashamed. I approached the job market with a lot more courage because of advice you gave me at a café in Ypsilanti. María, you continue to be an inspirational leader in Chicana feminist thought for me. I also have used you as a guiding star on how to approach comparative work, refusing to be pigeonholed into either one field or another. We can have it all, as you so often reminded me. Victor, even though Michigan wasn't always an easy place to work and learn, I was astonished by the level of care, attention, and effort you put into reading my work. I never quite appreciated the pressure you were under, and now, as a professor myself, I can see how extraordinary and uncommon your mentorship was. Deirdre, you are basically a model for how rigorous multilingual scholarship should be. I was and am so privileged to learn from you. Sarita, what can I say? You have been a stalwart, durable, and crucial support system for me as I have navigated academia. Your candor and generosity have been moving. At virtually every step of this process, from first year graduate student to job negotiations, you have been there without fail. I have also benefited from the tremendous mentorship and intellectual camaraderie of Jody Blanco, who pioneered an important path in the study of the Hispanic Philippines and made it easier for the rest of us. On that note, I'm grateful for the intellectual community of Ernest Rafael Hartwell, Matthew Nicdao, and Paula Park. We got this! I'm also grateful to Rocío Ortuño Casanova and Emmanuelle Sinardet for continued collaboration and for being thought partners.

There are a few people in my graduate school cohort that have left an immense impression on me. I am thankful every day for the friendship and ability to have learned from Yamil Avivi, David Green, Liz Harmon, Frank Kelderman, Jennifer Peacock, Mejdulene Shomali, and Wendy Sung. Mej, we've been through everything academic together. You taught me what it was to be a good teacher, friend, cook, and intellectual. All around you are my model for what it means to be confident in one's powers as a scholar and decent human being. Wendy, you are amazing; you are stylish, smart, and hilarious, and you go after what you want. I am also so grateful for the continued friendship and brilliance of Cass Adair, Tiffany Ball, Ava Kim, and Michael Pascual. You all are amazing, funny, and a reminder that friendship is the single greatest treasure of this life. To Jina Kim: I'm over the moon that we can be intellectual neighbors academically and geographically. Here's to our little but thriving community in the valley.

I was fortunate to have benefited from the Creating Connections Consortium postdoctoral fellowship program, generously supported by the Andrew W. Mellon Foundation. This program put the liberal arts college research and teaching environment on my radar (I had very little notion what liberal arts colleges were and what it would be like to work at one of them until this program). I was in what was then the Department of Spanish and Portuguese (now Luso-Hispanic Studies) at Middlebury College. This special department was affirmative and supportive in its mentorship of a young scholar that set out to study the Hispanic Philippines. This postdoctoral program changed my career and life; it gave me a foot in the door and helped me to establish the bona fides I needed to teach in a romance languages or Spanish department. I am especially grateful to Brandon Baird, Miguel Fernández, Enrique García, Nicolas Poppe, Fernando Rocha, Marcos Rohena-Madrazo, Patricia Saldarriaga, and Daniel Silva; my time in your department is unforgettable. I am also extremely grateful to Susan Burch for her amazing mentorship and guidance in the field of disability studies. Susan, you continue to be a champion for the field and your work has been pathbreaking for me.

I was fortunate to spend the beginning of my career in Tucson among amazingly generous and affirmative colleagues. The Department of Spanish and Portuguese at the University of Arizona took a rather courageous step in filling a position for a scholar in Latin American cultural studies with a Philippines specialist, and I admire that willingness to break with convention and geopolitical rubrics. I am so grateful to Bram Acosta, Katia Bezerra, Ana Maria Carvalho, Julieta Fernández, Lillian Gorman, Anita Huizar Hernández, Mary Kaitlin Murphy, and others in the department. I am also appreciative of the advice and goodwill that Malcolm Compitello shared with me when my path took me away from Tucson. I must give a special nod to Aditya Adiredja; you were my best friend and colleague during that blistering year in Tucson; yours is a friendship I continue to value and hold dear. You never knew this, but that year was a very low and depressing time for me. You were a light and a buoy.

The collegiality, support, and kindness shown to me by my colleagues at Amherst College is truly unmatched. I am so grateful to be in a community with passionate scholar-teachers. To my colleagues in the Spanish Department, it continues to be surreal that I can be an Asian Americanist professor of Spanish. This is not where I expected to be, but it is where I belong, and I feel that belonging more and more each day. An academic would be hard-pressed to find more dedicated and kinder colleagues than Sara Brenneis, Fiona Dixon, Carmen Granda, Catherine Infante, Jeannette Sánchez-Naranjo, Sarah Piazza, Paul Schroeder-Rodríguez, and Ilan Stavans. I am also indebted to the truly exciting work of colleagues in Latin American and Latinx and studies—thanks for letting me join the club. Again, being a Filipinx Americanist in a Latinx studies program is a learning experience, and I'm grateful to have found open-minded colleagues willing to learn with me; thank you, Solsi del Moral, Mary Hicks, Rick López, and Leah Schmalzbauer. And to the Michigan Mafia, it is wild that so many graduates of the same program in American Culture at the University of Michigan have landed at Amherst; it's always great to be in community with you, Lloyd Barba, Jallicia Jolly, and Kiara Vigil. I also want to convey my gratitude for the support and friendship of Abner Aldarondo. This book benefited from his attentive work as a research assistant.

At Amherst College, I am so grateful for the kind words and mentorship of the provost, Catherine Epstein, and the president, Biddy Martin. I am also especially grateful for the critical mass of Asian Americanists at Amherst; thank you Pawan Dhingra, Robert Hayashi, Franklin Odo, and Christine Peralta for your friendship and collaboration. I have also benefited greatly from the thought partnership of Sarah Bunnell, Riley Caldwell-O'Keefe, and Sheila Jaswal; I have grown immensely through our sustained and sustaining dialogue. I think that none of my flourishing at Amherst would be possible without the professionalism and skill of good academic department coordinators. Thank you, Eva Díaz and Lauren Gladu, for answering my questions and for your logistical support.

Without support networks, camaraderie, friendship, and no small amount of laughter would it be possible to thrive in the breakneck pace of academic work. It has been a lifeline and godsend to have built a diasporic community of queer Asian American professors to survive the tenure track with: Matthew Chin, Yuri Doolan, Kareem Khubchandani, Tom Sarmiento, Ian Shin, and James Zarsadiaz. To the Boy Luck Club, as we affectionately call ourselves, you have really made life in academia worth it. The mantra "work hard, but play harder" has been our call to not take ourselves too seriously and to approach all that we do as a gesture of friendship, love, and support. Ian, I think that you are for me a model of what an Asian American studies professor ought to be. If I continually ask certain questions—What would Ian do? What would Ian say?—I know that the answers will usually set me on the right path. James, I am so happy that we have become friends. You remind me that being a professor need not be a life of monastic deprivation. Thank you for making sure we are well fed and for allowing me the benefit of your exacting palate. Kareem, "you're a winner, baby!" No, but, you really are! I'm convinced that any Asian American studies text should come with the keywords *verve*, *style*, *taste*, and *avant-garde* and that your picture ought to be right there. Tom, I feel like we've be through so much together: graduate school, learning Tagalog together, almost always reviewing the same articles, and almost always contributing to the same anthologies; I don't think that I could find a better doppelgänger! Yuri, thank you for being a rock star and a reminder of why transnational scholarship is a priority. And Matthew, it has been such a pleasure that we have been able to have our paths cross so often, from being at Michigan together, on the job market together, and now in intentional community again. The Boy Luck Club summons a motif of luck that generally seems to be at play in my path toward this book. I am immensely lucky to count Elliott Powell as a constant source of levity, advice, and a sounding board for when I feel like the wheels are coming off. Thank you.

This book was made possible by generous institutional support. I am grateful to the research staff librarians at the Bentley Historical Library at the University of Michigan for their assistance with the archival research that made chapter 4 possible. I am also exceedingly thankful for the support of the staff of Amherst College's Frost Library, particularly that of Blake Doherty. A version of chapter 3 was first published as "Cripping the Philippine Enlightenment: Ilustrado Travel Literature, Postcolonial Disability, and the 'Normate Imperial Eye/I.'" *Verge: Studies in Global Asias* 2, no. 2 (2016): 138–62. I thank the University of Minnesota Press for permission to republish it here.

This book is a love letter to my immediate family. The more I'm alive, the more, it seems, our love for one another has grown. It's a love that seems effortless, that seems natural, that seems to be the foundational architecture of the world. To my siblings, Jeffrey Bolton, Brandilyn Hadjuk, Ashley Mejías, and Danica Malo: it is unreal, the supremely amazing people that you have transformed into. To my father, James, words cannot travel to where I need them to go to express the simple idea that you are my hero. You are a template for wit and grit. I find that as I get older that I am surprised that I am not a wholly terrible person and that I even have positive qualities like humor, cleverness, and deep reserves of energy, dedication, and resiliency. I look at you, Dad, and I see why. You might be the best human being I have ever met or that any person will ever meet. To my mother, Charlita, I know that it has not always been easy living in a place where you perhaps never truly felt that you belonged. But you carved out an impassable and incorruptible space of love and belonging for me even while it took me so long to feel like myself or to be completely truthful. I thank you and I love you, *mahal kita*.

Dave, it's hard to find the words to go there. I've known you through so many different versions of myself, both nurturing and self-destructive. Seasons change and we do too. I look at your face, and it's nice to know that spring always comes.

Crip Colonial Critique

READING MESTIZAJE FROM THE BORDERLANDS
TO THE PHILIPPINES

Then there were my fights at Chinese school. And the nuns who kept stopping us in the park, which was across the street from Chinese school, to tell us that if we didn't get baptized we'd go straight to hell like one of the nine Taoist hells forever. And the obscene caller that phoned us at home when the adults were at the laundry. And the Mexican and Filipino girls at school who went to "confession," and how I envied them their white dresses and their chance each Saturday to tell even thoughts that were sinful.
—MAXINE HONG KINGSTON, *The Woman Warrior*

Confession

When I was a child, no more than nine years old, I was a new transplant to the midwestern United States. My formative years until college were spent living in a racially diverse working-class rural exurb about an hour due north of Chicago.[1] My white father was initially stationed at a naval base in Alameda, California, before work forced him to relocate somewhere near the city of North Chicago—the then and still current site of the Great Lakes Naval Base on Lake Michigan. I suspect that he deeply wanted a change after serving multiple tours of duty during the Persian Gulf War, tired of fighting over oil. Sometimes I mourn the loss of a life I could have spent as a denizen of the East Bay area of San Francisco, mostly because this move signaled a rather prolonged detachment from a connected Asian American or Filipino American identity normalized on the West Coast.[2] I was a mixed-race kid, growing up in the rural cornfields of northern Illinois, resentful of the itinerancy of my youth and yet craving global connections that would explain the brownness of the mestizo skin I saw reflected back in the mirror.

One of the clearest and first midwestern childhood memories I have is being recruited by my mother to move a piano across the living room shortly after our move to Illinois. This was a recent acquisition, as my parents thought it would be an enriching activity for my sisters to learn to play. My brother and I were forbidden from playing. I suppose because it was too artistic, was considered a feminine activity, or was "too queer." (It was awkward to have to disappoint my mother by coming out approximately ten years later.) With two of my sisters and me in tow to help push the impossibly heavy instrument, my mother coordinated our efforts by counting down in three languages: "Uno, dos, tres, *push*! Uno, dos, tres, *push*! Ulit."[3] Not being raised speaking Tagalog or Visayan at all, it was jarring for me to hear my mother utter what even I knew to be Spanish words. When we finally finished, physically spent, I reflected on the words my mother used to align her and her Asian American children's efforts. As I look back on this moment decades later, it is still curious to me that numbers in Spanish came to her more naturally. As an adult haggling at a *tiangge* (bazaar or market) in Quezon City, I relived that childhood curiosity when I discovered that Spanish numbers are almost always used in these negotiations. Might there be an unconscious association at play between Spanish and labor? Was it simply because reciting Spanish numbers was simpler than the multiple syllables of "Isa, dalawa, tatlo"?

The curiosity that this banal moment sparked has led me to become a professor of Spanish, which is somewhat surprising to me given that I consider my main field of inquiry to be Asian American studies. In some ways my intellectual trajectory is set into relief by Maxine Hong Kingston's observations in *The Woman Warrior* on the ways that the perpetual foreignness ascribed to Chineseness provokes the manifold indignities that she and her family had to endure. Notably, Kingston's memoir illustrates a truism in much multiethnic American literature, which, as literary critic David Palumbo-Liu has argued, presents narratives that are protagonized by racialized characters that harbor a defective, eccentric ethnicity that is rehabilitated by the hard work of American liberalism and assimilation. Authors like Palumbo-Liu and Allan Punzalan Isaac have demonstrated how the trope of the eccentric ethnic immigrant presents them as generally unhealthy, damaged, and ill-fitting aliens whose physical and intellectual labors do not contribute advantage to the United States.[4] Therefore, we could reasonably position the work of the genre of assimilation as itself the representational instantiation of a rehabilitative logic that ramifies and reengineers alien laborers to be compliant with the mandates of ableist racial capitalism.

These are indignities that Kingston famously litanizes for us in a stream-of-consciousness style in *The Woman Warrior* epigraph that opens this introduction. Even so, couched within these painful recollections is the intimacy drawn between Mexican and Filipina girls, whose Catholic devotion, however glib, ties them together in the practice of confession. This cross-racial intimacy stands out to me for the ways that, as Michel Foucault has argued, the transhistorical "scope of the confession" whose iterations across dogmatic cultures increased its rhythms in an effort to prompt and "impose meticulous rules of self-examination," though "above all . . . it attributed more and more importance in penance."[5] It's ironic that what troubles me in Kingston's words is the ways in which the colonial power of the ritual of confession—which presumes to know and hollow out the native claiming to divine their mind better than they—would indeed prompt autodisciplinary self-examination. This moment of confession, in one of the most famous books in Asian American literature, sticks out in my mind delineating a difference that Filipino American subjectivity brings to Asianness by way of their likeness and propinquity to Mexicans—an intimacy to which the Chinese American Kingston is only ever an observer but which hails *me* as a Filipinx American. *The Woman Warrior* foundationally introduces the ways in which the violence of American assimilation unfurls between China and a borderlands space in the US West. The echoes of Spanish colonial subjectification through Catholicism serve as a partial though unmistakable backdrop. These echoes ripple through the multivalent threads of the tapestry of Asian racialization within a US multiethnic imaginary.

Given this analytical vantage, the ironies of being a Filipinx professor of Latinx studies and Spanish in the United States do not escape me. I feel as if I restage daily the girlish literary confessions described by Kingston, seduced by the discursive power to name that which must remain unnameable. I teach in a liberal arts context in which close colloquy with students is quite routine. After I'd had an unusually successful semester teaching a Spanish language course on bilingual Latinx experience, a bright Cuban American student from Miami dubbed me an "honorary Latino"—definitely in jest, but also in recognition of the intellectual camaraderie that we had cultivated throughout the semester. I did include material about the Hispanic history and heritage of the Philippines as a way to bring my own identity and perspective into the conversations in order to demonstrate that I was not coming at the topic of the course as a total outsider. Yet any claims of mine to an "insider" bilingual Spanish identity are, *a fin de cuentas*, circumspect, even though I and some of my students heard our mothers chanting in a language that was introduced by the same historical and colonial processes.

When I was hailed an "honorary Latino," my anxiety peaked. "I want you to know that that's not my objective!" I explained; I did not want to assume a sameness between Filipinx and Latinx Americans that overwrote important distinctions in our experiences, relationships to the state, and migratory histories. I wanted to convey that racial drag was not the outcome that I desired and yet I *did* feel an affinity with my students and was indeed honored that they would entrust their experiences and vulnerability to me as was organic to the topic of a class on bilingual identity and autobiography—to be seen as a part of the same batch of peoples descended from colonial processes that were global in scope. I want my reader to understand that this affinity goes beyond a simple common experience of all of us being "people of color" in the United States. I told my students that I felt like we were *primxs*, cousins—*mga pinsan*. Much like Latinx peoples, Filipinx Americans live, work, and study at the intersection of contradictory origins of the same two imperial powers—a Venn diagram of which might feel more like a complete circle at times. While I don't want to assume Filipinx experience is exceptional in terms of the ambivalent racial meanings negotiated as a result of colonialism, I am also often confronted with how unassimilable Asianness is into what normatively constitutes "Hispanic" or mestizo identity. The Philippines simultaneously challenges and corroborates Asian exclusions from *mestizaje* (racial admixture, miscegenation) as an American racial landscape.

Every time I step in front of a class that I will be teaching in Spanish, I convey to my students that while I am not nor ever will truly identify as Latinx, Latin American, or even as the much broader Hispano or Hispanic, I do not come to stand before them simply because of an impersonal avid interest in the language, its literature, and culture. In any event, what are the stakes in claiming, cultivating, and protecting a hybrid bilingual identity elaborated at the intersection of the colonial languages of English and Spanish whose introduction to the Americas was fundamentally rooted in Indigenous displacement, slavery, and racial capitalism? Even so, I really do view the better part of the past two decades meticulously studying the Spanish language as an extension and exploration of my own *Asian American* heritage and history; I don't actually feel a keen attachment to a journey to claim

Hispanic identity even if, ironically, the mechanism of that exploration has been learning Spanish. While identity markers like *Asian American* and *Latinx* index very real and different political experiences, they can't always account for how some experiences and identities vex the stable identitarian delineations to which they sometimes aspire. A Filipinx American person and scholar who serves as a professor of Latinx studies and Spanish, who even *teaches* Latinx heritage students the Spanish language, is not there by accident. There are deep, colonial histories that have set the conditions of possibility such that this pedagogical encounter between Asian America and Latinx America is indeed somehow inevitable, even *necessary*. It is encounters like this one—and, more pointedly, the deep geographies that subtend them—that animate the study of race, colonialism, disability, and mestizaje in this book.

I neither propose recuperation of Hispanic identity for Filipinas, Filipinos, or Filipinxs, nor really advocate for the mere inclusion of the Philippines in "Spanish studies" or Hispanic studies such as they are. While I am struck, for instance, by sociologist Anthony Christian Ocampo's claim that Filipinos are the "Latinos of Asia," I cannot claim a shared objective of unearthing the ways that Filipinos sociologically confess to or come to claim *latinidad*.[6] The ways that queer studies is positioned as a critique of normativity rather than the archival excavation of factual LGBTQ people is rather analogous to the ways in which I think about Filipinx *hispanidad*. That is, rather than an empirical possession of or propertied relation to the Hispanic, what are the regulatory and disciplinary rubrics through which we come to know of ourselves in racial, ethnonational terms in the first place? How do we resolve the conflicting meanings forged in the crucible of contradictory colonial origins? Or, do we defiantly reject resolution wholesale? And, more pointedly to the frameworks that are animate in this book, for which bodyminds does Spanish colonial humanism and US liberalism serve as a refuge and space of enminded political power? Spanish—the language, the history, the people, and the culture—has perennially signified a bastion of intellectual power and racial aesthetic beauty through mixture, the intersection of which is readily encapsulated by the disability concept of the bodymind.[7]

Fetishizing a recovery of the Hispanic as an empirical fact about myself or people like me is rather beside the point, particularly given the multilingual archives that I prioritize in this book. Spanish *is* a Filipino language. The Philippines was a part of the Spanish Empire. These facts aren't really debatable from my vantage. Moreover, Filipinx Americans and Latinx Americans have lived together, worked together, and shared community with one another for more than a century—even longer if we consider the exchanges of the Manila Galleon Route. There are deep, overlapping histories that have brought these communities—across continents and oceans—into contact. I thus view Spanish colonialism, and its collusions with US empire, the Spanish language, and the abstract Hispanic mestizo identity it inspired, as part of a field of meaning making that secured ability, capacity, and privileges for some while relegating others to the underside of political modernity. The Spanish language nourished an intellectual discourse that attained robust cognitive capacity in the face of colonial debilitation by eviscerating native self-determination and autonomy.

The archive through which the contradictory origins of these multifarious political landscapes intersect continues to be the discourse and archive of mestizaje, which binds such diverse geographies together while simultaneously being the source of the radical differentiation among them. I confront the historical and cultural representations of mestizaje and its constitutive imbrications with disability as a colonial logic that proposed the rehabilitation of the native Filipino into a fully fledged democratic subject with the colonizer existing in a propertied relationship to ability itself. In what follows, I elaborate how the rehabilitation of allegedly diminutive native capacity was seen to be an effect of colonialism whose rationalizing and anchoring cultural logic was secured through mestizaje.

On the Queer Colonial and Racial Life of Disability

Crip Colony: Mestizaje, US Imperialism, and the Queer Politics of Disability in the Philippines is an interdisciplinary study engaging an ample archive in literature, visual culture, and historical analysis of Anglophone and Hispanophone texts, which proposes the analysis of disability and colonialism as a unified ideological structure. Temporally, I privilege the transition of the Philippines from a Spanish colony in the late nineteenth century to US imperial territory during the early twentieth century. I suggest that the ideology of colonial disability "hails" subjects to be rehabilitated through a colonial reform ethos while endowing others that are at the interstices of the modern civilized subject and "savage" Indian with the ability to rehabilitate. I mark and archivally locate such interstitial spaces within racial fusions that foment, as part of mestizaje's project, intermediary subjects at the crux of ostensibly monolithic racial identifications. For this reason, the transitionary period from late Spanish colonialism to early US imperialism is striking, as we can view a snapshot into how racial meanings shifted from one epoch to the next through an already ambivalent and multivalent discourse like mestizaje.

At base, I argue that Filipino mestizaje simultaneously becomes a marker of difference from the colonized *indio* and a vehicle evoking and evidencing their reform—the mestizo body then is the evidence, product, and agent of colonial rehabilitation. I thus claim that mestizaje is itself a *racial ideology of ability* marking a preference for able-bodied and able-mindedness aligned with the colonial project. More specifically, I contend that mestizaje is a liberal form of colonial ableism that adapts a preference for able-bodiedness through the projection and representation of a queerly deviant Indian in dire need of reform and rehabilitation.[8] Characterizing mestizaje as a racial ideology of ability similarly picks up on Chicana literary studies scholar Julie Avril Minich's contention that mestizaje functions like a "national prosthesis." That is, it serves as a unifying discourse that "bolsters the formation of national identity [through] a body politic predicated on able-bodiedness."[9] Blending disability analysis with Chicanx studies, Minich adapts David Mitchell and Sharon Snyder's critique of narrative structure in literature, in which a protagonist's autonomy is secured through the secondary disabled characters who serve as metaphorical scaffolds.[10] For my purposes, I will similarly argue that the mestizo architects of the political community of the nation are assumed to possess and are afforded the capacities of able-bodiedness and able-mindedness, thus authorizing their arguments for national cohesion. The so-called Indian is the crip presence that augments or prostheticizes the rational powers of the mestizo.[11]

Broadly speaking, Filipino mestizaje is a racial, political, and aesthetic discourse that blends Spanish humanist and US progressivist thought in order to identify adequate beneficiaries of colonial rehabilitation and capacitation.[12] The Filipino "mestizo mind" also becomes the actualizer of colonial rehabilitative mandates for an Indian from which it has evolved.[13] I suggest that Philippine mestizaje colludes with US benevolent reform by interiorizing settler colonial logics surrounding and producing the Indian. Through an attention to the Philippines, I seek to confirm what Chickasaw theorist Jodi Byrd suggests: that the "Indian" need not be limited to understandings of settler colonial violence only in North America. Byrd argues that "Indianness has served as the field through which structures have always already been produced . . . [it] moves not through absence but through reiteration, through meme."[14] US imperialism in the Philippines reiterates settler colonialism and, where the Filipino *indio* is concerned, Indianness is also a "transit . . . site through which US empire orients and replicates itself by transforming those to be colonized into 'Indians' through continual re-iterations of pioneer logics, whether in the Pacific, the Caribbean, or the Middle East."[15] Mestizaje is a troubling racial discourse through which its subjects aspire to the vaunted capacities of the colonizers while navigating being weighed down by an Indigenous past. Rather than slough this past off, they rehabilitate and re-semanticize it. In order to understand these dynamics, this book positions and aligns with Jina Kim's calls for a "crip of color critique" in order to actualize a trenchant reckoning with genealogies of Spanish humanism, US liberal progressivism in the form of "benevolent assimilation" (which I analyze in more detail in chapter 1), and their various entanglements within mestizaje.[16] I break, however, with the orientation of crip theory, which is often geographically limited to the United States. I hold in tandem the various intersections of disability and colonialism that conspire in the racialized management of the native. In doing so, this project develops a framework I denote as *crip colonial critique*.

Crip colonial critique is a queercrip heuristic through which we grasp the racial-sexual and racialized gendered relations of disability within the developmentalist telos of colonialism more broadly.[17] Crip colonial critique unearths and scrutinizes the ways in which disability discourses fundamentally inhere within, animate, and propagate colonialism generally. Relations and ideologies of ability are always imbedded in colonial relations of power. This analytical frame imagines a union of colonial critique and crip theory that draws on concepts of race germane to Latin American coloniality. The term *coloniality* was originally coined by Peruvian sociologist Aníbal Quijano in his canonical essay "Colonialidad del poder, eurocentrismo y América latina" (Coloniality of power, Eurocentrism and Latin America), which foundationally argued that the notion of race emerged at and developed from the founding moment of modernity: the conquest of the Americas. Race's purpose was to give a framework to hierarchize bodies racially; to categorize and justify the valuation of their labors; and to facilitate the hyperextraction of surplus value from said racialized labor in order to introduce and sustain the order of colonial capitalism as the prominent global economic system.[18] Building on this foundational concept in Latin American studies, I read the ways that disability inherently structures the mechanisms through which the political rights of sovereignty and autonomy were annulled in order to effect the colonial hierarchization of race in the first place. Relevant to *Crip Colony*'s racial framing, a powerful aspect of Quijano's original formulation is the ways that race underwent shifts with the introduction of a new labor class of racially mixed mestizos who had access to the wider freedoms and political advantages associated with wage labor rather than the abject dispossession that Indigenous and Black slaves experienced under the colonial system. This new fabrication of humanity would, as a group, later wield great political power in the nation-states that would form in the "postcolonial" era significantly, for the purposes of this study, as creole mestizo intellectuals.[19] This demonstrates the ways that sexuality, race, and labor blended as much as humanity did in the advent of modernity with conquest.

I contend that crip colonial critique is a queercrip frame because of the ways that mestizaje often emphasizes a heteronormative mestizo subject as the center of revolutionary history and as the intellectual architect of robust political futures for the nation-state that suffered the violence of colonial rule—futures that are often expressly imagined through a heteroproductive lens and which thus rely on the labor of reproduction. All of the case studies in this book focus on the queerness of disability that colonialism attempts to rehabilitate and normalize through either heteronormative marriage, liberal education, or racial capitalist political economy. Thus, my work with mestizaje seeks to confirm, in another global context, what Robert McRuer foundationally theorizes as the "construction of able-bodiedness and heterosexuality, as well as the connections between them" in which the production of "disability [is] thoroughly interwoven with a system of compulsory heterosexuality that produces queerness."[20] The developmentalist telos of the nation as sovereign, autonomous, and invariably "good" enmeshed the cultural discourse of race with the biological drive to ensure heteroproductive "better breeding" along idealized racial lines.[21] Mestizaje, as a liberal and colonial form of ableism, fabricates ideal norms for national embodiment through the projection and representation of a queerly deviant Indian in dire need of reform essentially replicating the hierarchies endemic to the coloniality of power as not only a question of race but also of sexuality.[22] Queer critique of this racial discourse becomes instructive because it connotes an explicit form of racial-sexual power, to again invoke the apt formulation coined by queer-of-color critic Victor Román Mendoza, in which mestizos are created through the reproductive mixing, often coerced and violent, of white Europeans and the Indigenous peoples autochthonous to the Americas.[23]

For the various iterations of rehabilitated Indigeneity evinced in Filipino mestizaje, the *indio* is an epistemic container, evolutionary departures from which demonstrate modernization from precolonial atavism. Significantly, the meanings of this atavism also rebound through an Orientalist logic that affirms not only the "savagery" of the *indio* but also the barbarity of Asia, usually in the form of an antimodern China. And yet the role that Chineseness fundamentally plays in articulating Philippine iterations of mestizaje demonstrates that a Filipino mestizo archive is decidedly different from American varieties. In short, "the Oriental" was too foreign and thus unassimilable into mestizo embodiment, unlike the *indio* who necessarily had to be. Nevertheless, in the mestizaje that I examine, Asian and Indigenous embodiment and identification intersect indexing complimentary forms of retrogression that the Filipino mestizo (who is defined, under colonial processes, as *both* Asian and *indio*) civilizes, thus differentiating Filipino Asianness as itself a form of Indigenous rehabilitation and philosophical distance from depraved Chineseness. Perhaps one compelling and laconic rendition of my argument is the following: mestizaje in the Philippines was circumscribed by a colonial ableism that recursively gained meaning between the native, tidally locked in a usable past, and the Orient, recalcitrantly impervious to much-needed Westernization.

I don't cast *Crip Colony* as a study of Indigeneity per se, as I limit my scope to the study of mestizaje. Nevertheless, because of the ways that mestizaje has fundamentally and problematically exploited Indigenous identity, it strikes me as necessary to define the ways I am engaging with the concept. In what follows, I want to identify briefly the ways in which I am theorizing Indigeneity and the *indio* as a recursive issue for the politics of colonial ableism. In this project's critique of the manifold ableist logics racially enmeshed in mestizaje, the *indio* is a historical and epistemological juncture that connects multiple sites marked by Spanish and US racial colonial violence such as the borderlands, Latin America, and the Philippines.[24] I take inspiration from Cherokee queer theorist Joseph Pierce's moving theorization of Indian identification as a "process that is imminently queer.... Not queer as an identity position, not a fixed claim of self, but as a relational possibility."[25] Because I aim to frame this study in a geographically expansive colonial state of affairs, the ways that Indigeneity emerges across various arenas structured by asymmetrical power can be frustratingly elusive. That is, I use terms such as *native*, *Indigenous*, *autochthonous*, *Indian*, or *indio* in ways that are specific to their etiology of emergence whenever it is known and possible. Oftentimes, however, there are slippages that are difficult to resolve due to historical context and differing ways that state or colonial powers narrowly, or even *expansively*, define the parameters through which Indigeneity emerges or what it constellates—parameters that we might want to militate against in order to perform a relational analysis but whose specifics we may also want to maintain and which can be diluted by the act of comparison. This slippage is part of the very epistemological problem that is at the heart of a colonial politics of ableism.

Philippine Recursive Indigeneity

Indigeneity, it seems to me, is—as a political and identitarian fabric quilting across wildly divergent yet intimately connected contexts—a recursive phenomenon. That is, what might appear to inhere as an error of identification or a misattribution of unearned Indigeneity is central to the obfuscating logic of imperialism. This is not to circumvent the ways that durable, meaningful, and politically valid modes of national tribal identification persist despite such obfuscating logics. Indeed, Mohawk anthropologist and Indigenous theorist Audra Simpson has written that her own fraught discipline of anthropology colludes with settler state power and "has very much been the domain of defining the political for Indigenous peoples historically, and in fact was the mode for constructing and defining Indigeneity itself."[26] I partly mean to pinpoint the ways that colonial processes of producing Indians, *indios*, and natives through territorial expansion across broad transpacific geographies puts sovereign processes of nationhood for Indigenous peoples in jeopardy.

My focus on the politics of mestizaje is intimately connected to the elaboration of Indigeneity as a colonial knowledge object that can be rehabilitated, but such a focus on mixedness actually evokes the ways in which the racial calculus of settler regimes produces benchmarks for piecemeal claims to Indian identity that collude with colonial governmentality's strangulation of sovereign practices. Again, to cite Simpson's book on the contrapositions and ethnographic refusals of the Mohawk, she affirms that "present-day Kahnawá:ke was a seigniorial land grant that became a reserve held in trust for the use and benefit of these 'footloose' mixed-blood Mohawks—Mohawks, who, I will demonstrate through the course of this book, are not 'mixed blood.'"[27] That is, "mixed blood" is a settler and eugenic category that amplifies settler power by downgrading the power of an Indigenous sovereign polity to determine the political life of its citizens and identify them as *nationals*. What should be a *political* question answered in the realm of sovereign denomination is transformed by colonialism into a *racial* question that delimits sovereignty. In the frame of crip colonial critique, it's important to come to terms with the reality that for many, Indigeneity is *not* racial but rather national; not cosmic but instead kinship; not statistical calculation of genetic inheritance but—in its place—the sovereign articulation of material citizenship. Nevertheless, mestizaje is a valuable framing in that it demonstrates the discursive colonial processes that import Indigeneity into a Western national form, delineating for us, with more analytical certitude, the ways in which the categories of Indigenous and postcolonial citizen-subject are viewed as incommensurate, thus necessitating the latter to rehabilitate the former. In Simpson's more clarifying terms, you can't claim to be "48 percent Indian"—that is, 48 percent of a whole national sovereign identity (in racial terms); you either are recognized as a national citizen or you are not.[28] This is decidedly counterintuitive to the ways that ethnic minority entitlements to citizenship are enmeshed with hyphenated claims to personhood that presuppose arithmetic identities coformed through stable "halves": Filipinx American, Mexican American, and the like.

In my study, Indigeneity and its material and philosophical confluences within mestizaje across various domains of encounter function as a form of recursion. In the context of mathematics, logic, and computing, a recursion is a "technique involving the use of a procedure, subroutine, function, or algorithm that calls itself one or more times until a specific condition is met."[29] In simpler terms, a recursive code is a problem in code that is solved by a piece of the very same code that introduced the problem in the first place—as though one used material from a machine to build a hammer to repair that very same machine. The problem and its solution are part of the same self-contained ecology, though permutations of this system are not always selfsame by definition. This metaphor helps to explain the ways that race, disability, and Indigeneity layer on one another; fold in on themselves and into each other; introduce polemics of racial identification and misidentification; and introduce slippages whose inconsistencies are resolved by antecedent codes that originated the problems to begin with. In this way we can approach an understanding of how it is possible that Filipinos, the Kanaka Maoli, and the Quiché Maya are all Indian in relation to each other in recursive ways made possible by the broad swath of racial classification interdigitated by colonialism. Yet—and I want to be very clear here—in examining the queer relationality of Indianness I neither mean to make a case for the Indigeneity of Filipinos as equivalent to American Indigeneities nor for evaluating others' claims to such identity. I neither hold the subject position to ethically argue such a point, nor is that the focus of my project's genealogical exploration of mestizaje, though terms such as *tribal* and *Indigenous* are indeed political categories that are assigned to Indigenous

Filipinos by the Philippine state, not unlike in North America.[30] This is all to say that there are relational possibilities to mine particularly for populations that were classified as *indio* under Spanish colonial rule and later assimilated into the US settler empire. Moreover, it is this notion of recursive Indigeneity that allows me to think ambitiously across geography and racial difference to elaborate a comparative ethnic studies analysis.

Despite the mining of such connections, there also exists major differences in these wildly diverse locations in which race and the political category of the Indian circulate. These differences provide a portrait that might be more interesting for its incommensurability rather than comparative overlap. Nevertheless, it is precisely the incommensurate nature of the "American" Indian, the Spanish American *indio*, and the Philippine iterations of both that adumbrates a transnational genealogy of the colonial and racial life of disability. Spanish colonial law itself was drawing these connections in order to make racial sense of the disparate, far-flung, and diverse peoples that populated its colonies.[31] This space of incommensurability, rather than being one of friction and separation, I consider to be a place of mutual recognition, affinity, and possibility across a recursive field of global Indigeneity managed by and resistant to imperialism and settler colonialism. There is queer resonance in the racial ambiguities that inhere within referents like *Asia* and *America* or fabrications like *the mestizo*. As far as hemispheric, transnational, and transpacific conceptions of American studies are concerned, my hope is that a crip colonial critique will allow us to crip the colony and, in so doing, may provide a language to think through the ways that the Spanish colonial embeds within the US racial imaginary a biopolitical construction and management of the *indio* across philosophical and geopolitical borders.

In order to understand the ways that colonialism and disability intersect in the landscape of mestizaje, it is important to understand the different racial outcomes for the peoples historically subjugated by British versus Spanish colonialism. Both Anglo-American and Spanish colonialism treated the subjects of racial mixture and native peoples distinctly. In a basic sense, the Spanish Empire incorporated the *indio*, while Anglo imperialism treated the Indian as separate and distinct. In discussion of the ways that mestizo Chicanx people may have historical claims to Indigeneity but who do not exist under the political sign of "Indian" as US ethnic minorities, Maria Cotera and Josefina Saldaña-Portillo explore the ways that Spanish imperialism considered *indios* political subjects of the Spanish crown, while this was not the case for Anglo imperialism, which considered Indians distinct political subjects though still beholden to the British crown. They suggest that this is one compelling reason why the nations of the United States and those of Latin America incorporated Indigenous peoples differently.[32] Because the Philippines sits at the intersection of these at times not complementary ideologies that span the Americas, it becomes necessary to contextualize how hemispheric American race relations would result in various nation-building projects in Latin America predicated on precisely that which would be considered anathema in what eventually became the United States: the mestizo or racially mixed person. This is not to say there are insignificant traces of racial mixture or mixed-race people in the United States. Nevertheless, the histories of the violent extremes to which efforts went to preserve white purity in the United States stand in contradistinction to Latin American nation-states such as Brazil, Cuba, Mexico, and Uruguay, whose national mythologies and cosmologies rely on Indian incorporation rather than explicit elimination.

For our purposes, the condition through which Indigenous peoples were variously, and oftentimes inaccurately, integrated or eliminated index profound concerns germane to disability. Mestizaje was a discourse that famously blended *indigenismo*, cosmology, and eugenics to project a future state whose ideal figure was the mestizo. But it is also important to recognize that the United States also integrated the Indian into American Western imaginaries of the frontier as an equally if differentially mythic figure that rationalized white American claims on the land and its resources.[33] While there are certainly vast visible differences in the ways that American Indigeneities were treated, imagined, and exploited, I also find much discursive similarity in the ways that the Indian is a figure that was mythologized. While the Philippines is in Asia, its histories of conquest tell similar stories that seem more germane to the borderlands and Latin America.[34]

I seek to clarify the mestizo archive of the Philippines and its relevance to transnational studies of disability; however, I want to make it clear that I approach the question of mestizaje as an Asian American critic invested in hemispheric race relations. Mestizaje has a pronounced and prominent archive across the Americas. The Philippines poses a productive epistemological challenge to the geographies and embodiments we typically might imagine with mestizaje. Facetiously, Spanish historian Antonio García-Abásolo characterized the racially mixed populations from the Philippines as "mestizos de un país sin mestizaje" (mestizos from a country without mestizaje).[35] Despite its relative paucity, mestizaje's cultural import in the Philippines is rather undeniable despite its divergence from American examples. Rather than a simple "Filipino twist" on a more established Latin

American or Latinx mestizo norm, I center the Philippines as a productive opportunity in "queering mestizaje" by embracing contexts, histories, and cultures that would fall more within the purview of Asian American studies.[36] Even so, because mestizaje has been treated with incredible levels of critical profundity in both Latin American and Latinx studies *and* being inspired by the Philippines' shared history of Spanish colonial rule, I find it ethically and critically necessary to engage with the archive of mestizaje as an Asian Americanist invested in analyses of comparative imperialism. Through a crip colonial critique, I turn to the mestizo Philippines to think through the ableism of colonial enlightenment, which fashions able-mindedness through the rehabilitation of a crip Indian that the mestizo does *not* wish to be but from whom he derives an authorizing kinship—an Indian shaped through ideologies of US American and Spanish humanisms. Troubling and expanding on canonical renditions of mestizo thought embroiled in ableist eugenic architectures provides greater clarity to the ways that Filipinx engagements with mestizaje deviate from and align with it in ways that I believe can productively remap Asian American studies, Latinx studies, and disability studies.

In calling attention to mestizaje's ableist preference, I crip the colony in order to explore the ways that sexuality, coloniality, and race interlock in shaping our often commonsense and underexplored notions of the body and its attendant, often wildly differential, capacities. Throughout this book I will maintain that the discrepancy between colonizer and colonized is one reasonably understood as a difference of imagined capacity—ability requisite for the material conditions of robust political existence, subjectivity, and independence. In making this argument, I suggest that the colonial relation is also a relation of disability embedded in a logic of relational racialization; indeed, rather than an inert term that describes a set state of affairs, I agree with scholars like Sami Schalk and Jina Kim that disability is a socially and politically constructed system of norms that actively produces a set of relations that predispose racialized bodies to vulnerability, injury, and debilitation.[37] By the same token, I suggest that colonialism constitutes and materializes a spectacular array of disablements that I seek to understand. Mestizaje is enmeshed within this array as both a critical apparatus that reads against its colonial grain while also being endemic to the power asymmetries that give it life.

The Philippines has an uneasy and discomfiting position in the Americas as a former Spanish and US colony. I position its mestizo archive within an expansive and transpacific vision of the Americas given the ways that both Spanish and US colonialism similarly mark Philippine historical experiences of race. Such experiences resonate with Latin America and the US borderlands. Thus, Latin American and Latinx studies provide helpful models of understanding the entanglements of Anglo-American and Hispanic empires while Filipinx American and Philippine studies stand to enrich a hemispheric American studies approach. What ties these seemingly disparate groups and fields of inquiry together is a cultural and philosophical reckoning with mestizaje. The Philippines represents a unique milieu to which these "American" liberal ideologies have been exported.[38]

Yet before Philippine mestizaje can be understood for the ways that it reifies colonial ableism, it is necessary to gain an understanding of the ways that mestizaje has been taken up by disability studies. Necessarily this requires an engagement with Gloria Anzaldúa, who has been recuperated by disability analysts as a foundational woman of color disability theorist. Her work is an indispensable crossroads where disability and mestizaje intersect that is imminently relevant for the field orientation of this book. While *Crip Colony* is not centrally a book on Chicanx border studies (as it is principally a critique of Filipinx mestizaje), because transnational disability studies is a main field of inquiry it is crucial to gain a clear picture of the ways in which mestizaje has been theorized in disability studies in order to establish the difference that Filipinx mestizo studies brings to crip critique. As I'll explain in the following section, Anzaldúa's own work unfortunately reentrenches some of the eugenic ideologies inherent to the pseudoscience of American mestizaje in ways that are not thoroughly engaged by feminist disability studies. This should be of concern to a robust theory attending to the intersection of colonialism and disablement.

Mestizaje and Feminist Disability Studies

In her pioneering text *Borderlands / La Frontera*, Gloria Anzaldúa argues that a new mestiza consciousness problematizes the extent to which both the Mexican and US nation-states could presume to accurately frame the cultural and political thinking of Chicana feminist experience. As I have stated, my deployment of crip colonial critique is certainly deeply indebted to the ways that Quijano offered a powerful lens to map the emergence of race through conquest and dispossession of Black and Indigenous peoples.[39] Nevertheless, Anzaldúa is an equally powerful interlocutor in linking and expanding my adaptation of coloniality to the material realities of not only racialized bodies whose labors were historically hyperextracted by settler colonialism and chattel slavery but also the profound imbrication of race and ability. In a passage often cited by disability theorists claiming Anzaldúa as a disability figure, she famously writes, in a way that explicates an ethos of mixture and mestizaje, that "the U.S.-Mexican border *es una herida abierta* where the Third World grates against the first and bleeds. And before a scab forms it hemorrhages again, the lifeblood of two worlds merging to form a third country—a border culture."[40] Moreover, she reflects on the "Tortilla Curtain" that euphemistically marks the imposition of the border as a

> 1950-mile-long open wound
> Dividing a *pueblo*, a culture,
> Running down the length of my body,
> Staking fence rods in my flesh,
> Splits me splits me
> Me raja me raja.[41]

The almost itinerant subjectivity of the mestiza produces a consciousness that deals with ambiguities and contradictions not as realities to be resolved into tidy categories but instead as part of innovative hybrid thinking. Anzaldúa relies on the figure of the mestiza as the product of and agent to materialize a hybridity evocative of a "border culture" that is the "lifeblood" of "worlds merging"—blood spilt by the violent division and cleaving of the "pueblo" (people) or nation. The injury of the "herida abierta" (open wound) evidences her subjectivity as "rajada" (split or torn); these are tears that are implicitly stitched by the merging of blood evocative of the racial fusions and merging worlds of mestizaje.

Because of the philosophical unfixedness of the Chicana mestiza body and its imbrication with (and physical harm caused by) a political environment emblematized by the border, it is unsurprising that many feminist disability theorists have tried to argue that Anzaldúa is a foundational feminist disability theorist. Such moves are demonstrative of disability literature that attempts to resituate some foundational feminist thinkers, prominent in other fields, as scholars or activists not only in movements for racial justice but also for disability justice (and also to question frameworks that would consider said movements as irrevocably separate). Suzanne Bost; Qwo-Li Driskill, Aurora Levins Morales, and Leah Lakshmi Piepzna-Samarasinha; Alison Kafer and Eunjung Kim; AnaLouise Keating; and Carrie McMaster have all encouraged engagement with Gloria Anzaldúa and Audre Lorde, for instance, as women of color feminists foundational to what Schalk and Kim have called a "feminist of color disability studies."[42] Keating, for instance, conducted interviews with Anzaldúa later in her life that have crucially established the explicit linkages the Chicana feminist made between her physical impairments and her borderlands feminism.[43] Dissonant with the more mainstream ways that Anzaldúa is taken up in Latinx, queer, and feminist studies, McMaster notes, "although I viewed Anzaldúa as a feminist, a Chicana theorist, and one of the founders of queer theory, I had not learned to also think of her as a woman with a chronic illness, a person with a disability."[44] She and Bost have established that Anzaldúa's life and understanding of her body were substantially shaped by her adult onset diabetes and a rare genetic hormonal imbalance that caused her to begin menstruation at three months of age.[45] This condition required her to undergo a hysterectomy in order to remove a mass in her uterus.[46] Bost goes as far as to state that Anzaldúa's ample figurative use of animals to describe her mental states, such as "la serpiente," evokes a posthumanist break with the human/animal divide tantamount to "embracing . . . madness," thus placing "Anzaldúa's worldview outside of contemporary critical or political discourse—yet also within contemporary disability discourse" that is allied, indeed, with mad studies.[47] In a similar vein, McMaster has argued that Anzaldúa's very-well-known "concepts of la facultad, nepantla and nepantleras, conocimiento/desconocimiento, El Mundo Zurdo, new tribalism, the Coatlicue state, the Coyolxauhqui experience, and spiritual activism contribute both ideological and pragmatic tools to our work" of disability studies and activism.[48]

Foreshadowing the recent intervention of feminist of color disability studies as a productive and deeply necessary revision of Rosemary Garland-Thomson's feminist disability studies, Kafer and Kim have argued that claiming figures like Anzaldúa as "crip kin" substantiates that

there is no monolithic "disabled person" or universal experience of disability, but rather experiences, conceptualizations, and manifestations of disability that vary widely by cultural, historical, and global context. Just as scholarship that fails to attend to disability is complicit in maintaining ableism, scholarship that attends *only* to disability, casting it as separate from processes of racialization or histories of colonialism, reproduces oppressive norms. . . .

Moreover, an additive approach fails to consider that *disability* will likely need to be reconceptualized when colonial relations or histories of sexuality are addressed.[49]

My stake in these debates is to address such "colonial relations," as well as Schalk and Kim's invitation for engagement with iterations of race and disability outside the United States, which they themselves point to as a limitation of their own framing of feminist of color disability analysis.[50] To wit, Suzanne Bost's US-centric engagement with disability may dangerously limit an understanding of the pitfalls of Anzaldúa in adequately addressing both the coloniality of mestizaje, which Anzaldúa romanticizes, and the settler coloniality of the United States in which her claims to mestiza consciousness structurally obtain meaning. This limitation is evident in a provocative question posed by Bost speculating on Anzaldúa's disabled subjectivity: "What does it mean to live like an Aztec goddess in the late twentieth-century United States?"[51] Perhaps inspired by the framing given by technofeminist Donna Haraway that characterizes women of color as political "cyborgs," this pivotal question posed by Bost in her influential essay suggests that the irrationality and spirituality of Anzaldúa's "shape-shifting" mestiza consciousness generate critical opportunities for questioning liberal humanism as the locus of ableist ideologies.[52] Bost contextualizes Anzaldúa's ostensible Indigenous deity status, elaborating that "by bringing the ontologies of Aztec thought into her writings about her own embodiment, Anzaldúa creates friction between temporalities and epistemologies; she undermines assumptions about human life and human history that are rarely questioned. What does it mean to live like an Aztec goddess in the late twentieth-century United States? We must use our imagination to answer this question because there is no historical or empirical model to draw on."[53]

Claiming that there are no "models" to draw on perhaps contributes to and speaks to the prevalence of the eliminatory logics that erase Indigenous peoples from the present. This has the effect of locking them in a past that Anzaldúa and contemporary feminist disability scholars can then rehabilitate for different political ends, advancing disability justice while ignoring settler violence.[54] Bost's exuberant desire to claim Anzaldúa as an Indigenous disability "goddess" speaks to the need for renewed calls for a rigorous transnational, comparative, and multilingual approach to what Josefina Saldaña-Portillo calls a truly "American 'American Studies,'" one differentiated from a superficial approach to the transnational that "steers clear of the difficulties and complexities of archival research, ethnography, multilinguality, and multiculturality required by this approach" and instead produces knowledge that is more tantamount to a kind of "intellectual tourism."[55] Relevant to the feminist disability claiming of Anzaldúa that I have elaborated on, Saldaña-Portillo has produced perhaps one of the more widely known critiques of Chicanx feminist recuperations of mestizaje. This is significant because mestizaje is one of the central devices through which Anzaldúa's disability story unfolds. Ultimately I agree with Saldaña-Portillo that Chicanx appropriations of an ancestral Indian as the point of origin for political and territorial claims are materialized "by claiming [that] Aztlán as an Indigenous nation [is] historically anterior to the founding of the United States." Moreover, when such ancestral claims are read within, for instance, the Zapatistas' critique of mestizaje as a harmful racial ideology that has oppressed Indigenous sovereignty, it is clear that "mestizaje is incapable of suturing together the heterogeneous positionalities of 'Mexican,' 'Indian,' and 'Chicana/o' that co-exist in the United States" instead relegating "the Indian [to] an ancestral past rather than recognizing contemporary Indians as coinhabitants not only of this continent abstractly conceived but of the neighborhoods and streets of hundreds of U.S. cities and towns."[56] The inability of Anzaldúa to connect modern Chicana mestiza identity to contemporary concerns that affect Indians relegates them to an ornamented past that is treated as "a kind of pastiche grab bag of Indian spiritual paraphernalia."[57] Saldaña-Portillo concludes that "[Anzaldúa] goes through her backpack and decides what to keep and what to throw out, choosing to keep signs of Indigenous identity as ornamentation and spiritual revival. But what of the living Indian who refuses mestizaje as an avenue to political and literary representation? What of the *indígena* who demands new representational models that include her among the living?"[58] That is to say, Chicanx invocations of mestizaje collude with the settler colonial project positioning Indians on what Denise Ferreira da Silva calls the "horizon of death," even if such claims point to a process of "mourning" vis-à-vis an Indigeneity—the connectivity to which has been erased due to colonial violence.[59] For this reason, it is important to keep in mind the ableist eugenic framework in which mestizaje was initially articulated.

Bost's claim that Anzaldúa's feminist disability bona fides are anchored in her status as an "Aztec goddess" advances disability justice as a form of settler violence. I contend that it is absolutely vital that disability studies not replicate these settler patterns of colonial violence that rely on an Indian that mestizaje has rehabilitated in order to advance the goal of "diversifying" disability. Without considering Indigenous peoples among the living and the very real "historical and empirical model" that they indeed do bring to the present, disability studies will run the risk of succumbing to a multiculturalist logic that only very shallowly includes racial critique as a central aspect of its analytical operations.[60] Placing Anzaldúa at the center of a rapprochement between disability studies and racial hybridity shows an uncomfortable yet productive paradox. What happens to the celebrated status of Anzaldúa as "crip kin" when brought into the context of critiques of her appropriative and reductive "postnationalist" uses of mestizaje? Foregrounding the ways that settler colonial ideology manifests itself through discourses of debilitation demonstrates how they are reliant on the image of a crip Indian to be rehabilitated by and as a technology of colonial ableism. Disability theory that is not attentive to these realities actually then *propounds* disability as an effect of settler colonialism. In a sense, Anzaldúa's postnationalist feminist frame, which she announces through the visibility of the epistemic and physical "open wound" of the border, similarly recuperates an ancestral Indian to then be evolved *into a Chicana* with hybrid cognition. This furthers the violence of colonial ableism as a form of settler colonial appropriation in its rehabilitative attachment to an Indigenized *frontera*.

Rather than a radical disability justice framework, what we are left with in this context is a settler colonial disability studies. One way in which borderlands feminism in Anzaldúa's articulation capitulates to what Jessica Cowing calls "settler ableism" is by decontextualizing the deep eugenic quagmire in which mestizaje is embedded.[61] Anzaldúa recuperates the cosmic race by ultimately misunderstanding José Vasconcelos's arguments around a "fifth race" as a "theory . . . of inclusivity," similarly endorsing pseudoscientific arguments romanticizing a "hybrid progeny [as] a mutable, more malleable species with a rich gene pool." In a celebratory tenor she extols the exciting hybrid character and epistemological possibility of the cosmic race: "José Vasconcelos, Mexican philosopher, envisaged *una raza mestiza, una mezcla de razas afines, una raza de color—la primera raza síntesis del globo.* He called it a cosmic race, *la raza cósmica,* a fifth race embracing the four major races of the world. . . . From this racial, ideological, cultural and biological cross-pollination, an 'alien' consciousness is presently in the making—a new *mestiza* consciousness, *una conciencia de mujer.* It is a consciousness of the Borderlands."[62] Anzaldúa actually seems to trumpet the ideal of Vasconcelos's cosmic race, which one would be very hard-pressed to do after a careful reading of his essay. I want to leave open the possibility, however, that it may certainly be conceivable to retool a problematic ideology and infuse it with new political meanings. Nevertheless, given the ways that Anzaldúa liberally reaches back into time to resuscitate a lost Indigenous heritage grounded predominantly in Aztec spirituality, it is fair to pose the question of what it means to recuperate a past decoupled from its granular specific historical conditions and contexts—in this case, the historical development of the race sciences and eugenics through which mestizaje (by Anzaldúa's own citational protocol) obtains its meanings. The conversation that Anzaldúa initiates with Vasconcelos in her canonical and significant contribution to women of color feminist thought (and, by proxy, feminist disability studies) forces us to come to terms with a contradiction at the heart of mestiza consciousness as a concept that is born from the traumas of historical exclusion while also propounding foundational exclusions of Black and Indigenous peoples central to the cultural discourse of mestizaje. Questioning the ableism of mestizaje as a political discourse is in tension with the recuperation of it as a mode of productive though arguably heavily romanticized "hybrid" thinking that, similar to Vasconcelos's theory, attempts to recast the Chicanx and the Mexican uncomplicatedly within a field of Indigenous identification: "I am visible—see this Indian face—yet I am invisible. I both blind them with my beak nose and am their blind spot. But I exist, we exist. They'd like to think I have melted in the pot. But I haven't, we haven't." Read alongside her acknowledgment that "this land was Mexican once / Was Indian always / and is. / And will be again" there is a desire to articulate the mestiza consciousness as emergent from the status of an individual that we are encouraged to consider, for many intents and purposes, a detribalized Indian.[63] While this is a generalization, casting the Chicana mestiza as an unmoored Indian appears to be at least one of the implications of Anzaldúa's mestiza consciousness.

While reifying the lens of "mestizos" to read social reality better than the rest of us is not something that I wish to do in the space of this book, I do think that analyzing the politics and representations of Filipino mestizos can communicate something important about the colonial politics of ableism. At base, what is true about all the historically divergent contexts of Latin America, the Philippines, and the borderlands is the broad articulation of mestizaje as a discourse shaping identity, nationalism, and cultural politics. Mestizaje emerges from the contact between Spanish colonizers and the Indigenous colonized. As such, it is indelibly and inescapably a colonial reality that is shared across various diverse geographies and temporalities. However, mestizaje is also a philosophical and cultural theory pertaining to the complexities of hybridity. The Philippines is not an exception to this. This book indeed foregrounds some works by Filipino *hispanistas* for their challenges to coloniality, on the one hand, while also taking a critical posture to the ways in which they calcify mestizaje's racial and colonial ableist assumptions, on the other. In this way, the pitfalls of Anzaldúa's work offer a helpful historical resonance of similar entrenchments of asymmetrical power in the mestizo Philippines.

Filipinx Mestizaje: The Reorientation of an American Concept

The Philippines' colonial history is a marginal "peculiar" case for Spanish historical studies while being a central case study for American studies' understanding of US foreign policy shifts at the turn of the twentieth century.[64] I am buoyed to see that this is shifting.[65] Nevertheless, Spanish historian Josep Fradera originally remarked on the "peculiaridad" (peculiarity) of the Philippines as Spain's only Asian colony solidifying an Orientalist register in the articulation of Spanish colonial history vis-à-vis its mysterious and exceptional Asian experiment. And although he was highlighting a fundamental inassimilable quality of the Philippines into normative chronicles of Spanish historiography that more regularly include its American colonies, he might not be too far off the mark on the ways in which the archipelago presents differences that must be accounted for as strange, peculiar, and even queer.

The Philippines was first "discovered" by Portuguese explorer Ferdinand Magellan in 1521 during his famed and apocryphal circumnavigation of the globe.[66] Coincidently (though perhaps fated), this was the same year in which conquistador Hernán Cortés defeated Montezuma in the Aztec city of Tenochtitlán, completing the *conquista* of what today is Mexico. The Philippines officially and administratively became a Spanish colony when its first colonial outpost was established on the island of Cebu in the central Philippines in 1565. The Philippine islands became a far more ecclesiastical colony rather than a well-established military outpost, as was observed in the colonies of New Spain and in other parts of Latin America. Its positioning as an *ultramar* (overseas) territory of the Spanish Empire was significant, however, on the Manila Galleon Route, which connected the port cities of Acapulco, Mexico; Granada, Spain (notably the last Muslim stronghold to be conquered by the Catholic monarchs Ferdinand and Isabel in 1492); and Manila in the Philippines, as well as many other economic hubs controlled by the Spanish crown. In fact, the Philippines was administered on behalf of Spain by the viceroyalty of Mexico City from 1565 until 1815, when the Galleon Route was ultimately ended by the Mexican War of Independence. In this administrative sense, the Philippines was actually a part of Mexico; this historical relationship has inspired the necessary conversation with aspects of Chicanx studies in this introduction. There were many cultural, intellectual, linguistic, and political exchanges, as well as the trade in commodities, foods, and bodies, between the Americas and the Philippines through this route, attesting to the inherent global nature of Philippine culture and politics.[67] Despite such exchanges, the Catholic priests evangelized by transcribing Indigenous Philippine languages with the Latin alphabet, and the Spanish language never saw widespread use nor was it systematically imposed—this is perhaps one of the most convincing historical explanations for why the Philippines is not a Hispanophone country today.

Nevertheless, many Filipinos (nonpeninsular Spaniards born in the Philippines) and peninsular Spaniards liaised with Natives, producing a creole class of Filipinos who later reclaimed the term for the native-born, autochthonous peoples of the islands. These *ilustrado* (intellectual) Spanish-speaking mestizos were instrumental in the Philippines' own revolutionary, nationalist period of consciousness raising in the late nineteenth century, fitting a pattern of independence movements that transpired in Latin America during that century. Philippine historiography dates this period from the execution (on the charge of sedition) of three native-born Filipino Catholic priests, Mariano Gómez, José Burgos, and Jacinto Zamora, in 1872 until the beginning of the Philippine Revolution in 1896.[68] Known by the portmanteau of their last names the GomBurZa execution fomented widespread resentment and suspicion of Spanish authority—and particularly of the Catholic Church. Such anticlericalism became a central political sticking point for mestizo intellectual José Rizal, seen by many as one of the central figures of the so-called Philippine Enlightenment and the revolution though he was mainly a reformist who believed in a continued relationship with Spain.[69] A central figure of study of this book project, Rizal, a *sangley* or Filipino-Chinese Hispanic mestizo, represents an anticolonial striving for political and intellectual self-determination in the face of Spanish malfeasance and debilitation, on the one hand, and a contentious avatar for a Philippine mestizaje that integrated and replicated colonial rehabilitation, on the other.

The Philippine Revolution (1896–98), following Rizal's execution by a firing squad of the Guardia Civil (again, on the charge of sedition), gained an ally in the United States, which ensured its triumph, though the victory was short-lived. The United States entered into war against Spain following the sinking of the USS *Maine* in the Bay of Havana and defeated the weakening colonial power in a matter of months in a conflict remembered in history as the Spanish-American War (1898). Custodianship of the Philippines passed to the United States after a negotiation with Spain following its defeat at the Treaty of Paris, despite the Philippines' protestations and hard-fought grassroots independence movement. Thus began the colonial period under the United States following the Filipinos' defeat in the Philippine-American War (1899–1902)—a period that endured until 1946. United States control was characterized as "benevolent assimilation" and tutelage in the modern franchise of democratic self-government. As I will explore in chapter 1, benevolent assimilation assumed the inability of Filipinos to self-govern, and thus the Philippines became a custodial population of the United States—indeed, *sold* to the United States by Spain.[70] While such political rationalizations of the annulment of sovereignty were certainly metaphorically staged, they were also deeply entwined with evaluations of the literal cognitive capacity of the colonized. While I suggest that the asymmetrical power dynamics between the colonized and the colonizers are partially shaped as a function of perceived ability, these are also ideologies that are internalized and replicated within colonial society. Accompanying disablement is the desire to rehabilitate; and such rehabilitation not only involves mestizo and colonial uplift of the *indio* but also the ways that the Orient is cast in disabled terms.

Rizal is evocative and emblematic of a crucial difference indexing a profound departure of American mestizaje from Filipinx iterations of it: Chineseness, China, and the corresponding ways that Orientalism manifests within the development of hybridity. While I have described Rizal as a *sangley* mestizo, this, according to Philippine historian Richard Chu, would cause confusion given prevailing historical Spanish legal categorizations whose "colonial regime used a three-way classification system to segregate the people under its rule. The '*sangleyes*' or the 'Chinese' comprised one group, and the *mestizos* (the creole offspring of 'Chinese' men and local women) and the '*indios*' (the natives) comprised the other two."[71] Later the United States would simply classify mestizos and *indios* as "Filipinos" while the Chinese were regarded as "alien," demonstrating the ways that Chinese exclusion influenced US colonialism in the Philippines. When compared to Latin America, it's important to note that the variety of mestizaje that is central to Philippine national mythography integrates (however contentious and illusory that integration may be) Chinese racial identity into the Filipino national body despite these exclusions. Yet this exists alongside anti-Chinese animus, which also animates Philippine mestizaje not as a unifying racial nationalism but as a racial-colonial hierarchy scaffolded by an abiding Orientalism. Cultural and literary studies scholar Caroline Hau has asserted that contemporary Filipino racial politics evokes this Orientalist historical dialectic of "inclusion and exclusion [that] highlights the unsettled and shifting meanings not only of 'Chinese' and 'Chineseness,' but of mestizoness, 'Filipino,' and 'Filipinoness' as well."[72] One need not look further than the *pambansang bayani* (Philippine national hero) José Rizal who, as a Hispanic Chinese mestizo, was demonstrative of a kind of mestizaje that was crucially oriented in an Asian context bridging East Asian and Southeast Asian hybridities. Yet Rizal, like other *sangley* mestizos, would likely not have identified strongly with Chinese identity, particularly during a nationalist period in which a general Filipino identity was solidifying. Indeed, during the US period, evidence suggests that Filipino intellectuals utilized Spanish culture (partly, though not exclusively, in the form of the Spanish language) and US anti-Chinese rhetoric to distinguish the Philippines as a modern, "Americanized" nation vis-à-vis China, which was scripted as a container for depravity, ruin, queerness, and disability (see chapter 3). The hybridity evocative of mestizaje is especially complex in the Philippines in that it can be difficult to determine where Asia is, who's Asia, and whose Asia? Asia in the Philippine articulation of it is at once American, Asian, and Spanish, amalgamating multifarious cultural formations that vex stable identification and categorization.

The mestizo Philippines is an important case study rounding out Asian Americanist engagements with mestizaje in the Americas, which has not paid too much attention to the archipelago as it does not fit neatly within critical race study historiographies that prioritize histories of migration *from* Asia. In American instantiations of mestizaje, critics like Jason Oliver Chang, Ana Paulina Lee, and Lisa Lowe have shown that unlike the ways that Indigenous peoples, and to a much lesser extent Black peoples, were folded into mestizaje and ostensibly integrated into the mestizo national body, Chinese laborers during and after the period of the liberal abolition of slavery were articulated as foreign presences.[73] "Chinos" were largely considered unassimilable into the national identities that were forged in the independence movements of the nineteenth century from Spain. Independence from European powers galvanized American republics (including the United States) to cast the Orient as irrevocably foreign even though today many of these nations pride themselves on being inclusive multicultural havens. Performance and food studies scholar Tao Leigh Goffe, for instance, has offered important readings against the grain of the liberal multiculturalism of the Americas using the amalgamated tastes of the dish chop suey as an analytic to track the ways that Afro-Asian intimacies are configured as "surplus" and therefore obfuscated by a Black-white dyad.[74]

Afro-Asian, Chinese, and Indian (as in from India) subjectivities are often left out of critical conversation in the multiethnic landscapes of American experience, particularly as these Asian laborers "replaced" Black plantation labor. Significantly, the substitutive function orchestrated by colonial racial capitalism of Chinese and South Asian laborers seems to have also solidified a persistent forgetting of hemispheric Asian Americas, which concerns the mestizo archive centered in this book. For instance, Chang has demonstrated that Chinese laborers were subjected to an *antichinista* discourse that was fundamental to the consolidation of a Mexican national identity, particularly in the early twentieth century after the Mexican Revolution.[75] While this could be said to be beyond the scope of the ways that a cultural "disability" theorist like Gloria Anzaldúa engaged with multiraciality by consistently commenting on the Black, Hispanic, and Indian identities that compose her mestiza consciousness, the backdrop of *antichinismo* in Mexican identity is completely absent from the mestiza consciousness in ways that prompt questions about what precisely composes the renditions of Mexican national history that are then innovated by Chicana feminist thought. Similar to the ways that Asian Americans in North America are configured as perpetual foreigners differentiated even from the most liberal and pluralistically multiracial instantiations of national identity, the Asian racial form was jettisoned out of the "inclusive" clutches of mestizaje. Paulina Lee has tracked similar ways that Orientalist sentiments have shaped the supposedly racially democratic and plural Brazilian national identity.[76] In all of these cases, the mestizo racialized body consolidated its meaning around its fundamental difference from the Asian body. Unfortunately, these historical, economic, and discursive articulations of the manifold Asian exclusions that quilt across American experience are corroborated in the foundational literature of mestizaje philosophy.

There is evidence of an enduring, constitutive, yet undertheorized Orientalism in perhaps the most infamous text on mestizaje—that of Mexican statesman and politician José Vasconcelos. I want to cover Vasconcelos briefly because his eugenic outlook is relevant to the disability analysis of this book and, moreover, the ways in which he excludes Asia mark the fundamental difference that Filipinx racial politics brings to the scholarly conversation on mestizaje that must fundamentally include Asianness. In his book of essays *La raza cósmica* (The cosmic race, 1925), Vasconcelos is well known for arguing that mestizos are a "cosmic" master race that should inevitably be the future outcome for humanity. The foundational character of mestizaje utilized the Orient as a discursive space in which disability and pathology are situated. This is important because it economically, culturally, and racially indexes the extent to which Chinese people were inassimilable into the mestizo frame. To this point Vasconcelos writes,

> Ocurrirá algunas veces, y ha ocurrido ya, en efecto, que la competencia económica nos obligue a cerrar nuestras puertas, tal como hace el sajón, a una desmedida irrupción de orientales. Pero al proceder de esta suerte, nosotros no obedecemos más que a razones de orden económico; reconocemos que no es justo que pueblos como el chino, que bajo el santo consejo de la moral confuciana se multiplican como ratones, vengan a *degradar la condición humana*, justamente en los instantes en que comenzamos a comprender que la inteligencia sirve para refrenar y regular bajos instintos zoológicos . . . si los rechazamos es porque el hombre, a medida que progresa, se multiplica menos y siente el horror del número, por lo mismo que ha llegado a estimar la calidad.

> It shall occur at times, and in effect it has already, that economic competition will obligate us to close our ports, as the Anglo-Saxon has, to an immeasurable eruption of Orientals. But in doing so we are only following economic rationalizations; we realize that it is not just that nations like that of the Chinese, under the holy counsel of Confucian morality would multiply like rats, would come to *degrade* the human condition, when we have just begun to understand that our intelligence would influence us to refrain from base animal instincts . . . if we reject them it is because man, as he progresses, will procreate less feeling the horror of overpopulation and because he has begun to understand quality (over quantity).[77]

This passage illuminates for the reader that the national mestizo body possesses an able-bodiedness through the uplift of the autochthonous native. Indeed, the purpose of "inteligencia" is to refrain from base sexual depravity, thus linking cognitive ability and sexual respectability on the screen of Yellow Peril. Mel Chen has established the profound linkage of disability and the Asian racial form in ways that demonstrate that Orientalism, as one of the engines of mestizaje's ableism, was part of a global eugenic norm rather than an exception to the rule. While "mongoloidism" (the racist initial term for Down syndrome) is not mentioned by Vasconcelos explicitly, it is difficult to extricate the conceptual and deep ontological relation of the term from Vasconcelos's reference to the racialized "mongol." This demonstrates the extent to which Asian racialization has been deeply imbricated in the understanding of disability as a product of global processes of colonial encounter.[78] Insofar as disability discourses are concerned, the body indexes likewise the extent to which qualification of ability transpires within the frame of sexuality ("se multiplican como ratones"). The founding identity of the mestizo shores up its meanings through its fundamental dissimilarity from the Asian body.

Mapping the Book

The Philippines' experience as a Spanish colony and its particular history as a "mestizo" nation are definitely outliers to the more tried-and-true paths worn in the Americas. American genealogies of mestizaje have been analyzed by many scholars in Latin American studies and Latinx studies, as I've demonstrated in this introduction. While there are certainly exceptions, mestizaje as a political and social engine of the Latin American republic is understood in contradistinction to US American varieties of multiculturalism that expressly foreground racial fragmentation and segregation over that which is imagined and understood in the Caribbean and Latin America. What I aim to do is establish canonical mestizaje alongside more peripheral idealizations of it in the Philippines as it transitioned into the rehabilitative framework of US benevolent assimilation. Indeed, José Vasconcelos conceived of his own framework of mestizaje as a direct response to US imperialism's own global expansionist efforts, wherein the Louisiana Purchase and the subsequent acquisition of the previously Mexican territories of the Southwest ensured an accumulation of wealth without which "no hubieran logrado adueñarse del Pacífico" (they wouldn't have taken over the Pacific).[79] Because Mexican philosopher and state builder Vasconcelos was so global in his account of mestizaje, I in turn seek a similarly expansive account that would contextualize epistemic flashpoints of mestizaje and its various meanings in concert with wildly divergent geographic arenas—specifically, the mestizo nation of the Philippines that was acquired by the United States when "se adueñó del Pacífico" (it overtook the Pacific), as Vasconcelos has observed.[80]

The first two chapters of Crip Colony seek to understand Philippine mestizaje within such global framings as Hispano-Philippine culture collides with US imperial statecraft. In chapter 1, "Benevolent Rehabilitation and the Colonial Bodymind: Filipinx American Studies as Disability Studies," I resituate the US colonial discourse of benevolent assimilation within disability analysis. By cripping this particular genealogy, I argue that

Filipinx American studies has, in all but name, propounded its own deep understanding of the mutual constitution of race and disability in its deconstruction of the supposedly "benevolent" empire of the United States. Filipinx Americanists have already critiqued the ways that benevolent assimilation assumed and imposed colonial subjects' incapacity for self-rule. I suggest that this was rooted in a belief in the native's cognitive incapacity for robust and full-fledged sovereignty. Therefore, benevolent assimilation was implicitly designed to rehabilitate the native in order that they acquire the capacities that they sorely lacked. To home in on the colonial disability discourse of US imperialism, I dub this form of assimilation arguably more accurately as *benevolent rehabilitation*. The intervention of this chapter is a historiographical and genealogical expansion of Filipinx American studies to contemplate its already prodigious consideration of disability while also insisting on a fuller embrace of some of disability studies' foundational theories. Additionally, I suggest that disability studies more intentionally consider the Philippines and Filipinx America, which have been foundational case studies precipitating American studies' moves to think about US history and culture as the historical formation of an empire.

As we'll see in chapter 2, "Mad María Clara: The Bastard Aesthetics of Mestizaje and Compulsory Able-Mindedness," similar difficult entrenchments are likewise advanced in canonical Philippine renditions of mestizo thought in the writing of José Rizal. Departing from Mexico's centrality in terms of the meanings and prominent conditions through which mestizaje as a philosophical discourse materializes, I seek to analyze Filipino recursions of it in Rizal's canonical novel *Noli me tángere* (Touch me not, 1886). I suggest that colonial society in the Philippines was ineradicably structured through a "compulsory able-mindedness," drawing on the theory of "compulsory able-bodiedness" suggested by crip theorist Robert McRuer. I argue that the literary aesthetics of mestizaje bring together the institutions of heterosexual marriage, nationalist patriotism, and disability in order to establish that full national status as a citizen-subject turned on a heteronormative identity that spurned or rehabilitated cognitive debility. I suggest that Rizal's famed and hapless heroine, María Clara, the paramour of the patriot protagonist Crisóstomo Ibarra, runs afoul of dutiful patriotic Filipina femininity. While Ibarra is the architect of revolution, the mestiza María Clara ends the novel having gone insane, wailing skyward for a nation that must forsake her. While this chapter's arguments might seem counterintuitive to this book's claim that mestizaje marks out subjects that are rehabilitated and thus able-minded agents of colonial violence, this process was not invariable. Variations of it exist when we are attentive to gender and think feminism and queer critique alongside mestizaje's domestication of the colonial bodymind.

In chapter 3, "Filipino Itineraries, Orientalizing Impairments: Chinese Foot-Binding and the Crip Coloniality of Travel Literature," I return to the question of mestizaje's relationship with China. Perhaps surprisingly, similar notions of Vasconcelos's "Oriental" degeneracy exist in Filipino interpretations of mestizaje despite the Philippines' location in Asia. The chapter argues for a reading method that critiques colonial travel narration as a genre that discursively proliferates itself through what I call a "normate imperial eye/I." I align crip theory and postcolonial criticism to mount a critique of the often-studied colonial genre of travel literature. Teodoro Kalaw's Spanish-language travel narrative *Hacia la tierra del zar* (Toward the land of the czar, 1908) advances Philippine national interests at the intersection of competing imperial projects—the Japanese in Taiwan, Czarist Russia in Manchuria, and the United States in the Philippines. Kalaw morally reforms Philippine modernity through the deformation of the Chinese female body and its bound feet, demonstrating how the Filipino mestizo intellectual, or *ilustrado*, participates in the complex systematic normalization of the able-bodied subject as invisible/benevolent translator of space, place, and other bodies. In so doing, I establish that the mestizo writer actually demonstrates that he is the benevolently assimilated Americanized Filipino—the Hispanic mestizo product of US benevolent rehabilitation advancing its imperial aims throughout a disabled Asia from which he is ontologically and corporeally distinct.

In chapter 4, "A Colonial Model of Disability: Running Amok in the Mad Colonial Archive of the Philippines," I examine the ways that US settler colonialism and its transpacific migration indelibly shaped the administrative colonialism of the Philippine archipelago. I examine archival evidence of the curious case of Indigenous Muslim, or "Moro," Filipinos who, in dozens of cases in the late 1920s and early 1930s, would "run amok" on a vengeful killing spree, typically with a machete, that lasted until they were killed by Philippine Constabulary officers trained by the United States. Philippine and US colonial officials characterized these cases as acute states of madness in which uncivilized Filipinos went insane, even though these same officials connected such incidents to a premeditated religious rite targeting sworn enemies. It was theorized that this racialized form of madness particular to the "Malay race" was the result of an illiberal religious worldview, the pagan practice of slavery, and, significantly, the custom of plural marriage or polygamy. These cases of "mad" Filipino Indians running amok became a litmus test for potential Philippine independence provisionally granted in the 1934 Tydings-McDuffie Act. If civilized Filipinos couldn't handle their own Indians like the United States did, it was reasoned, then they were not ready to join the civilized nations of the world as a truly independent nation. The chapter demonstrates that the introduction of benevolent rehabilitation earlier in the twentieth century would recur in civilized Filipino police management of "uncivilized" Indigenous Filipinos decades later.

All of these case studies demonstrate the ways in which ideologies of ability ramify through and as racial discourses that anchor the liberal promise of sovereign ability to the liberal product of the uplifted racially mixed body. Because different racialized bodies have been shown to have differential abilities ascribed to them, there is sound reason to think through mestizaje as itself an ideology of ability navigating the pressures of colonial reality. What I observe in all is an unerring faith in the rehabilitative powers of racial mixture and the intellectual prowess of the mestizo class in championing the liberal cause of self-determination. Through engagement of prominent and emblematic examples of Filipino cultural and intellectual thought, I show that mestizo politics in the Philippines propagated mestizaje itself as a colonial discourse of the rehabilitation of the colonial body and mind of the native and thus participated in an (anti)colonial politics of disability. In short, what would it mean to examine mestizaje as a racialized colonial "ideology of ability"?[81]

One

Benevolent Rehabilitation and the Colonial Bodymind

FILIPINX AMERICAN STUDIES AS DISABILITY STUDIES

Filipinx American studies has, in all but name, propounded its own critique of the ways that ability and racialization condition imperial logic.[1] Central (though perhaps surreptitiously so) to Filipinx American criticism is a profound engagement with the dialectic between race and disability. The development of Filipinx thought, I argue, emerges significantly out of an insistent interrogation of colonial ableist logics inherent to the historical discourse of "benevolent assimilation," which justified US colonial occupation of the Philippines in the name of liberal democratic values that Filipinos were ostensibly unable to embody. At base, I argue in this chapter that the confluence of political constructions of Filipinos' mental fitness for self-government and the campaign of US imperial war in the Philippines is evidence that the US colonial project was a structural and colonial imposition of disablement. This colonial disablement revolved simultaneously on both the destructive proliferation of genocidal warfare and an ableist ideology that annulled political sovereignty and the perceived capacity for independent thought.

By uncovering this underrecognized disability genealogy, I seek to push it further to consider the ways that the intersection of disability and Indigeneity have conditioned Filipinx colonial racial formations. Toward this end, this chapter has a deliberately promiscuous archive that is born from the transitionary colonial periods shaping the Philippines' historical experience of race and its connection to disability. I find inspiration in queer diaspora theorist Gayatri Gopinath, who advances a queer cultural studies reading practice that she denotes as a "scavenger methodology" to read presumably heteronormative texts against their grain via the lens of a queer subject whose relationship to national heteronormativity is qualitatively and perspectively different.[2] In a similar manner, I advance a *crip colonial critique* against the grain of the colonial logics of imperialism through a similarly diverse archive, including the poetry of Rudyard Kipling; a political cartoon, "School Begins"; President William McKinley's 1898 executive order on benevolent assimilation; and José Rizal's 1891 political essay *Filipinas dentro de cien años*. I have elected to stage the critique and archive in this multifarious manner partially to reflect on the fact that empire consolidates its power in an interdisciplinary fashion without regard for the borders placed between genre and discourse.[3] The visual, the textual, and the discursive work conjunctively to sediment the global reach of colonial ableism. It's my hope that my framing of Filipinx critique as vitiations of colonial "benevolent rehabilitation" will inspire and advance further granular analysis across many disciplines and archives that connects imperial violence against the Filipinx body with the colonial abrogation of the perceived capacity for independent thought and autonomy.

This confluence, or intersection, of the mind and body obtains as a useful unit of analysis of crip colonial critique that is most aptly identified, I suggest, as a "colonial bodymind."[4] As far as Filipinx thought is concerned, this colonial bodymind is an emergent critical heuristic that advances intellectual and cultural production deconstructing colonial violence while also centering Filipinx embodiment as the racialized product of innumerable physical and epistemic wounds. In sum, classifying the racial body as primitive, incapable, and dependent predisposes it to physical harms, in part functionalized by the assumption of its cognitive deficiency to participate in democratic political arrangements. This intersection is the colonial bodymind. The field of Filipinx American studies has shown the ways that the dispossession of autonomy and political determination as mental attributes of democratic subjects are coconstituted by regimes of imperial war and violence that would predispose the colonial body to harm, injury, and impairment. One political reality affecting the mind cannot truly be separated from those that affect the racialized body.

A crip colonial critique of benevolent assimilation locates an emergent racialized colonial genealogy of ability that I capture via the tongue-in-cheek term *benevolent rehabilitation*—reading intentionally against the false promise of assimilation.[5] Such a move is meant to demonstrate the ways that Filipinx

American studies participates in disability studies *as an emergent form of crip of color theory* though it is never explicitly named as such. Because this field is animated by a disidentification with the turn of the twentieth-century progressivist discourse of benevolent assimilation, it runs contrary to the colonial presumption and imposition of incapacity. Filipinx postcolonialism is itself a genealogy of crip analysis, which aids us in partially historicizing the social and colonial construction of cognition itself. One of the main claims that I seek to advance through the case study of benevolent assimilation–cum–rehabilitation is that cognition is not merely a biological reality inherent to the human but instead is a historical and social phenomenon that we produce and continue to reproduce. Moreover, the lion's share of its discursive and aesthetic construction obtains in colonialism.

Through visual and discursive analysis, I pivot from the US colonial discourse of benevolent assimilation to José Rizal's *Filipinas dentro de cien años*, which preceded its invocation. This essay is widely considered a centerpiece of the mestizo enlightenment of the Philippines. In his sociopolitical analysis, Rizal attempts to wrestle with the Philippines' future political prospects given that the nation is in the crosshairs of multiple colonial powers. This essay, sometimes translated as "The Philippines, a Century Hence," is notable for its predictive, even prophetic, observations on US imperial power at the turn of the twentieth century in addition to its biting criticism of Spanish colonialism. The essay, despite being written in Spanish, is a welcome and necessary addition to the archive of Filipinx Americanist criticism of US imperialism as a "benevolent" reform of the hapless native. The discourse of benevolent assimilation is drawn most notably, for the purposes of this chapter, from President McKinley's executive order on the topic as a way to frame colonialism through an affect of friendship and tutelary support for the new Philippine nation. Less than a decade prior to the presidential announcement of this colonial "friendship," Rizal is particularly concerned with growing US interest in foreign conquest and is keenly aware that US eyes are set on the Pacific region. Rizal's essay puts forward the Filipino mestizo class as the avant-garde of anticolonial thought positioning the mestizos as, what he calls, "el cerebro de la nación" (the brain of the nation).[6] Placing this text in conversation with benevolent assimilation clearly demonstrates a counterindication to the ways that US imperialism ethnologically entrapped Filipinos into the debilitated state of the disabled Indian. This is a state that, Rizal argues, Philippine society has and from which it should advance, unfortunately reifying the settler presumptions inherent to colonial ableism.

Yet because of the politics of racial mixture that is inflected in Rizal's essay, I am compelled first to turn to the visual grammars of rehabilitation and capacitation. This visual turn allows a productive and necessary rapprochement of Philippine *mestizaje* (racial admixture, miscegenation) vis-à-vis US multicultural racial formations domestically and in the Pacific. For this task *Puck* magazine's iconic cartoon "School Begins" (1899) visually concretizes the colonial disability logics of rehabilitation as an emergent property not only in the colonization of the Philippines but also in direct conversation with domestic racial formations of anti-Blackness, settler colonialism, and anti-Chinese racial animus presaging similar multifarious racial formations that would appear in José Vasconcelos's *La raza cósmica* (The cosmic race), which I analyzed briefly in the introduction. In so doing, we can establish that the eugenic etiologies of mestizaje have a global reach. Indeed, as I will demonstrate in this chapter, Rizal's essay mortgages Philippine independence on and through a logic that iterates what Saidiya Hartman has called the "afterlives of slavery."[7] For a colonial context that leverages reform, rehabilitation, and the presumed mental deficiencies of the colonized, the visual allegory in "School Begins" of US empire as a classroom is apt. Rizal's attention to US foreign policy and emergent status as a global power, I suggest, necessitates a thorough meditation on the domestic US racial formations that inform its colonial apparatus abroad and with which Rizal contends.

"School Begins": The Queer Aesthetics of Racialized Disability

In this section, I attempt to render more concrete the physical differentiation and racial hierarchies implicit in mestizaje and multiracial formations rooted in perceptions of capacity. The field of Filipinx American studies, in its critique of US imperialism, grapples with the historical reality that the Philippines entered the American racial imaginary as a consequence of the colonization of the US Southwest and at the same time that territories in the Hispanic Caribbean were acquired. Such a diffuse global encounter with race renders a complex portrait of racialization whose convergences and divergences lend themselves well to the analytical moves endemic to mestizaje. I'd like to take Alicia Arizzón's contribution toward queering mestizaje further to consider how a transpacific encounter between the borderlands and the Philippines is a cultural landscape where the meanings of race mixing have embedded political aims into ideals of human capacity

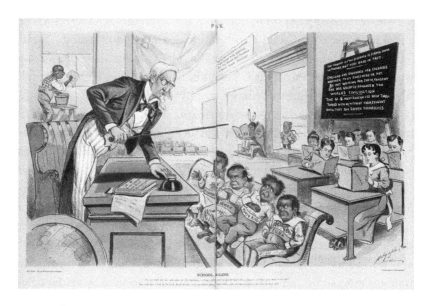

FIG. 1.1. Illustrator Louis Dalrymple's "School Begins," a *Puck* magazine political cartoon from 1899. The illustration depicts the project of US empire as a classroom setting; Uncle Sam is a towering figure at the head of the class, teaching new "students" from (left to right) the Philippines, Hawaii, Puerto Rico, and Cuba, who are depicted as children. "'School Begins' in Large Format." Accessed June 21, 2022. https://peter schmidt.domains.swarthmore.edu/school-begins-lg.htm. Dalrymple, Louis. "School Begins." Still image, 18990125. https://www.loc.gov/pictures/item/2012647459/.

as they were constructed and shaped in US imperialism.[8] To clarify these abstractions, the pedagogical image in "School Begins," a satirical political cartoon published in the humorist magazine *Puck* in 1899, not only stages an encounter between the Hispanic Caribbean and the Philippines but also shows US domestic racial formations furnishing a portrait of American ability whose consolidation coincides with the acquisition of colonial territory.[9] Similar visual tropes of race, colonialism, and the doubt cast on the ability of the colonized to govern themselves are live ideas in many colonial images produced during the advent of US imperialism in the late nineteenth and early twentieth centuries.[10]

The turn of the twentieth century saw the visual representation of empire produced in thousands of highly graphic political cartoons whose level of detail and quality are unparalleled in the contemporary moment. Scholars such as Alfred McCoy, Victor Román Mendoza, and Alfredo Roces, as well as artist Ellen Sebring, have all contributed analysis on the ways that such images gave a visual grammar to racialization through images whose circulation did considerable work in inculcating and diffusing a racial imaginary with impressive global reach.[11] Mendoza has done pioneering work analyzing the ways that US ideas of Blackness were a filter through which the visual rhetoric of empire shaped the understanding of the Filipino body, thus attesting to the transnational interchange between US racial forms and their "exportation" to the Philippines. McCoy and Roces have foundationally looked at the ways that cartoonists in the Philippines attempted to visually represent racial unity and provided a visual archive that demonstrates the ways that Filipinos navigated US imperialism by fighting for a free Filipino press.[12] Despite this very important local focus, in a similar transnational ethos to Mendoza, I turn toward the ways in which the United States attempted to make sense of Filipino racial embodiment as it worked to incorporate its new custodial population. Such incorporation was marked by domestic racial formations informed by settler colonialism, Jim Crow, and anti-Chinese animus and thereby shaped the ways that US tutelary imperialism apprehended the "native" embodiment and cognitive capacity of Filipinos.

The punitive imposition of Uncle Sam at the head of the classroom provides clues to fleshing out the cognitive hierarchy at play. Providing useful historical context, Sebring has noted that much of the inspiration of such images pivoted on a conciliation between England and the United States, both of which saw a reinvigorated international political relationship through their common commitment to the colonial project. Given this background, it is chilling to observe the ways that US benevolent assimilation manifested through and alongside Rudyard Kipling's colonial poem "The White Man's Burden," which encouraged the United States in its colonization of the Philippines by poetically entrenching problematic assumptions of the ability of the native. With striking eugenic flourish, Kipling encourages the United States to

> Take up the White Man's Burden—
> Send forth the best ye breed—
> Go bind your sons to exile
> To serve your captives' need;
> To wait in heavy harness,
> On fluttered folk and wild—
> Your new-caught, sullen peoples,
> Half-devil, half-child.[13]

The "half-devil, half-child" is evocatively on display in the front bench at the center of "School Begins," presumably at the start of the class whose lesson is self-government. The white man's burden is at least partially an educative one, to serve their "captives' need" to be brought up by the "best [the empire] breed[s]."

Considered intertextually with Kipling's estimation of Filipinos as devil children, I suggest that "School Begins" is a particularly iconic representation of colonial ableism. The disabilities of the colonized partially inform the colonizer's "burden" to expand and extend the "blessings of 'civilization and progress' to barbaric non-Western, non-Christian, non-white peoples" through which the "Indigenous man will be brought out of ignorance through the inescapable march of progress in the form of Western civilization."[14] The trope of the "half-devil, half-child" does not immediately or intuitively connote disability; yet, intertextually connected to "School Begins," we see that this "devil child" is one that requires rehabilitative tutelage so that it does not remain a disabled Indian. To wit, this image from *Puck* stages an evolutionary and didactic portrait whose racial and ableist logics demonstrate, to use the framing of Lisa Lowe, the liberal-colonial intimacies between the borderlands, the Atlantic, the Caribbean, and the Pacific.[15]

"School Begins" sardonically illustrates many of the same discourses of normality of interest in disability scholarship by presenting racial types in an American progression of human development. In the right of the image, at the back of the classroom, we observe the assimilated mostly whitened United States, depicted as Anglo, though most are probably white Mexican students (mestizos); they have achieved the aims of US colonial reeducation that, in turn, are visually shaped by evolutionary logics of human development. I speculate that some of these star students might be white Mexicans because they are representations of states in the US Southwest—from left to right, Texas, Arizona, California, and New Mexico. Given that these were previously part of Mexican territory acquired by the United States following the Mexican-American War (1846–48) and the Treaty of Guadalupe Hidalgo (1848), these states' personification as upright, studious, and white speaks to the ways in which the Spanish colonial reflects within the US racial state in the production of novel comparative racial meanings. To prove their modernity and civilization, mestizos chose to be white. That is, historically many mestizo Mexicans did choose whiteness when they found themselves in US territory operating under the rules of a different racial state: many previously Mexican nationals and mestizos marked themselves as white in order to maintain their properties, as only whites could be landowners at the time.[16] These racial histories and shifts pivot around the question of the disabled Indian as a foil on which the prospect of statehood represents a rehabilitated political and racial status. Such a status revolves around the implied capacities required to be a property owner and a proper steward of land. In the same row, on the far left, next to Arizona, is Alaska—represented, curiously, as a darker-skinned and perhaps Indigenous girl. Her studiousness and uncommon focus foreshadow the front of the class seated on the bench, those "intermediary" new racial subjects recently "acquired" by US empire. It remains to be seen if they will move (up) to the back of the class to be a white borderlands subject or be relegated to the status of abject racial failure, which constitutes those figures in the image's background.

The background of the image depicts a Jim-Crowified African American laborer, a North American Indian, and a Chinese "coolie" laborer as defective human types that are stuck in an evolutionary past and deficient intellectual state from which even US colonial education's ability to free them is specious. Because of their relationship to American capital and labor, all are visual citations of US racial capitalism whose logic renders them empty embodiments, and therefore idiotic and unintelligent in the context of the classroom; they are not students—or, at least, in the case of the Indian, not good students. Yet their bodily labors can still be exploited within the context of the colonial reeducation of the United States' new custodial populations of (from left to right in the foreground) the Philippines, Hawaii, Porto [Puerto] Rico, and Cuba. The Black body labors in the classroom cleaning the windows. The Chinese coolie outside the doorway, marked perversely by his queue, is a potentially queer contaminant that must be segregated from the space of the classroom—a clear allusion to the Chinese Exclusion Act of 1882.[17] And the North American Indian, who stupidly holds his book upside down, represents an intriguing connection between how societies imperially expand through a logic of industrial rehabilitation. Though it is notable that the rendering of the upside-down book is erroneous; if it were to be turned right side up, the cover would read "C B A." It's unclear if this is just an artistic oversight or if it is part of the image's visual critique of the erroneous and "backward" content that is meant to be conveyed to the Indian, perhaps signaling a colonial education that is meant to fail.[18]

The Indian, seated by the door frame through which the coolie is visible outside, indisputably occupies the role of the classroom dunce, but instead of the dunce cap this figure wears a feathered headdress—a head covering that clearly marks his masculinity in opposition to the more feminized "Indians" in the center of the image (more on that later). According to the

Oxford English Dictionary Online, and as many are well familiar, the dunce cap or dunce's cap (the latter in British English) is "a tall, cone-shaped paper hat formerly put on the head of a schoolchild who made too many mistakes in his or her work or misbehaved in a minor way, as a punishment or a sign of disgrace." Other extended uses of the term include reference to "a person who is slow at learning or of low intelligence; a stupid, dim-witted person; an idiot."[19] Rather than refer to stupidity and cognitive delay in a general sense, "School Begins" explicitly racializes the dunce, who continues to fail the test of civilization and is thus placed on a "time-out" as newer, similarly Indigenized, subjects enter the class—new subjects of empire that are central in the image and prospectively ushered into a different temporality of modernity.

Writing on the ways that the framework of the politics of recognition reifies colonial state power, Indigenous theorist Glen Coulthard has remarked on the ways that such ostensibly equitable mutual recognition "in its contemporary liberal form" between the settler colonial state and First Nations governments militates against native self-determination by prioritizing assimilation into the settler state.[20] For Coulthard, the colonial residential schooling system was one of—though not exclusively—the most important and damaging technologies of such forced assimilation. The "School Begins" classroom resonates with these settler colonial educative directives in a US imperial context that foregrounds the benevolent assimilation of new colonial territories at the turn of the twentieth century. Indeed, the presence of the Indian dunce links the status of stupidity and colonial reeducation to a broader settler colonial ideology of Indigenous reeducation emblematized for many by the Carlisle Indian Industrial School, which was in operation in Pennsylvania from 1879 to 1918.[21] Not unlike civilizational logics of mestizaje beginning with the Spanish colonial period wherein the Indian was civilizable, the establishment of places like the Carlisle School was rooted in the belief that the North American Indian could be rehabilitated into the cultural mores of Western civilization. Rooted in American progressivist ideals of human perfectibility and liberal progress, from which benevolent assimilation derived its own origins, the Indian would be reshaped, hollowed out of their culture, and integrated into American society as an industrious (concordant with the school's naming) productive laborer. Here the violent extraction of culture is a capitalist tactic of value extraction. Such extractive politics speak to the ultimate objective of benevolent rehabilitation. "School Begins" sardonically visualizes the dubious results and expectations of the intelligence of the subjects of such education programs. At the turn of the United States' imperial century, the new *indios* (Cubans, Filipinos, Hawaiians, and Puerto Ricans) are represented as the incoming class that is visually placed within a settler regime of colonial reeducation whereby America's ability to truly uplift the native would allow an opportunity to reshape expectations for Indigenous intellect. Nevertheless, it is crucial to engage with the ways these racial hierarchies of intelligence are mapped through deviant genders and sexualities.

The suspicion of the native children's deficient intellectual abilities is registered through their relative femininity and queerness. As I have mentioned, in the cartoon we see in the back of the classroom the personages that embody the US Southwest—the dutiful white or fair-complexioned mestizo students are assiduously studying the art of civilization. We know the contents of their studies. On Uncle Sam's desk is a textbook whose title reads "US First Lessons in Self-Government." The fastidiousness through which we gauge their scholarly focus and, consequently, the relative success they have achieved as self-governing subjects, is demarcated through normative racial, sexual, and gendered cues. They are respectably and conservatively dressed, with clean coiffures. Significantly, this is the only space in the imperial classroom that is clearly coeducational, following normative markers of Western American masculinity and femininity. The normative racial-gendered demarcations of the bodies of these whitened mestizos correspond to the geographic demarcations of an expanding empire. The annexation of new territories, and their evolution into statehood for some, signals success in the craft of self-government clearly marked by their assimilation of respectable racial and gendered identities. Strong intellectual prowess is partially a function of the performance of normative gender and sexuality.

We can track the ways that nonnormative gender and sexuality align as a technology of colonial ableism particularly by comparing the racialized Indigeneities of the Philippines and Hawaii as they are presented on the bench, conveniently right next to one another. The Filipino character in the cartoon, in pink and with a particularly sour countenance, strongly resembles General Emilio Aguinaldo, an *insurrecto* dissident who countered orderly colonial society. He was the leader of the Philippine independence forces against the United States after they unlawfully annexed the archipelago following the Spanish-American War. *Insurrection* was a term that was widely used by the US colonial forces in order to delegitimize the Philippines' sovereign anticolonial movement for independence in such a way that disenfranchised Filipinos of the ability for self-rule, thus necessitating their tutelage. Aguinaldo was also represented in an 1899 cartoon in *Judge* magazine as a female pickaninny, drawing on US domestic tropes of Black racialization and dehumanization.

Judge

OUR NEW TOPSY.

Topsy (Aguinaldo)—"I's so awful wicked there cain't nobody do nothin' with me. I keeps Miss (Sam) a-swearin' at me oalf de time, 'cause I's mighty wicked, I is."

FIG. 1.2. Illustrator Victor Gillam's "Our New Topsy," an 1899 political cartoon from *Judge* magazine, which depicts Uncle Sam as a maternal figure in a dress (left) and General Emilio Aguinaldo, the leader of the Philippine independence forces (right). Aguinaldo is depicted in a familiar Jim Crow artistic style fashioned after the "pickaninny." NYPL Digital Collections. "Our New Topsy." Accessed June 21, 2022. https://digitalcollections.nypl.org/items/510d47e0-fb90-a3d9-e040-e00a18064a99.

The deviant sexuality of the Filipino body and the civilization of the Filipino mind are both understood via visual racial scripts through which US Blackness at the time was constructed, further corroborating the fluid and dynamic interaction of racial formations evoked in "School Begins." Indeed, Jim Crow visual grammars of race are one mode through which we can understand the condescending racist depictions of Cuba, Hawaii, the Philippines, and Puerto Rico in the US imperial classroom. Kanaka Maoli political theorist Noenoe K. Silva has convincingly analyzed the ways that media representation of Filipinos and Hawaiians, during the late nineteenth-century conflicts of the colonial coup of Hawaii and the Philippine-American War, were "rooted in American racism against Africans, and used to justify the continued subjugation of African Americans in the post–Civil War period."[22] Silva's analysis is particularly noteworthy here because right next to Aguinaldo in "School Begins" is likely a representation of Queen Lili`uokalani, the rightful sovereign of the Hawaiian people who was deposed in January 1893, just three years before the start of the Philippine independence movement against Spain. We can note the ways in which both Aguinaldo's and Lili`uokalani's gendered representations deviate vastly from the back of the class of whitened Mexicans. Silva has noted how "the black stereotype of the 'pickanniny,' notably in the drawing of frizzy hair and the use of the exaggerated contrast in color between the dark skin and white eyes," is part of a visual grammar of racist representation that advanced not only segregation but also settler colonialist expropriations of native Hawaiian lands and imperial annexation of the Philippine archipelago.[23] "School Begins" is not exceptional in this regard, making evident the ways that a whole inventory of racist anti-Black signifiers recursively appear in the representation of the Indigeneity and thus the disqualification of sovereignty of the new class of US empire, marked here, curiously, by a queer infantilization. In essence, Aguinaldo and Lili`uokalani, as well as the characters representing Puerto Rico and Cuba, are "foolish, children . . . from a savage and cannibal 'race.'"[24] Despite Lili`uokalani's well-documented resistance to occupation, actually *following* the precepts of Western international law to stage her complaints as a competent and worthy sovereign, she was subjected to "detailed representation[s] of [herself] as childlike, incompetent, desirous of tyrannical power, and violently vengeful."[25]

To wit, the caption of "School Begins" reads: "Uncle Sam (*to his new class in Civilization*)—Now, children, you've got to learn these lessons whether you want to or not! But just take a look at the class ahead of you, and remember that, in a little while, you will feel as glad to be here as they are!" All this is to say that the borderlands of the United States, what was once the fringe of the normative center of US power, receives high marks. Nestled under the textbook on self-government is the immediate concern in the developmentalist pedagogy elaborated in "school": sheets of paper hang out with the words "The New Class: Philippines Cuba Hawaii Porto Rico." It is safe to say that these new students, these new *indios* of American expansion at the turn of the twentieth century, do not adequately conform sartorially nor racially to the standard set by their more advanced heteronormative classmates. This marks their Indigeneity differentially from the other *indios* present in the image. The complex interplay and mixtures of races evoked in the school delineates ability itself as a property of whiteness—a by-product of colonial expansion and incorporation. Disability is a form of racialized distribution of vulnerability projected into racial forms whose capacities are demarcated partly as a function of their colonial racialization and deviation from heterosexuality. The mixture of races and gestures toward assimilation and incorporation are of great interest in the effort to offer a diverse genealogy of racialized ability through the frame of mestizaje.

To crip mestizaje in this constellation of texts means understanding the limitations of mixed race as a framework, particularly when working with an archive that reflects on US transatlantic and transpacific expansion into spaces in which the idea of the Indian and the mestizo obtain differently. That is to say, mestizaje as a racial discourse in the Hispanic Caribbean is not collapsible into or equivalent with similar ideologies of mixture in the Philippines or the US borderlands—all territories portrayed in "School Begins." Nevertheless, racial mixture as it is evoked in mestizaje opens up different questions for comparison that would not be entertained in the monolithic referent *Asian*—or *Asian American*, for that matter. Far-flung places are connected under the tentacular expansions of US empire building and, indeed, their visualization in "School Begins" adumbrates the scopic capture of psychophysical variation along a eugenic and ethnological racial spectrum. Embedded in the image, and the ideology of benevolence that informs US imperialism, is an evolutionary developmentalist schema that frames the liberal progress narrative central to modernity. Notions of sovereignty, autonomy, and self-determination are bound up within a developmentalist timeline wherein those that have inherited and internalized the political subjectivity of liberalism can in turn rehabilitate those they have deemed as worthy inheritors of such enlightened patrimony.[26] This turn—of the rehabilitated becoming rehabilitators—is one of the hallmark functions of benevolent rehabilitation, which I analyze here, but also in greater depth in chapter 4. The charity discourses that have shaped disability welfare have a very striking linkage to ethnoeugenic discourses of rehabilitation central to imperial benevolence. Largesse manifests as a political phenomenon in colonial logics, wherein to rehabilitate an "idiot savage" takes on peculiar importance to consolidating a robust articulation of American ability. This ability, nevertheless, is bound up with colonial capitalism.

What is productive about "School Begins" is the difference that it brings to discussions of mestizaje as simultaneously a pivot point around which disability is measured and as a crip analytic in itself. While mestizo nations like Mexico or Uruguay historically have had discourses that promote abstract national unity through biological racial mixture, the racial diversity of the United States, by contrast, has historically been marked by a pronounced racial segregation that is at odds with the "cosmic" racial unities that characterize many Latin American nations. Because of the immense anxiety to protect Anglo-Saxonism from degeneration, the purpose of the race sciences, eugenics, and ethnology was to hierarchize racial difference into discrete categories in order to preserve their separation. And yet they are also all mixed together in the imperial classroom, implying that one raced group could blend into or evolve into another, ostensibly achieving whiteness. There is no one racialized figure around whom the discursive and disabling technologies of empire exclusively circulate. The disabled Indian with his book upside down, the queer coolie laborer banished from the classroom, the Black laborer furtively looking toward the center of the class where Uncle Sam disciplines the new colonized students whose racial embodiments appear to be the summative patchwork of colonial projects that have laid siege to the class's failures: settler colonialism, echoes of enslavement, Chinese labor exploitation, and the conquest of the borderlands inform the United States' imperial advance and the ways in which it apprehends the racial, cognitive, and physical capacities of its new populations. Despite the multifarious racial conditions emblematized in the first US class on civilization, it's clear that it gestures toward progress. To be sure, atavism as an evolutionary concept was "intimately connected to the western notion of progress."[27] Such progressive narratives deployed disability in order to constitute racial difference. Disability historian Douglass Baynton corroborates the often underexamined mutual constitution of disability and race:

> By the mid-nineteenth century, nonwhite races were routinely connected to people with disabilities, both of whom were depicted as evolutionary laggards or throwbacks. As a consequence, the concept of

disability, intertwined with the concept of race was also caught up in ideas of evolutionary progress. Physical or mental abnormalities were commonly depicted as instances of atavism, reversions to earlier stages of evolutionary development. Down's syndrome, for example, was called Mongolism by the doctor who first identified it in 1866 because he believed the syndrome to be the result of a biological reversion of Caucasians to the Mongol racial type.[28]

The result is that ethnological racial "types" emerged via attributions of impairment of ability in order to render commonplace, for instance, the notion that "African Americans lacked sufficient intelligence to participate or compete on an equal basis in society with white Americans."[29] This is clearly depicted in "School Begins" with the caricaturized representation of the African American working to keep the classroom clean. He is in the classroom, but he is not subjected to or worthy of the colonial reeducation that US empire promises. The cartoon is just as much about the juridico-political separation of Black people from white people inaugurated by the US Supreme Court case *Plessy v. Ferguson* (1896) as it is about the consolidation of a US imperial identity following the Spanish-American War (1898). Jim Crow violence amends and elucidates the meanings of anthropological race in and around the Hispanic Caribbean and the Pacific.[30] The corporeal difference of the racialized body assembled a panoply of racial scientific discourses that measured human psychophysical capacities whose variations are knowable partly because of the debilitated Black bodymind. I suggest that we see a visual snapshot of such psychophysical anthropometrics represented in the colonial classroom in which colonial logics of imperial capitalist expansion are rendered rehabilitative—yet some candidates for colonial capacitation are not always successful.

Central to the visual cultures of eugenic anthropometry as demonstrated by a superior Uncle Sam looming over infantilized defective "natives" is the laboring body. The supposedly "industrial Indian" sets the landscape for the ways that settler colonial ideologies of Indigenous savagery in the US transpacific context are convoked in the multiracial imaginaries of an American empire trying to make sense of race. For instance, are Filipinos "Asian," like the coolie? Are they Hispanic, like the Cubans and Puerto Ricans? Or are they Indigenous, like the Hawaiians or the Indian? And yet US transpacific expansion relied on a biopolitical and eugenic statisticalization wherein the labor and the coherence of the bodies that perform it simultaneously draw on disability tropes of disqualification that differentially (yet universally) affected Asian, Black, and Indigenous bodies. US empire naturalizes divisions of racialized labor via an economy of debility that asymmetrically orders different peoples' ability to inhabit the abstraction we call cognition, which indexes the practical reasoning required to self-govern. The multifarious racial histories indexed in the imperial classroom demonstrate domestic US reckoning with race as it expanded abroad but also beg for a contextualization of race and ability within a global framework. Part of that project involves giving greater context to the US imperial discourse of benevolent assimilation.

Benevolent Rehabilitation and the Colonial Bodymind

The visualization of cognition in "School Begins" integrates conceptions of relational racialized embodiment, territorial acquisition, hyperexploitation of labor, and eugenic configurations of intelligence. These conceptions are coordinates on a map whose orientations are plotted by US benevolent assimilation. In this section, I shift the scavenger archive of colonial ableism from the poetic and visual to the discursive. President McKinley's declaration of benevolent assimilation was predicated on an assumption of the Filipino's incapacity for autonomous self-rule. While the deconstruction of the "benevolent" empire of the United States does not, in any way, completely exhaust or explain Filipinx American studies' interventions, benevolent assimilation remains an enduring colonial reality for the field. As I established in the introduction, US imperialism trafficked in a persistent assumption of native inability, excluding natives from robust sovereignty. The ability to participate and author political arrangements and social contracts as a sovereign subject produced the mind of American racial ability through a deficient Filipinx body. The Filipinx colonial bodymind then becomes the evidence of colonial disability—deemed too irrational and lacking the cognitive capacity to be a robust political subject. Such moves have antecedents in US settler colonialism's braiding of the transpacific project of US imperial expansion with the dispossession of Indigenous peoples in North America. Unfurling this disability logic of empire reorients Filipinx American studies to reassess its own already prodigious contributions to global disability histories.

Benevolent assimilation was tantamount to a public relations campaign famously declared in an executive order that then president William McKinley issued after the United States' victory over Spain in 1898. Following an extraordinarily quick victory over the Spanish Empire for control of its last colonies, the proimperialist presidency was almost equally quick to unequivocally argue that the US annexation of these territories (Cuba, Guam, the Philippines, and Puerto Rico) would be unlike the violent colonialism of European powers. US rule in the Philippines was decidedly not another colonial epoch of Philippine history. Rather, it was a moment of progress for both the development of the Filipino people and the consecration of a world power indexed by its self-declared beneficence. Worth quoting at length, McKinley's executive order (often referred to as the Benevolent Assimilation Proclamation) makes US intentions clear—that we come in peace and as friends:

> With the signature of the treaty of peace between the United States and Spain by their respective plenipotentiaries at Paris on the 10th instant, and as a result of the victories of American arms, the future control, disposition, and government of the Philippine Islands are ceded to the United States. In the fulfillment of the rights of sovereignty thus acquired and the responsible obligations of government thus assumed, the actual occupation and administration of the entire group of the Philippine Islands becomes immediately necessary, and the military government heretofore maintained by the united states in the city, harbor, and bay of Manila is to be extended with all possible dispatch to the whole of the ceded territory.
>
> In performing this duty the military commander of the United States is enjoined to make known to the inhabitants of the Philippine Islands that in succeeding to the sovereignty of Spain, in severing the former political relations, and in establishing a new political power, the authority of the United States is to be exerted for the securing of the persons and property of the people of the islands and for the confirmation of all their private rights and relations.
>
> It will be the duty of the commander of the forces of occupation to announce and proclaim in the most public manner that we come, not as invaders or conquerors, but as friends, to protect the natives in their homes, in their employments, and in their personal and religious rights....
>
> Finally, it should be the earnest wish and paramount aim of the military administration to win the confidence, respect, and affection of the inhabitants of the Philippines by assuring them in every possible way that full measure of individual rights and liberties which is the heritage of free peoples, and by proving to them that the mission of the United States is one of Benevolent Assimilation substituting the mild sway of justice and right for arbitrary rule. In the fulfillment of this high mission, supporting

the temperate administration of affairs for the greatest good of the governed, there must be sedulously maintained the strong arm of authority, to repress disturbance and to overcome all obstacles to the bestowal of the blessings of good and stable government upon the people of the Philippine Islands under the free flag of the United States.[31]

Not to be misconstrued as invasion or conquest, the US assimilation of the Philippines was in line with the ideals of extending the "full measure of individual rights and liberties." Military occupation becomes coextensive with the securing of rights for or on behalf of Filipinos who cannot do it themselves.

The thesis of benevolent assimilation was presented as a way to secure individual rights, as is the "heritage of free peoples." Part of McKinley's argument concerns the protection of private property, particularly the home ("to protect the natives in their homes"). While not about industrialization per se, the identification of property and the home as bourgeois values to be protected at the expense of the native's ability to consent to intervention demonstrates the extent to which logics of racial capital inform McKinley's "benevolent" assertions. The gendered divisions of labor within the "tribal" family and home, as elaborated by Roderick Ferguson in his critique of Karl Marx, come to mind in understanding the ways that benevolent empire postulated itself through a pedagogical function to rehabilitate the native away from the "sway of arbitrary rule," which no doubt referred to the insurrection, as it was called, during the Philippine-American War (1899–1902).[32] Native consent (whether it is given or not) hurts the protection of such bourgeois rights, even as it's the attribution and qualification of consent that would attest to the validity of the contractual capacities of the native to be rehabilitated. Paradoxically, it is the responsibility of imperial culture to bequeath the patrimony or "heritage" of freedom on the natives. The space of the imperial classroom as it is depicted in "School Begins" corroborates the gesture of largesse that is embedded in the rehabilitative project of imperialism meant to reshape the native mind to approximate the levels of intelligence that are enshrined in liberal ideals of freedom, possession of private property, and the reproduction of a particular home life meriting the protection of a heteronormative colonial force. The classroom as a scene of benevolent rehabilitation into respectable citizenship and civilization, as I have been establishing, is a visual economy of psychophysical variation that captures the textured realities of eugenic thought as it circumscribes the moral justification of imperialism—a justification that ramifies through an affect of benevolence. Indeed, it has been established by various disability studies scholars that "morality" itself was a cognitive faculty not only in the United States but in other parts of the world.[33]

It is the affirmation of American ableism, the ability to perform a series of tasks for a population, that is easily swayed by arbitrary and ultimately false rule in order to ensure the "greatest good of the governed." The "mild sway of justice" is a competing vision of the "good" that is conveniently disposed of. No doubt the Philippine insurrection lead by General Aguinaldo would have been on McKinley's mind as he invoked US occupation not as aggression but rather as temperate and even peaceful negotiation. It should be noted that Indigenous insurrections in the south of the archipelago far outlasted the "official" end of the Philippine-American War.[34] By "Indigenous" I mean those largely non-Christian nations in the southern part of the archipelago who largely and enduringly escaped Spanish influence and whose ancestors in the current historical moment exist under the political category Indigenous in the Philippines.[35] The supposed inability of Filipinos to properly govern themselves provides the logical framework through which a movement for independence against a new ruling power can be reclassified as an insurrection. The end goal of the imperial project is clear: "the bestowal of the blessings of good and stable government upon the Philippine Islands under the free flag of the United States." Liberty, the "good," and the political sovereignty concordant with a "stable government" are simultaneously and paradoxically the "heritage of free peoples" and a gift one can bestow.[36] What might explain how this logical contradiction can exist? Can one rob the freedom of a people and thereby ensure their liberty? Must a nation pass through a stage of unfreedom in order to arrive at autonomy?

This contradiction is where I locate a disability logic that explains how one can enfranchise another with rights to which they are entitled to as ontologically free. Mimi Thi Nguyen has critically argued that US foreign policy has historically and routinely placed itself in the position of giving people the "gift of freedom"—a contradiction in terms.[37] I suggest that through the case study of US colonization of the Philippines, arguably when such contradictory gifts were exported in earnest, we can see how the positions of gift giver and recipient are understood through perceived mental capacity to understand the contents of the gift. As we can see in McKinley's order, freedom is measured equally through the legitimization of violence in the name of security of "persons and property" as much as it is through perceived capacity. Ability is a condition of freedom and property granted paradoxically by colonial imposition. I'd venture to further suggest that the separation of Filipinos from property, the rationalization of which is grounded in the incapacity to self-rule, establishes that ability itself is a form of property—and white imperial property at that. If this is the case, then rehabilitation of the native is logically an effect of their colonial dispossession, which also ontologically conditions what constitutes normative ability in the first place.

One of the most foundational treatments of benevolent assimilation is Stuart Creighton Miller's pioneering *Benevolent Assimilation: The American Conquest of the Philippines, 1899-1903*.[38] In no uncertain terms, Miller reveals that US foreign policy at the turn of the twentieth century could not be understood outside clear racism. Several scholars have contributed similar critiques, ushering in a stage of American and ethnic studies scholarship that views US history not through an exceptionalist triumphalism but rather as the development of military empire. Historians like Warwick Anderson, Gail Bederman, Kristin Hoganson, Paul Kramer, and Vicente Rafael, as well as cultural theorists like Amy Kaplan, Victor Román Mendoza, Dylan Rodríguez, and Sarita See, have rendered the Philippines and the Philippine-American War not as marginal episodes worthy only of being footnoted in the grand narrative of American civilization.[39] Instead these scholars' work has amply demonstrated the Philippines as a foundational though not exceptional case study precipitating the imperial or global turn of American studies. An important aspect of this work, most notably introduced by Kramer from a historical perspective but certainly also highlighted by Miller, is that US domestic racial issues are not divorced from imperial expansion. Kramer explains how colonial ideologies introduced by the United States were ramified within the Philippines by many Filipinos jockeying for control in the administrative structures of colonial bureaucracy.[40] In addition to Kramer, scholars like Mary Renda (whose work is in Haiti) demonstrate the extent to which cultural forms within the United States helped to facilitate Americans' identification with the mission of imperialism even though most would never set foot in these acquired colonial territories.[41] In the case of the Philippines, world's fairs like the one in St. Louis in 1904 displayed "primitive" Filipinos such as the Aeta (popularly and problematically known as Negritos) and the "Igorot" to emphasize the civilizing mission of the United States—fairgoers could affectively identify with such a mission, convincing themselves that US expansion was an undisputable good. Additional work by Kaplan contributes to the ways that domestic spaces within the United States played an enormous role. The feminine labor of making the "home" was instrumental in supporting the more masculine labor of imperialism abroad.[42] Rafael intervenes in such "manifest domesticity" by articulating the ways that empire was also an extension of "white love" rooted in the foundational institutions of white femininity and heterosexuality.[43] Pseudoscientific discourses of ethnological comparativism, and their underwriting of such institutions of heteronormativity as the nuclear family, heterosexual marriage, and American "manliness," conspired to create a perverse colonial underclass of the Filipino.[44] In doing so, the Filipino was identified equally as a primitive object of scorn and one of sympathetic care ripe for uplift to become a stable and mentally sound practitioner of the art of governance.

Other generations of Filipinx scholars who personally and intellectually have been affected by US imperialism have reflected on how US "care" and tutelage have shaped Filipinx American politics.[45] Some, such as Rodríguez, go as far as stating that a definition of Filipinx American "culture" without a thorough recognition of the violence of US imperialism means the project of Filipinx America is doomed to fail.[46] The memory of violence, its historical impact, and its invisibility have demonstrated the extent to which US history is articulated through a culture of compulsive omission: we forgot that we forgot about US empire and the Philippine-American War, as See has so eloquently argued.[47] Significantly for a disability studies analytic, See has also analyzed the ways in which visual artistic representation in Filipinx American art has often trafficked in the imagery of "grotesque corporeality—torn bellies, spilling hearts, and headless, defecating corpses" in order to demonstrate a "dramatic pattern of wounds that is rooted in the traumatic history of colonial violence and loss."[48] She has, perhaps in a way that mirrors Gloria Anzaldúa's queer theorizations on the violence of the borderlands, conceived of this trope of Filipinx mourning through aesthetic self-mutilation as an "open wound."

The historiographical and theoretical conglomeration of this cadre of scholars, intellectuals, and activists deconstruct the ingrained colonial assumption that US care uplifted its objects of tutelage as much as it enacted violence on the natives that empire was meant to save. Conservative estimates of the death toll of Filipinos at American hands during the Philippine-American War number in excess of one million. This would account for nearly one-fifth of the total population of the Philippines at the turn of the twentieth century.[49] Delimiting the intellectual potential of Filipinos to govern themselves by exaggerating their "primitivism" through racially biased Western scientific categories worked in tandem with exposing the population of the archipelago to injury and premature death. The US endowed itself with the right to scientifically classify the dregs of humanity and the right to maim it.[50] This confluence of the assumption of intellectual deficiency (and thus the inability to self-govern) and the genocidal campaign of US imperial war following a just and autonomously fought war for independence against Spain, renders the US colonial project in the Philippines as a structural imposition of disablement that revolved simultaneously on both the destructive proliferation of genocidal warfare and a political ideology that annulled political independence and the capacity for sovereign thought.[51]

To conclude this chapter's analytical scavenger hunt in a way that is germane to the transitionary emphasis of this book as a whole, I turn to a Hispanic Philippine cultural archive in which we can locate the aestheticization of racial "cognition" as an inherent ability to the human. Here I turn to José Rizal, one of the main mestizo intellectuals of the so-called Philippine Enlightenment. Rizal was a doctor, political essayist, and novelist who, in no uncertain terms, characterized the Filipino colonial condition under the Spanish in medicalized terms. He allegorized the Filipino social dynamic under colonialism, as well as political responses to it, through corporeal terms whose ethos, I claim, can help us to re-semanticize extant framings of embodiment and disability. In his novel *Noli me tángere* (Touch me not, 1886), which is the central object of analysis for chapter 2, he likened Spanish Catholic malfeasance to a "social cancer" that had to be cut out of Philippine society. Provocatively, he would characterize the mestizo class as the "brains of the nation" that would no doubt be best suited to perform such a procedure.[52] Here I foreground an engagement with his canonical political essay, *Filipinas dentro de cien años*, in which we can flesh out a multifarious archive of the colonial bodymind and highlight epistemic moves of colonial capacity building that Filipinx American studies ought to read against.

"Embrutecimiento" and Mestizo Cognition

For those that are familiar with it, it might be evident why I would choose to give a close reading of Rizal's essay *Filipinas dentro de cien años* (1889–90).[53] Yet it would also be unsurprising that many Filipinx Americans might not be aware of this essay given the US domestic and inward orientation of ethnic studies. Rizal's is an uneasy legacy for the project of Filipinx America as a field of thought, agency, and autonomy. He is the progenitor of the problematic heritage of "mestizo enlightenment" in the Philippines, which did as much work to calcify racial and class hierarchies within the archipelago as it did to make passionate, convincing, and vital arguments for a more independent Philippines (even if such independence, if many *ilustrados* like Rizal had their druthers, would have resulted in a reformed colonial relationship with Spain).[54] It was Rizal who argued in "Cien años" that the *ilustrado* (intellectual) class of Chinese-mestizo elite Filipinos was the "brains of the nation." Their vaunted intellectual capacity ensured that they knew best how to chart a path forward for their beloved *patria* (homeland). Rizal's reasoning and training resulted in a medicalized corporeality for the nation wherein the body and mind were unified—both were raced as mestizo. And yet such racialized meanings for the body and mind—what I am calling a colonial bodymind—were paradoxically effaced in his quest for a postcolonial independence.[55] Rizal casts this bodymind in animalistic terms: colonialism is a process that makes a "brute" of the Filipino. In conjunction with the racial visualization of cognitive capacity for consent and self-government in the *Puck* cartoon "School Begins," Rizal's essay on the future prospects of Filipino sovereignty offers us a vista into the cultural and political construct of cognition. Commonsense understandings of cognitive capacity would lead us to think that it is wholly housed within the body as a "fact" of what bodies and their minds can do; nevertheless, it has a racial life as a product of colonial discourse.

"Cognition" is a cultural production and social phenomenon that has been historically brought about in the crucibles of racial war and imperial statecraft. Those that are easily seduced by "the right for arbitrary rule," as McKinley argued, are imagined to be the "half-devil" children unable to participate in political arrangements as an equivalent actor. Implied in this colonial logic is the relative mental unfitness of the colonized. Thus, rather than only a physiological and biological capacity consigned to the human, the literal ability to cognize phenomena is historically enmeshed in unequal power relationships. Bear with me as I make a fine point of this: the mass of neurons we collectively identify as the "brain" outside the body is a network of pathways transmitting information. What I mean by "outside the body" is that thoughts and concepts brought to bear on corporeality (the brain included) originate from the body while simultaneously attaining a life of their own not reducible to embodiment. My meaning here is not too dissimilar from Cartesian dualism. Within a body, however, the brain and our notions of what it can do cognitively bear the social traces of bodies defined in the racialized "contact zones" of imperial encounter.[56] While it is the argument of this chapter that US colonial discourse justified acquisition of the Philippines irrespective of sovereignty because of the enduring incapacity of the native, it is important that we understand how who was being dispossessed of such ability understood the cultivation and intellectual development of their own capacities. While his scope is limited, Rizal offers us such a multi-perspectival vista into the ways that (dis)ability is a deeply rooted and global colonial mentality—particularly within the framework of mestizaje. No doubt drawing on his training as a medical doctor, Rizal offers us a metaphorical and enminded construction of the Philippine nation from his mestizo perspective. Rizal notably calls his class of *ilustrados* "el cerebro del país"—the brain (or cerebrum) of the nation.[57] In arguments he first authored in 1889 and 1890, Rizal declares that this anticolonial cerebrum is waking up:

> Hoy existe un factor que no había antes; se ha despertado el espíritu de la nación, y una misma desgracia y un mismo rebajamiento han unido á todos los habitantes de las Islas. Se cuenta con una numerosa clase il-ustrada dentro y fuera del Archipiélago, clase creada y aumentada cada vez más y más por las torpezas de ciertos gobernantes, obligando á los habitantes á expatriarse, á ilustrarse en el extranjero. . . . Esta clase, cuyo número aumenta progresivamente, está en comunicación constante con el resto de las Islas, y si hoy no forma más que el cerebro del país, den-tro de algunos años formará todo su sistema nervioso y manifestará su existencia en todos sus actos.

> Today there exists a factor that did not exist before: the spirit of the na-tion has been awakened, and the same misfortune, the same abasement has united all the inhabitants. Now factor in a numerous enlightened class [*clase ilustrada*] within and outside the Archipelago, a class created and propelled to grow in ever greater numbers by the bungling efforts of certain governors, who force [the country's] inhabitants to expatriate, to educate/enlighten themselves [ilustrarse] in foreign lands. . . . This class, whose number grows continually, is in constant communication with the rest of the Islands, and if today it forms no more than the country's cerebrum, in a few years it will form the entire nervous system and will manifest the country's existence in all its actions.[58]

The description of the country's mestizo intellectuals as if they were neurons in "constant communication" with elements throughout the entire archipel-ago and the evocative metaphor of a cerebrum with an ever-complexifying "nervous system" are unsurprising given Rizal's training in medicine. Body and mind find a productive union in his description of a country whose existence was manifesting against a hard-headed religious authority whose superstitious and corrupt governance paled in comparison with the reasoned and rational approach of the scientific Filipino *ilustrado* (a topic I'll elaborate on in chapter 2). Significantly, during the final years of the Spanish colonial period of the late nineteenth century, Rizal described the "frail-ocracía" (friarocracy) over those past three centuries as dulling the mind of the Filipino national—a process he called "embrutecimiento" (literally, the rendering of one into a brute). Rizal describes this process as follows:

> Llegado á este estado el rebajamiento moral de los habitantes, el desaliento, el disgusto de sí mismo, se quiso dar entonces el último golpe de gracia, para reducir á la nada tantas voluntades y tantos cerebros adormecidos, para hacer de los individuos una especie de brazos, de brutos, de bestias de carga, así como una humanidad sin cerebro y sin corazón.

> Having arrived at this state of moral degradation of the inhabitants, their despondency, their disappointment in themselves, it was decided then to inflict the last coup de grace, in order to reduce their wills and sleeping minds to nothing, in order to reduce these individuals to a kind of body [literally, "arms"], to brutes, to beasts of burden, as if they were a kind of humanity without a brain and without a heart.[59]

The disabling "embrutecimiento" of the Filipino is a characterization of the native subject as being "morally degraded" by the violence of colonialism. They are wholly and only a body "without a brain." The positioning of the mestizo Filipino as a nationalist intellectual de-emphasizes and, I would suggest, writes against the colonial inertia that renders the Filipino a brute, objectified as pure body—a "beast of burden" shouldering the encumbrance of colonial rule. "Beast of burden" is an interesting phrase indicating colonial parameters for the material conditions of labor for Filipino colonial subjects living under Spanish rule. It indicates the extent to which the idea of sovereignty and self-possession—hallmarks of able-bodied self-sufficiency and robust political existence—recede away from the colonial body. The Filipino "brute" is prized only for the physical labor that it may perform rather than any intellectual contribution to democratic self-rule. Rizal deftly connects the realities of the mind and body, helpfully elaborating an example of the disability concept of the bodymind in a colonial context.[60] In elaborating this lamentable condition, he advances an ethical argument foregrounding intellectual labor of the colonized mind. As far as Rizal's text goes, mestizos serve as an intermediary figure between a native past and a postcolonial future. We can observe in this passage echoes of similar ideas advanced in other mestizaje philosophies, such as that of José

Vasconcelos, wherein it is problematically argued that Indigenous embodiment must be modified to encompass a different subjectivity more attuned to the realities of dispossession. Nevertheless, in much the same way that we may desire to compare the case of Filipino colonial race relations with Latin American iterations of mestizaje, it is necessary to perceive the ways that the question of Filipino Indigeneity and mestizaje are not articulated in a political vacuum separate from other racial formations.

The rehabilitation of the native body from laboring beast to luminary "brain of the nation" embeds Philippine mestizaje in a global network of colonial race relations. Rizal's "estudio politico-social" (politico-social study), which ponders what will become of the Philippines a century hence, charts a path for a modern Philippines with a rehabilitated Indigeneity partially through an entrenchment of the colonial anti-Blackness of the time notably before the outbreak of the Philippine war for independence from Spain:

> Si las Filipinas consiguen su independencia al cabo de luchas heroicas y tenaces, pueden estar seguras de que ni Inglaterra, ni Alemania, ni Francia, y menos Holanda, se atreverán á recoger lo que España no ha podido conservar. El África, dentro de algunos años, absorberá por completo la atención de los europeos, y no hay nación de los europeos, y no hay nación sensata que por ganar un puñado de islas aguerridas y pobres, descuide los inmensos territorios que le brinda el Continente Negro, vírgenes, no explotados y pocos defendidos. Inglaterra tiene ya bastantes colonias en el Oriente y no se va á exponer a perder el equilibrio; no va á sacrificar su imperio de la India por el pobre Archipiélago Filipino.

> If the Philippines acquires its independence after tenacious and heroic battles, you can rest assured that neither England, Germany, France, nor Holland, will risk recovering what Spain will have not been able to keep. Africa, within a few years, will completely absorb the attention of the Europeans, and there is neither a European nation nor a sensible one that would relinquish the defenseless unexploited virgin territories of the Black Continent for a handful of war-torn and destitute islands. England already has several colonies in the Orient and won't open itself up to a loss of control; it won't sacrifice its empire in India for the poor Philippine Archipelago.[61]

Significantly, we can clearly observe that the partitioning of Africa that transpired in the Berlin Conference of 1884–85 greatly influenced Rizal's thinking about the future of the Philippine nation, as it was primed for revolutionary upheaval in just a few years after the publication of his essay. If Rizal represents one of the brightest minds of the Filipino nationalist movement, then it appears that such a critical mind would have to reconcile the ways that Philippine anticolonialism meaningfully obtains through the installing of colonialism as a global project. That is to say, if we would praise Rizal for his foresight regarding the impending imperial desires of the United States (about which he was correct), it is also crucial to understand that the solidification of a Filipino revolutionary and intellectual enlightenment from a mestizo perspective forsakes solidarity with the African continent. Need the Filipinx critic not concern themself with Africa? While Rizal's text is filled with stupendous insights on the ways that Spanish colonialism greatly inhibited freethinking, sovereignty, and progress—again, what Rizal dubs the "embrutecimiento" of the Filipino pueblo—it appears that national freedom is a prospect that is mortgaged on the unfreedom of others.[62] The "Oriente" and the "Archipiélago Filipino" would pass from repute in the following century—a century that seemed like it would be structured by the territorial and economic exploitation (yet again) of Africa. While we cannot necessarily fault Rizal for a historical context in which the Philippines was not an independent nation in a world that was free from colonialism, it appears that he is emblematic of a Filipino mestizo subjectivity that derives authority through the oppression of "el Continente Negro."[63] What might it mean to read Philippine mestizaje and Rizal's moving case for its intellectual virtues within the context of an approaching US colonialism that itself was a by-product of a racial state built through transatlantic slavery? It seems that one answer to this question as far as Rizal's politics are concerned is that a Philippine independence movement is not a form of anticolonialism that is etched in transnational solidarity with other colonially dispossessed peoples. Ostensibly, the major colonial powers would be too busy with their partitioning of the "Black Continent" to worry about the Philippine archipelago. And it seems that Filipino philosophies on individual freedom in the face of a stultifying colonialism were equally disinvested from dispossessions occurring a world away.

In a reading that is reminiscent of Lisa Lowe's "intimacies of four continents" and mirroring similar more obvious critiques of the relationship of Latin American mestizaje and slavery, it likewise seems difficult to think about Philippine mestizaje separate from the history of liberal abolitionism and its failures. Rizal is writing in the era after the illegalization of slavery in many parts of the world.[64] And yet despite such progressive developments banning the sale and trade of human beings, the acquisition of territory via colonial fiat reaches a fever pitch at the Berlin Conference, which began a series of conquests of African nations from 1884 until 1914. Such colonial developments circumscribe the anticolonial sentiments extolled by the mestizo thinker Rizal, offering another vector of analysis for thinking about how continents across the globe share an underelaborated historical intimacy with one another. For instance, Lowe's work explicitly anchors histories of Asian migration to the Americas to histories of abolitionism. She avers that after the Haitian Revolution the prospect of exploiting Black bodies for plantation labor was increasingly dubious. According to Lowe's analysis, plantation owners felt that they were too freethinking and radical to be productive and reliable laborers. So capitalist enterprise transformed other racialized bodies into the flexible and cheap labor that it required. Extractivist industries sought out coolies and other Asian laborers as model laborers who were more dutiful and less radical. The historical and political economy of the model minority myth notwithstanding, rather than view as discrete the geopolitical referents we dub *Africa* and *Asia*, it seems they indeed exist as racial formations that mutually inform one another—a dynamic that Lowe captures through the term "intimacies."[65]

We can observe in *Filipinas dentro de cien años* a similar intimacy in which the formulation of an Asian liberal modernity in the Philippines is inextricable from the shifting labor demands and racial ideologies of colonial capitalism. Specifically, and perhaps surprisingly, at play in Rizal's treatise on Filipino independence and intellectual freedom is the reality of transatlantic slavery. To put it bluntly, Rizal's sociopolitical study is structured and enabled by the unfreedom of Black peoples in the epoch following the emancipations of slaveholding nations across the world. How might we reframe the nascent political and intellectual movements of mestizo Filipino culture within the sociopolitical context of late nineteenth-century abolition and, more specifically, its failures? It is then not only the dispossession and rehabilitation of a Filipino *indio* that is the object of care of a mestizo elite but also the imbrication of this settler paradigm on the substrate of the echoes of slavery. If European colonialism of Africa is itself a manifestation of abolitionism's failures to truly emancipate from the structural violence of global anti-Blackness, it seems an apt critique of Rizal to suggest that anticolonial Philippine politics against Spain and the United States might measure its own struggle for freedoms over and against the relative unfreedom of the descendants of such a system of colonial anti-Blackness.

This global "intimate" framework fundamentally shifts the ways that we understand race and racialization during a period of incipient nationalist consciousness in the mestizo Philippines.[66] I argue that Rizal's lack of solidarity suggests that the mestizaje that structures the gains of Filipino nationalism in the late nineteenth century is politically adumbrated by transatlantic slavery and its aftermath. I would suggest that Filipino liberationist politics and its supposed if uneven abrogation of Spanish colonialism is articulated under the shadow—and perhaps as partially an afterlife—of transatlantic slavery. While Philippine nationalism cannot be completely determined by the politics of slavocracy, it can serve as a node through which we can entertain a more thorough communion of the transatlantic and the transpacific as geopolitical lenses through which global racism and racial capitalism produce "odd bedfellows."[67] Rizal's seemingly epiphenomenal mention of the African partition is another trajectory through which US imperialism can be more fully understood. To wit, in a prophetic tone that resembles that of José Martí in "Nuestra América" (Our America), Rizal similarly warns of a burgeoning US imperialism:

> Acaso la gran República Americana, cuyos intereses se encuentran en el Pacífico y que no tiene participación en los despojos del África, piense un día en posesiones ultramarinas. No es imposible, el ejemplo es contagioso, la codicia y la ambición son vicios de los fuertes . . . pero ni el Canal de Panamá está abierto, ni los territorios de los Estados tienen plétora de habitantes, y caso de que lo intentaran abiertamente, no le dejarían paso libre las potencias europeas, que saben muy bien que el apetito se excitó con los primeros bocados. La América del Norte sería una rival demasiado molesta, si una vez practica el oficio.

> Perhaps the great American Republic, whose interests lie in the Pacific and which does not participate in the despoliation of Africa, will one day think of overseas possessions. It's not impossible, such a phenomenon is contagious; greed and ambition are vices of the powerful . . . but the Panama Canal is not open, nor do US territories have a plethora of inhabitants, and in the event that they were to expand openly, they would inhibit European encroachment. They know very well that the appetite intensifies after the first few bites. North America would be a troublesome rival if it were to expand its reach.[68]

As Rizal accurately surmises, the dawn of US imperialism represents a moment in which US power redefined itself globally in the decades following its civil war and the racial failures of Reconstruction. US expansion into the Caribbean and the Pacific represented a shift in power wherein Europe declined or at least made room for another global player. Many scholars in American studies and ethnic studies have openly resisted the historical segmenting of domestic racial developments of the United States and the more international shifts in its foreign policy that saw the acquisition of Spain's last colonial possessions. Many scholars have explicitly linked the two periods. The United States' "splendid little war" in the Philippines, commonly known as the Philippine-American War, was a cultural response to the declining Civil War generation in the United States that was dying out. Establishing a direct cultural link between the American civil war and nascent imperial expansion, historian Kristin Hoganson has argued that a masculinist anxiety around the lack of battle-hardened American men created the seductive desire for war to reinvigorate manhood and thus created a foreign enemy on whom such white masculinity could be violently enacted. Rizal's observations seem to confirm that out of such a cultural milieu, the United States would naturally set its sights on the Pacific ("la gran República Americana, cuyos intereses se encuentran en el Pacífico").

Methodologically speaking, US empire studies scholars have productively questioned a unidirectional model of historical work in which the domestic United States is separated from its colonial possessions. Similar to recent Asian American studies scholarship that tracks Asian racialization vis-à-vis Black and Indigenous modernity, they have contended that domestic racial ideology is not simply exported abroad. Rather, domestic racial issues actively shifted in response to the United States' expanded colonial purview. Some scholars have provocatively analyzed the contradiction of, on the one hand, the historical separation of Black people and other people of color from the full privileges of US citizenship within the United States and, on the other, the annexation of territories with "savage" Brown people.[69] That is, that Black people continued to be viciously excluded from full and robust political life while Brown people were simultaneously assimilated into and as US nationals represents a paradox that existed in logical noncontradiction. For instance, US annexation of the Philippines saw a sharp increase in Filipino labor migration to Hawaii and the West Coast, furthering the settler colonial designs of the United States in these areas. These Filipino laborers traveled as US nationals with American passports.[70] While US citizenship did not affirmatively include the Philippines, it is clear that the franchise of citizenship supplely expanded, thus affecting migration patterns and demography at a time when domestic space segregated along a Black-white binary.[71]

Given such inquiry on the matter, my framing that links Rizal's liberal anticolonialism to the historical aftermaths of transatlantic slavery is not so farfetched. Equality through separation of the races seems to ideologically exist as a parallel to the colonial intimacies that proliferate through imperial expansion. Is it really simply coincidental that the United States begins its campaign to annex some of its first colonial territories in 1898, just two years following the legal ruling of *Plessy v. Ferguson* in 1896? Might Rizal help us materialize a postcolonial reading of the Jim Crow era? Or might Filipino nationalist consciousness be an underestimated vector through which the contradictions of American liberalism can be more thoroughly vetted in a global encounter?

Rizal represents an uneasy and unintuitive archive for Filipinx American critique of colonialism. There are good reasons for this. The Spanish-language origins of the archive of the *ilustrados* makes access in the original difficult for the largely non-Hispanophone Filipinx population and its diaspora. Philosophically, working in Spanish might mean recentering Spanish coloniality in some form (though the assumptive role that English plays in the field might be something we should interrogate). We see that Rizal's work, in many ways, served as a counteragent to the processes of the "embrutecimiento" of the native. And yet the Filipino *bruto* or "beast of burden" is enmeshed in the historical, political, and economic shifts constitutive of the "afterlives of slavery."[72] The *ilustrados* and their Propaganda Movement effloresced to affirm that the "beast of burden" did have a mind of its own and, indeed, was the cerebrum of the entire nation. Nevertheless, the mestizaje through which such a bodymind materializes in Rizal's reading also problematically duplicates colonial ideologies and internalizes them.

Rizal and the *ilustrados* represent a bourgeois, landowning, class of colonized intellectuals whose efforts were to create a broad national Filipino identity that would transcend ethnic and tribal differences. While Philippine mestizaje has enabled problematic colonial and racial dynamics within the Philippines that have not historically been useful for an Asian American movement with broad appeal, mestizaje ironically gets at the historical racial fissures of the nation and ethnicity that can be conveniently sublimated in the name of a politics of unity. In terms of methodology, such epistemological processes of uncritical political and ethnic unity make comparative work across difference, geographies, languages, and colonialisms difficult. On the granular analytical level, I have attempted to read against the grain of Rizal's colonial ableism even as he also presents a "mestizo consciousness" that similarly and powerfully questions the "embrutecimiento" of Spanish colonialism and foreshadows US imperial designs on the Pacific. At root, I claim that disability analysis permits a remarkable hermeneutic grasp of the ways that Indigeneity, empire, and Filipinx American critique intersect.

The Historical Construction of Cognition
as Racial Dispossession

Within the colonial context, disability and race are analogous (though not interchangeable). Filipinx American studies has established that the political justification for colonialism in the Philippines was erroneously grounded in the inability of the Filipino nation to self-govern. It is perhaps somewhat expected, then, that the critical impetus of Filipinx thought would be to recuperate agency by abrogating arguments levied against the self-determination of the colonized. I want to caution against this impulse. This might imply that the implicit subject of Filipinx political agency is or should be able-bodied, thus potentially leaving uninterrogated the ableism of colonialism. This tension is particularly apt for a study of the mestizo enlightenment of the Philippines in which *ilustrados* provide archival and textual evidence to the intellectual ability of the colonized reading against such colonial ableism. For this reason, this chapter has included a discussion of José Rizal because of the ways that he explicitly corporealized the experience of colonialism in ways that are unsurprising given his background in medicine.

The linking of race theory to disability studies presents an epistemological problem in the form of a catch-22 of sorts. Does embracing "disabled identity," as much disability studies and politics suggests, mean a detraction from offering a full-mounted critique of colonialism that assumes the disability of the native?[73] That is, would employing disability analysis inevitably do work to solidify the colonial presumption of the incapacity of the colonized? I suggest that this might show the limitations of only focusing on disability identity rather than a structural critique of ableism. For this reason, crip colonial critique as a critical exercise that militates against the ableist normativities within institutional and, in my view, colonial logics seems a more likely opportunity to read colonialism, race, and disability in tandem. Typically, disabled identity as the centerpiece for disability politics in the West would not take into account the realities of colonialism, thus potentially replicating such logics in the name of disability justice as a narrowly domestic project—one that would seek accommodation from a state while misunderstanding or ignoring its colonial history. Nevertheless, we might also point to an extant ableism that runs unchallenged in minority theory wherein we assume that the agentive subject that would speak against the colonial must be able-bodied in order to be truly resistant. Yet because colonialism in the Philippines in the form of what I have been calling "benevolent rehabilitation" assumed the disabled condition of the Filipino as a fully self-governing subject, the project of reclaiming "disability" as part of reclaiming an identitarian agency is not equally available to anticolonial and colonized subjects. It seems irresponsible to blame this on an unquestioned ableism without considering the colonial conditions under which such a move would be made in the first place. In any event, it is not my interest to lay blame on one side or the other. My purpose is to offer an alternative genealogy for disability and crip analysis in Filipinx American studies while also encouraging Filipinx thought to more seriously interrogate disability and its relationship to colonial racism.

As I have demonstrated, in the cartoon "School Begins," eugenic and ethnological visual representation of the Black laboring body and the Chinese coolie lend credence to a crip colonial critique of racialized normalization. That is, colonial capitalism required the norming of embodiment to accommodate standardized units of labor time, and bodies that could perform them, in order to facilitate the extraction of labor. This has clear ramifications for disability studies, whose analyses center around forms of embodiment whose variations vex such standardization. Adding to Lennard Davis's argument that "statistics is bound up with eugenics because the central insight of statistics is the idea that a population can be normed," I center the context of imperial biopower and the colonial proliferation of ideologies of ability as they pertain to the values of industrial societies.[74] In doing so we can shed light on the ways that evolutionary theory, race science, and discourses of defect inform the racialization of colonial subjects as deviations from implicit norms. Eugenics, being an idea that is connected to the seductive concept of "a perfectible body" that can undergo "progressive improvement," demonstrates the ways that US benevolent assimilation was a rehabilitative logic that combined ethnological comparativism with eugenic betterment.

The presence of these two figures of colonial capitalist labor exploitation, the perverse coolie and the stereotyped Black laboring body, gives us insight into the ways that capitalist labor abstraction and the ideas around a perfectible human body articulate in the realm of colonial anthropology. These bodies represent the limits of abstraction in that a racial type needs to emerge to globalize such biopolitical ideologies. Racial defectives are constructed as objects of charity and even care, wherein colonial "benevolent" notions of rehabilitation of defect justify occupation of territory.

A clear way that this manifests in "School Begins" is through the linked psychophysical capacity of self-determination and autonomy—or political sovereignty. Because the racial colonial subject reaches the diagnostic threshold of defect, imperial expansion transforms into an evolutionary discourse wherein the United States can actually leverage its own failures of racial integration in the form of the historical failures of Reconstruction, Indian "industrial" reformation, and Chinese exclusion to establish itself as a rehabilitative and benevolent force. Disability rhetorically functions as marking an essential inequality between the colonizer and colonized. This is crucial so that the United States can avoid the contradiction of ensuring the freedoms of the Philippines when it failed to "integrate" the racial "defects" of the coolie, Black person, and Indian. That is to say, disability allows racial inequality, in the presence of liberal freedom, to exist in logical noncontradiction.[75] US benevolent rehabilitation, given its visual and discursive links to eugenics, ethnology, and evolutionary science, is a global rupture and important archive in untangling the meanings of disability and its enmeshment with race.

In chapter 2, I explore the ways that rehabilitative and capacitating discourses were already present in the late Spanish colonial Philippines prior to the US age of benevolent assimilation. Philippine Hispanic culture was primed to internalize these ableist logics into extant ideologies of mestizo reform. I extend my engagement with José Rizal, which began in this chapter, to what is considered his masterwork, the novel Noli me tángere. In it we see how the colonial bodymind of the Filipina mestiza was of central importance in Rizal's liberal notions of reform and anticlericalism. A crip colonial critique of Noli me tángere demonstrates how the mestiza shoulders the colonial burdens of disablement, and her excision from the nation that must forsake her charts pathways for mestizo enlightenment and colonial capacity. Yet the Filipina mestiza's queerness registers a mode of resistant reading and agency that articulates against the grain of colonial masculinist ableism.

Two

Mad María Clara

THE QUEER AESTHETICS OF MESTIZAJE AND
COMPULSORY ABLE-MINDEDNESS

José Rizal's *Noli me tángere* (Touch me not, 1886) is the most famous modern Filipino novel. Specifically, it is a noted and biting anticlerical critique of Catholic malfeasance in the church's rule of the Philippine Islands. Rizal effectively positions Filipino intellectuals as the harbingers of reason and enlightenment by representing Spanish religious authorities as bound by superstition, outdated tradition, and colonial orthodoxy. It is told through the perspective of its mestizo protagonist, Crisóstomo Ibarra, beginning with his return to the Philippines from a stint abroad following the death of his father. Ibarra sets to the patriotic task of building a school, believing that the Filipino people will benefit from a modernized education. This significantly foreshadows the educative function of US benevolent rehabilitation as it manifests in the allegory of the colonial classroom, which I analyzed at length in chapter 1. Ibarra's educational plan is foiled when he learns of a plot to assassinate him during the laying of the cornerstone of the school. This attempt on his life and the discovery that Padre Dámaso, the main antagonist that represents the corruption of the Spanish Catholic order, orchestrated events that led to the death of his father causes Ibarra to lash out against the Spanish friars. Ibarra sets on one, almost murdering him. Yet his childhood love interest, María Clara, stays his hand, begging for mercy. This move in the plot produces an irresolvable conflict between María Clara and Ibarra—a gendered difference in the mestizo rational and national project meant to contravene the duplicity of the Catholic order. This conflict is the central tension in the racialized and gendered relations of Filipino *mestizaje* (racial admixture, miscegenation) that is examined in this chapter. For many, *Noli me tángere* articulates a national identity and culture through Spanish letters based on the unrequited heterosexual romance between Ibarra, an ardent and modern patriot, and María Clara, the hapless product of the union of Dámaso and a native Filipina.

In short, María Clara is a bastard. She is the very fruit of the corruption Ibarra (and Rizal) seeks to vitiate. The enlightened Filipino mestizo Ibarra and the compromised heritage of the bastard María Clara form an antinomy that embeds within the racial logics of mestizaje a gendered and sexual order. The mestizo *ilustrado* (intellectual) is the beacon illuminating a corrupt colonial order through noble efforts to educate his comrades. The mestiza bastard, María Clara, is the wretched hybrid byproduct of ill-fated parentage. Therefore, the "foundational romance," to paraphrase Doris Sommer, of a heterosexual union among Filipino mestizos does not ensure the sociopolitical unit of the nation.[1] Instead, this union is withheld from bastard subjects that are incommensurate with its goals. To paraphrase scholar John Blanco, María Clara is the bastard of the unfinished revolution of the Filipino nation.[2] She is mestizaje wrought wrongly, and thus heterosexuality as patriotic virtue and national feminine duty is denied; it seems that racially she is incapable of performing the task. Perhaps such denial represents a reproductive logic unto itself that is meant to literarily clarify that which should be excised from the strategic breeding of a modern nation.[3]

Asylum as Convent

María Clara is the childhood love interest of the most famous character in Philippine literature. Crisóstomo Ibarra, the hero and protagonist of *ilustrado* José Rizal's narrative, returns to the Philippines from his long years abroad having imbibed the liberal ideals of a European education—a characterization similar to the biographies of many of the Filipino mestizo elite of the late nineteenth century.[4] Indeed, Ibarra's growing disenchantment with the colonial order mirrors Rizal's later years, thus giving readers a vista into what a modern and cosmopolitan Filipino subjectivity is. As scholar Raquel Reyes has aptly demonstrated, within the anticolonial modernity of the *ilustrados*, the intellectual and the libidinal intertwined often in the disciplining of female sexuality.[5] For this reason, Ibarra's role in Filipino political representation is not only important but also significant in his relationship with María Clara. Readers no doubt avidly look toward the reeducation of the Filipino as an overriding ethos of the anticlerical *Noli me tángere*. Equally at stake, however, is whether Ibarra and María Clara will rekindle their romance—a heterosexual coupling foundational for the narrative of a viable Filipino nationalism based on responsible governance and not superstitious religious orthodoxy.[6] Rather than securing the passage of property through the institution of marriage, the conception of a child that would herald the coming of a renewed nationhood, or simply the blissful nuptial existence wherein the family is the bedrock of the national project and its continued reproduction, Ibarra and María Clara are not to be; their romance is doomed from the start. Ibarra, betrayed, must flee the country that he loves. Reviled, María Clara must live out the rest of her days as if she were a ghost haunting the very religious superstructure held in such utter contempt by her paramour. As we will see, she chooses this cloistered existence for herself, but let us not doubt that Rizal placed her—confined her—there, constraining her ability to decide for herself and any agency we might attribute to her. At the novel's end, Filipino soldiers regard María Clara, almost a fantastic figure, trepidatiously:

En efecto, a la brillante luz del meteoro había visto una figura blanca, de pie, casi sobre el caballete del tejado, dirigidos al cielo los brazos y la cara, como implorándole. ¡El cielo respondía con rayos y truenos! Tras del trueno se oyó un quejido triste.

¡No es el viento, es el fantasma!—murmuró el soldado como respondiendo a la presión de mano de su compañero. . . .

¡No, no es fantasma!—exclamó el distinguido;—la he visto otra vez; es hermosa como la Virgen . . . ¡Vámanos de aquí y demos parte!

Indeed, through brilliant meteoric light the solider saw a white figure, standing almost on the edge of the [highest point or ridge of the] roof, her arms and face extended toward the sky as if she were imploring the heavens. The sky responded with lightning and thunder. Following the thunder, a sad groan could be heard.

It's not the wind, it's a ghost!—the solider muttered, responding to the compression he felt from his companion's hand. . . .

It is not a ghost!—he exclaimed;—"I've seen her before; she is as beautiful as the Virgin . . . Let's take our leave of this place![7]

Despite the rather moribund circumstance, she is admired for her virginal beauty. While such beauty is attractive, it belies the danger she seemingly represents. The soldiers flee ("demos parte"), perhaps unsure of what misfortune such a vision might portend. Rizal seeks readerly engagement with this ostensible phantasm through a series of questions: "¿Quién gime en medio de la noche, a pesar del viento, de la lluvia y de la tempestad? ¿Quién es la tímida virgen, la esposa de Jesucristo, que desafía los desencadenados elementos y escoge la tremenda noche y el libre cielo, para exhalar desde una peligrosa altura sus quejas a Dios?" (Who groans in the middle of the night, despite the wind, the rain, and the storm? Who is this timid virgin, Jesus Christ's betrothed, that defies the unbridled elements from such dangerous heights directing her protests to the tremendous night sky?)[8]

Of course, we come to find out that it is not a ghost, as the solider is quick to point out. It is how the story concludes for María Clara. Instead of being married to Ibarra, she is "la esposa de Jesucristo" (the wife of Jesus Christ)—a euphemistic way of referring to this virgin's station as a nun, though one who wails at the night sky rather than engaging in contemplative prayer. Rizal's rendering of this wretched figure screaming her grievances to a God that, naturally, cannot hear her, has perhaps two meanings in the world of *Noli me tángere*. First, it is punishment for wrongs that she unwittingly committed against our hero. She is one of the main reasons that Ibarra is accused of sedition and must expatriate himself, their personal correspondence serving as evidence for the treacherous and deceitful Padres Salví and Dámaso—character representations of the "frailocracía" (friarocracy) poisoning Filipino society. Moreover, Ibarra and María Clara's unrequited love indicates an impossibility for freedom and happiness for the Filipino nation writ large. Second, this baleful sight indexes the unlivable and untenable circumstances that Filipinos must truck under Spanish colonial rule. María Clara's is a tragedy that allegorizes the plight of the nation doomed to madness.

This tragic scene is the epilogue to Rizal's novel. This foundational romance ends not in an idyllic heterosexual union marking the advent of a new national age but instead on the rain-laden steps of the convent in which María Clara will spend the rest of her days.[9] Surprisingly, clinical language is used to describe her predicament. She is a patient of the convent. The fantastical and the medical intertwine in the ghost story about this disabled subject. And she is not cognitively disabled in a metaphoric sense; Rizal uses precise diagnostic language here. Her diagnosis is uttered first in the ultimate lines of the novel by the abbess charged with the nuns' care:

. . . La abadesa decía que era una loca.

El hombre no sabría tal vez que en Manila hay un hospicio para dementes, ó acaso juzgaría que el convento de monjas era sólo un asilo de locas, aunque se pretende que el hombre aquel era bastante ignorante, sobre todo para poder decidir cuándo una persona está en su sano juicio ó no.

Cuéntase también que el general señor J. . . . pensó de otra manera, y que cuando el hecho llegó á sus oídos, quiso proteger á la loca y la pidió.

Pero esta vez no apareció ninguna hermosa y desamparada joven, y la abadesa no permitió que se visitase el claustro, invocando para ello el nombre de la religión y de los Santos Estatutos.

Del hecho no se volvió á hablar más, como tampoco de la infeliz María Clara.

Fin.

. . . The abbess said that she was insane.

The man wouldn't know perhaps that in Manila there is a hospice for the demented, or perhaps might judge the convent to be an asylum for insane women, although it's assumed that that man was quite ignorant, especially in regards to determining when a person was in their right mind or not.

It's also said that Mr. J. . . . thought differently, and when the news reached his ears, he wanted to protect the insane woman and asked for her.

Yet this time no beautiful defenseless girl appeared and the abbess did not permit visitations to the cloisters, invoking the name of religion and the Holy Statutes.

This case was not spoken of again, and neither was the hapless María Clara mentioned.

End.[10]

The convent may be, by Rizal's admission in his final lines, an asylum. The fungibility of the convent and asylum may indicate the extent to which religious institutions and theocracy are vestigial remnants of a colonial architecture meant to be transcended. That is, it symbolizes a confinement that needs to be breached. María Clara is confined where the nation must never go. Rizal's anticlericism might hinge, at least literarily, on this very moment of María Clara's tempestuous wailing. If the ilustrado is a figure of reason over superstitious faith, then the colonized's incapacity and perceived deficiencies need to be displaced from the mestizo national bodymind.[11] I suggest that this displacement happens through the feminization of madness confined to the body of María Clara and so shackled to the walls of the convent—her mestiza body is rendered the "colonial bodymind" attesting to the *ilustrado's* rehabilitative powers. Whereas, in chapter 1, I posed the colonial bodymind as a submissive subject position that intersected with Indigeneity, Rizal's representation is distinct here. Paradoxically, María Clara's body is also that of a mestiza, but, in *Noli me tángere* the aesthetics of her mestizaje emblematize what the protagonist Ibarra calls the "social cancer" of colonial society.[12]

Her mestizaje does not indicate a productive mixture extolling the virtues of intellectual culture but its colonial obverse: a colonial imposition that produces demented subjects in need of rehabilitation. And while María Clara's mestiza body represents the debilitations of coloniality, it's her presence in Philippine literature that paradoxically indicates a pathway for the *ilustrado* to cure the ills of his society. If one can represent social subjects disabled by colonialism, one then can transcend one's own debilitations through *their* rehabilitation. In a way, *Noli me tángere* represents an epochal moment in the Philippine development of literary genres of diagnosis whereby the presence of the disabled madwoman, or the otherwise incapacitated, signals the elaboration of benevolent rehabilitative powers through their very representation in colonial literature. Indeed, just a few years following the publication of *Noli me tángere*, Rizal would write about how Spanish colonialism "embrutece" (renders [into] a brute) the Filipino (a subject I covered in chapter 1).[13] We need only see that in his first novel the "brute" is the iconic and tragic María Clara.

It takes María Clara's imprisonment and desolation to demonstrate, at least within this vein of Philippine intellectual culture, that diagnosis is the substrate on which questions of sovereignty are staked. There can be no equivocation since the verb *era* (she was), as seen in the passage above, "era una loca" (she was a madwoman), is utilized to indicate a permanent state of insanity that would coincide with a more medical diagnosis rather than "estuvo loca," which would translate more like "she was acting crazy" or "she was acting like a crazy person." María Clara is diagnosed as crazy, and not insignificantly, by the abbess. Dispelling all doubt, there is reference to "un hospicio para dementes" (a hospice for the demented) in Manila, demonstrating that there was certainly a discourse around which the mental variations that modern culture would classify as "insanity" were managed through cordoning them off from the rest of the society.[14] Given this reference, it appears that Philippine society during the late colonial period was not too dissimilar from developments in how Europe and other parts of the West classified and treated the insane. Clear in Rizal's novel is a society predicated on a social division between rational subjects and those that are "demented."

The representation of the convent as an asylum—in conjunction with the capital city, the "center" of Philippine civilization, as a place that possessed institutions for the medical treatment of the insane—elaborates a spectrum of mental ability through the aesthetics of mestizaje. That is, Ibarra is the revolutionary mestizo rehabilitating society against the disablements of colonialism. María Clara is the bastard mestiza whose mixture does not avow hybrid thinking or complex subjectivity but rather corruption. Rizal conveys for us a logic and aesthetic of mestizaje that is hewn by a patriarchal hierarchy of mental ability. If Rizal's *Noli me tángere* is an emblematic text of the tradition of mestizo Filipino writing, it avers to show a passionate yet no less rational depiction of colonial society spearheaded by an intellectual vanguard. The so-called Philippine Enlightenment or Propaganda Movement was widely populated with scientists and medical doctors, as well as artists bursting with cognitive ability. They demonstrated the contractual capacities befitting an anticolonial intellectual movement wherein the subject of social protest was categorically not disabled. While entrenching problematic aspects of ableism constitutive of anticolonial and intellectual vanguardism, especially evident with the presence of María Clara haunting the articulation of such a movement, strategically contesting pernicious presumptions of native incapacity was ideologically significant.

Mestizaje then obtains as an aesthetic field in which different configurations of bodyminds can thrive to contest the conditions of colonialism. And yet, it is also a cultural, intellectual discourse that disciplines subjects that do not cohere properly to its norms. María Clara is evocative of the underside of the cognitive and rehabilitative aesthetic of mestizaje. Hers is a mestizaje that shows the compromised and polluted aspects of racial mixture that come with the imposition of colonial rule. She is a mestiza that is "demasiada blanca" (too white); she complicates the narrative of mestizaje as a discourse of uplift and instead demonstrates the complicated racial landscape wherein the feminization of cognitive impairment evokes a double standard whereby mestizaje uplifts mestizos with an ability to generate critical claims about society and engage in negotiations about the material conditions of colonialism, yet mestizas are rendered artifactual presences laying bare the systematic imposition of disability.[15] It appears reasonable to claim that the management of Filipina sexuality materialized also through a dividing line between sane and insane.[16] Mad María Clara may serve as the foundation on which the sane, judicious, and intellectual project of Philippine nationalism is articulated by Rizal and his contemporaries. The unrequited and impossible heteronormative love of Ibarra is what drives her crazy.

Rendered painfully explicit are the linkages between madness and death or dying; Manila places its demented in the hospice. Because of this linkage, it is not difficult to imagine that María Clara will die here or that she is actively dying demonstrating a necropolitical dimension to insanity and the institutionalizations that proliferate to contain madness. It is certainly from a dangerous height (*altura*) that María Clara wails, giving a suicidal impression. In short, madness here represents a colonial death sentence reflecting a state of affairs of terrific calamity for an unfree Philippines. It is the convent as asylum that explicitly links colonialism as exacting a cerebral toll and imposing mental disabilities on the colonized. Despite its depressing nature, this scene is perhaps the most modern of all in the pages of Rizal's work. While all the action of Rizal's novel takes place within the Philippines, it is clear that Michel Foucault's historical narrative on the ways that the "insane" came to be classified and then confined from the rational resonates here. Nevertheless, it would not be common, I suggest, to find a line in European literature in which the convent "se juzgaría como asilo de monjas" (would be judged as an asylum for nuns). This is so because Europe had specialized institutions for that. In the "age of reason," as it is dubbed by Foucault, reason has—through the definition of a subrational class of persons—emerged as a constitutive feature of civilization.[17]

The fact that Rizal finishes this novel, *the* Filipino novel, in Berlin shows that while this story features a local, if very elite, portrait of Philippine colonial society, this is a cosmopolitan narrative—one that ends with "la infeliz María Clara" (the hapless María Clara). Her confinement to the convent-cum-asylum is foil to the freedom of movement of the *ilustrado*. The *ilustrado*'s intellectual ability is directly tied to a literal physical body with the capability to traverse and cross borders (this is a dynamic that will be explored at length in chapter 3). Philippine intellectual culture as the "cerebrum of the nation" can be read as a rehabilitative culture so that the Philippines can avoid the fate of María Clara. Given this framing, she is a figure that demonstrates the feminization of madness, thus carrying a significant cognitive burden in the development of an intellectual anticolonial society that might participate in negotiations or intellectual exchanges with the colonizers about the conditions of their colonization as equal interlocutors. While there certainly existed palpable impositions on the sovereignty of many Filipino authors and thinkers of Rizal's era, the cloistered walls of the convent do demonstrate a backward and impeded Filipino society stunted by Spain. María Clara is a figure meant to inspire such a reading—her confinement perhaps meant to emblematize the confinement of the entire archipelago. Her madness ("era un loca") allegorizes the frustration of a people. And yet hers is a madness that neither overdetermines nor nullifies the intellectual capacities of the *ilustrado* elite. While Philippine colonial society under Spanish religious authority might be likened to an asylum, it does not indicate that the mestizos that bring you this story are crazy themselves.

Reference to the infrastructure dealing with the "mad" dovetails with the slippage between convent and asylum that transpires in these closing lines. It seems that Rizal might be making an implicit claim about the state of Philippine civilization. If madness exists as a qualified psychosocial disorder and there exists an institutional apparatus to manage it, clearly the society in which the mad appear would speak to the robust civilization of that society. This is an important point, as it would, constitutively, abrogate claims of barbarism. Hence, a generous reading of an institute for the "demented" would be an abundant social beneficence extended to the "subrational" sectors of Philippine society—a beneficence no doubt extolled by mestizo intellectuals themselves. Paradoxically, the presence of madness as a qualified, scientific, and clinical category of personhood does work to undermine an assumption of the "native incapacity" of Filipinos as a group without reason or intellect. In other words, in a novel that reflects the colonial context of the Philippines, the constitution of civilization through the management of madness is further clarified. Civilization's existence is affirmed by the presence of a madness that is managed institutionally. This reading has major limitations, naturally. The exposition of an anticolonial sovereignty through a hierarchy of mad and rational does not articulate a society based on the precepts of freedom and autonomy. When anticolonial freedom and expression is read via a crip colonial lens, we see that it is paradoxically the presence and proliferation of carceral spaces that index a legitimate stake and claim to sovereignty. Such a paradox confirms Filipino studies observations on the problematic aspects of mestizo elite society in the Philippines and the real limitations of reentrenching colonial ideologies within colonized society.[18]

What might we make of the fungibility of the convent with the asylum? Was the convent a place for the worship of God? Or "acaso se juzgaría que el convento de monjas era un asilo de locas" (perhaps it could be determined that the convent of nuns is an asylum for crazy women). I'd like to elaborate in more detail on mestizaje as an aesthetic field through which the representation of a racial spectrum of humanity indexes a psychophysical division of mental capacity.

Bastard Genealogies of María Clara

Contesting Eric Hobsbawm's redefinition of nationalism in the age of political revolutions in the late nineteenth and early twentieth centuries, John Blanco identifies a typically ignored "mutually determining" aspect of nationalism. That is, envisioning or reclaiming a national patrimony in response to "and [in] defense against the emergence of modern imperialism." Rightfully so, Blanco points out the extent to which Hobsbawm fails to account for the ways that colonialism bore out anticolonial nationalisms provoked by what Hobsbawm points out as burgeoning imperial powers during what he calls "the age of empire." It is within this context of "alternative modernities" that Blanco maps the undertheorized affinities between José Martí and José Rizal in his 2004 essay "Bastards of the Unfinished Revolution: Bolívar's Ismael and Rizal's Martí at the Turn of the Twentieth Century." He does so around the figure of the colonial "bastard" as the inheritor of a perhaps compromised and impure legacy. These common themes and character tropes in revolutionary literature, Blanco claims, "do not so much assert the existence of an 'imagined community' . . . as they ceaselessly announce their future possibility." To wit, Blanco reflects,

> The title of my essay aims to highlight two important themes in the late colonial literature of Cuba and the Philippines . . . embodied in the figure of a bastard son or daughter in various novels and poems. The first theme is the recovery of a lost legacy, patrimony, or the intimation of fate, which reconfigures the ethical and political decisions of the colonial subject on the eve of revolution. The second is the bastard's anomalous identity, which prefigures the colonial subject's abandonment by the society that engendered the colonial condition, but also gives her or him the relative freedom to break with the familial or paternalistic past by criticizing it and by announcing the advent of historical self-assertion in the colonial world.[19]

Despite this incredibly insightful argument, María Clara, the feminine "blanca" bastard who represents the foil to the masculine bastard of liberal revolution, is not even mentioned by name in Blanco's brilliant essay. And yet, by his own compelling admission, she is the central tension around which Rizal's disenchantment with the liberal revolution is articulated.

Blanco summarizes Rizal's novelistic oeuvre in contradistinction to Bolivarian parallels in Latin America thus: "Across the Atlantic Ocean . . . colonial expatriate of the Philippine archipelago (and soon-to-be national martyr and hero) Dr. José Rizal produced his two novels *Noli me tangere* (Do Not Touch Me) and *El filibusterismo* (Will to Subversion), around a woman whose bastard origins catalyze the hero's unjust persecution and recourse to revolution against the Spanish colonial government."[20] She is both traitor and "catalyst" for revolution. As we saw in the previous section, the woman with "bastard origins" is María Clara. That she is rendered a nameless archetype and doomed catalyst for the protagonist's trials and travails speaks to the broader conversation on the ways that gender and sexuality shape the racial narratives that subtend the "recourse to revolution." To be fair, the protagonist, Crisóstomo Ibarra, is also unnamed in the sentence from Blanco that I have quoted. I would chalk this up to a stylistic choice in the introductory matter of Blanco's article rather than any jarring or problematic gaps in his analysis. Indeed, his conceptualization of the bastard trope animates my own analysis in this chapter. I am deeply curious about the "woman whose bastard origins catalyze" a complication of the autonomy garnered through the recovery of patrimony.[21]

It seems one bastard genealogy permits a transoceanic meditation of Latin Americanism and Philippine republicanism, while another feminized bastard inheritance is better left forgotten as it, unsurprisingly, does not seem to command the same proclivity for uncovering lost global affinities. By thinking through those "mutually determining" aspects of nationalism, we can observe that within its literary corpus hierarchical racialized-gendered relations based on intellectual capacity and sanity obtain.[22] In so doing, the trope of the bastard represents for some a fruitful subjectivity from which different critical questions about colonial reality can be entertained for revolutionary ends. Meanwhile, the feminized bastard serves more as the catalyst for these more important national and transnational conversations rather than being the subject of them. I suggest that this affirms a rational and—not to equivocate—sane mind. Notably, this is a "bastard" mestizo mind. The underside of this recuperation of the mestizo bastard, simultaneously embodying a "lost legacy" and a "break with the familial or paternalistic past," is the representation of an impurity that is neither hybrid innovation nor ever-complexifying modern subjectivity in the face of imperial dispossession. Instead, María Clara's is a bastard mind that goes insane—confined from the society for which an alternative modern sensibility ushers forth "future possibility."[23]

I certainly do not dispute the exceedingly relevant and important work of uncovering the strange affinities between anti-imperial Philippine literature and Latin American parallels, both engaged in disidentifications with North American expansion. That such an admirable project means reading intellectual genealogies wherein Filipino bastards are not unlike or, indeed, "akin to [Simón] Bolívar's Ishmael—a lost and illegitimate bastard of a problem defined specifically as American" gives me productive pause.[24] This is a critical pause that makes me want to engage with Rizal's *Noli me tángere* with an eye toward the less romantic feminized bastard of ill-fated parentage. María Clara is not announced as a political subject suffused with a masculinist energy and revolutionary bravado such that her subjecthood can mark an intellectual genealogy that crosses oceans, continents, and multiple empires. She doesn't seem to inspire political crossings that allow mestizo *letrados* to consort and commune with one another through time and space. Mestizaje and the bastard subject positions that it births seem to allow such genealogies to flourish . . . for *men*. Rather than read the perhaps parodic send-up of Bolívar in the form of Rizal's "Simoun" (a significant pseudonym of Ibarra) in his second novel, *El filibusterismo*, the "less romantic bastard" of María Clara serves as the catalyst and subject of the queer and feminist analysis of this section.

I will attempt to prove that María Clara is a queer subject that can offer important queercrip tools for understanding the elaboration of disability within colonial society. As I have alluded to, in *Noli me tángere* a plot is fabricated against the hero, Crisóstomo Ibarra. An uprising against the Spanish authorities is staged by the duplicitous Padre Salví, who succeeds in attributing the leadership of the revolt to Ibarra through a personal letter he, through intimidation, obtains from his childhood love, María Clara. Significantly, this framing and its cover-up takes place after Ibarra is excommunicated after an altercation leads him to threaten the life of a friar, Padre Dámaso, for insulting his deceased father. María Clara stays Ibarra's hand, no doubt saving him from execution in the process. Extant, however, is the less generous reading of María Clara as a naive dupe expressing loyalty to the friar. Following the excommunication, who we come to know as María Clara's father, Capitán Tiago, is forced to cancel María Clara and Ibarra's engagement; she is then arranged to marry a Spaniard selected by Dámaso. We later find out that Dámaso is María Clara's true biological father. In a moving scene following Ibarra's escape from prison that is facilitated by Elías, the outlaw dissident and a friend, Ibarra is able to see María Clara on the night of a fete thrown in her honor to celebrate her engagement. In a much-anticipated scene, Ibarra reproaches María Clara for her betrayal but, since he is a man of honor and magnanimity, decides to forgive her. In a rare agentive moment for María Clara she pleadingly convinces Ibarra of her innocence, but not before being admonished by our hero and terminating their relationship for all time:

—¡Crisóstomo!—murmuró llena de terror.

—¡Sí, soy Crisóstomo!—repuso el joven con voz grave:—un enemigo, un hombre que tenía razones para odiarme, Elías, me ha sacado de la prisión en que me han arrojado mis amigos.

A estas palabras siguió un triste silencio; María Clara inclinó la cabeza y dejó caer ambas manos.

Ibarra continuó:

—¡Junto al cadáver de mi madre juré hacerte feliz, sea cual fuere mi destino! Pudiste faltar á tu juramento, ella no era tu madre; pero yo, yo que soy su hijo, tengo su memoria por sagrada, y a través de mil peligros he venido aquí á cumplir con el mío, y la casualidad permite que te hable á ti misma María, no nos volveremos á ver; eres joven y acaso algún día tu conciencia te acuse... vengo a decirte, antes de partir, que te perdono. Ahora ¡sé feliz y adiós!

—Crisóstomo!—she murmured, full of terror.

—Yes! I am Crisóstomo!—The young man spat back bitingly:—an enemy, a man for whom there are many reasons to hate, Elías, he aided my escape from the prison that my friends placed me in.

A sad silence followed these words; María Clara bowed her head and let both of her hands fall.

Ibarra continued:

—On my mother's grave I swore to make you happy, no matter what may become of me! You were able to go back on your oath, she was not your mother; but I, being her son, hold her memory sacred, and through many travails I've come here to fulfill my promise. Chance has permitted me the opportunity to speak with you directly, María, we will not see each other again; you are young and perhaps one day you may feel remorse... I come here to say to you, before I leave, that I forgive you. Now: Be happy and farewell![25]

Notably, Ibarra cites parentage and honoring his mother's memory as the source of his honor and integrity in his condescending diatribe toward María Clara. Tellingly, he informs her that she is not bound by the same oath that binds him, since his mother "no era [su] madre." The oath to which he refers is probably not exclusively a promise of love and fidelity between two young lovers. Ibarra's promise is tied to a lineage and patriotic heritage—or "patrimony," to use Blanco's language—that exclude María Clara. She neither shares the same parentage nor is bound by the same commitments that circumscribe Ibarra's love; indeed, the love of the true son is where Rizal wishes to focus our attention. There is a clear national genealogy articulated in Ibarra's admonishment. These are not avenues of patrimony that are available to María Clara; indeed, the whole project of constructing a national patrimony that would be honored and protected by its citizens is foreclosed to María Clara. Her existence may even be inimical to them.

The family drama Ibarra has laid out for us makes family loyalty coextensive with national duty. His mother stands in for the nation. Irrespective of the fact that he is not racially a completely "native" son, the native mother secures a national bond materialized through the articulation of an oath (*juramento*). Nevertheless, the mestizo prodigal son possesses the hybrid and modern subjectivity that confers the knowledge necessary to understand the stakes of such a bond, irrespective of whether or not racial mixture might diminish the possessive relationship to it. The mestiza María Clara does not enjoy the same political privilege of cosmopolitan hybridity reserved for the *ilustrado*. In her case, mestizaje is a field in which certain kinds of political claims are made and aesthetic judgements are articulated about the individuals that would ideally comply with such claims. Such subjects gravitate toward thoughts not of complex modern subjectivity but rather impurity. This reading is consistent with María Clara's own understanding of her unfortunate heritage and her own mother. Pleading with Ibarra to have sympathy for her, she furnishes proof that she is the luckless progeny of a mother that did not want her and, by extension, a nation:

La joven sacó de su seno dos papeles.

—¡Dos cartas de mi madre, dos cartas escritas en medio de sus remordimientos, cuando me llevaba en sus entrañas! Toma, léelas y verás cómo ella me maldice y desea mi muerte . . . ¡mi muerte que en vano procuró mi padre con medicinas! Estas cartas las dejó él olvidadas en un cajón . . . sólo me las entregó a cambio de tu carta . . . para asegurarse, según decía, de que no me iba a casar contigo . . .

The young woman furnished two papers from her breast.

—Two letters from my mother, ones she wrote in the midst of her many regrets, when she carried me in her womb! Take them, read them and you will see how she cursed me and desired my death . . . my death, that my father attempted to orchestrate in vain through the use of medicines! My father left these letters forgotten in a drawer . . . he only gave them to me in exchange for your letter . . . in order to be assured, as he said, that I would not be marrying you . . . [26]

This anticolonial politic, derived from an inherited legacy of indisputable familiar genealogy, is foreclosed to María Clara precisely because of those institutions that Ibarra (and Rizal) set themselves on in critique. She is perhaps a victim that they cannot recognize. And yet she speaks for herself: "Crisóstomo!—dijo—Dios te ha enviado para salvarme de la desesperación . . . ¡óyeme y júzgame!" ("Crisóstomo!" she exclaimed, "God has sent you here to save me from despair . . . hear me and judge me!") Despite her vociferous desire to be heard, Ibarra states, "No he venido a pedirte cuenta . . . he venido para darte tranquilidad" (I've not come here to listen to you . . . I've come to give you peace"). But, in an agentive moment, she refuses:

—No quiero esa tranquilidad que me regalas; ¡la tranquilidad me la daré yo misma! ¡Tú me desprecias, y tu desprecio me hará amarga hasta la muerte! . . .

—. . . una de las dolorosas noches de mis padecimientos, un hombre me reveló el nombre de mi verdadero padre, y me prohibió tu amor . . .

Y murmuró al oído del joven un nombre en voz tan baja que solo él lo oyó. . . .

—¿Qué me quedaba ya? ¿podía decirte por ventura quién era mi padre, podía decirte que le pidieses perdón, á él que tanto ha hecho sufrir al tuyo? ¿podía decirle á mi padre acaso que te perdonara, podía decirle que yo era su hija, á él que tanto ha deseado mi muerte? ¡Sólo me restaba sufrir, guardar conmigo el secreto, y morir sufriendo! . . . Ahora, amigo mío, ahora que sabes la triste historia de tu María, ¿tendrás aún para ella esa desdeñosa sonrisa?"

—I do not want the peace that you give me; peace is something that I'll give to myself! You who discounts me and your disdain for me will embitter me until my death! . . ."

—In one of the many painful nights of my sickness, a man revealed to me the name of my true father, and he forbade me your love . . ."

She whispered the name into Ibarra's ear in a voice that was so quiet that only he heard it. . . .

—And so what was left to me? Could I have by chance simply told you who my father was, could I have told you to ask him for forgiveness, from him who has caused you to suffer so? Could I have asked my father that he, perhaps, forgive you revealing to him that I was his daughter, he who so desired my death? The only option I had was to suffer, to keep the secret, and die in anguish! . . . Now, my friend, now that you know the sad story of your María, would you still show her that disdainful smile?[27]

This moment is tremendously evocative: María Clara calls Ibarra out for his myopic view, unaware of the many injustices sedimented in Philippine society—injustices that, frankly, only a robust feminist analysis of the material and discursive conditions of Spanish colonialism would be able to ascertain. María Clara expresses the impossible position that she has been placed in through the revelation that Dámaso is her father. The lie that implicated Ibarra was caught in a web of far deeper falsehoods, the revelation of which would fly in the face of the colonial structure of knowledge. The truth from her lips—indeed, a truth that actually never audibly leaves them from the readers' perspective—would never obtain as fact in an environment in which duplicity is so routinely and easily orchestrated. She is only able to "murmur" the name of her father without it being articulated directly. The reader never positively knows in this scene who her real father is; it is revealed later in the novel. Thus, the knowledge of her true parentage is disarticulated and disaggregated from her. It seems, then, only fitting that in the next scene in which we see María Clara, she chooses imprisonment in a convent rather than an arranged marriage—a compelling scene that I'll discuss in more detail.

In this imposed silence, she reveals her double bind: being held to a standard of silence in a Catholic power structure that controls discourse and truth, on the one hand, and being held to a standard of complying with a feminine and heteronormative loyalty to the nation that does not consider the intersection of patriarchy and colonial power, on the other. That is to say, *María Clara's agency in this moment exceeds the authorial intent of Rizal*, even despite his efforts to silence her in the very scene in which the truth of the friarocracy is revealed. In fact, María Clara's rejection of Ibarra's tranquility and peace, which she would claim for herself and give to herself, is uttered in silence—a silence rhetorically illustrated for us by Rizal himself. Only Ibarra can know from her lips "en voz tan baja que solo él lo oyó" (a voice so soft that only he heard it). Hers is a truth about the critique of the friarocracy that reverberates only as a "broken dialogue" whose final articulation is mournful shouts to a thunderous sky and a God who does not hear.[28] This mimics Foucault's insight on how the insane are cordoned off from society. While we see her literal imprisonment in the novel's end, within this scene we see a more metaphysical containment in which, stunningly, María Clara's loud remonstrances are expressed through debilitating silences.

This is a poignant moment of gendered, perhaps feminist, self-reflection on the operations of colonial power vis-à-vis what and who is heard, as well as the heteropatriarchal restrictions that place María Clara in a double-bind of fulfilling the feminine duty of unwavering loyalty for a nation from which she is, through no fault of her own, excluded. While Rizal certainly represents an idealized Filipina archetype that readers are meant to admire because of her beauty and self-sacrifice for a nation that would hold her in contempt (indeed, I think that this is the entire point of Rizal's novel), she has principally functioned in the ways that Denise Cruz has diagnosed: "Maria Clara was symbolic of a certain type of Filipina femininity ... she was fantastic ... an apparition produced to serve multiple purposes, a woman who appeals to other characters in the novel because of her disconcerting and extraordinary mestiza beauty." Cruz, not unreasonably so, is more forgiving in her analysis of *Noli me tángere* and the feminine archetype of María Clara, claiming that Filipino nationalist thinkers in the early twentieth century misread the satire with which Rizal rendered "her weakness, isolation, lack of political consciousness, and her dutiful acceptance of patriarchal rule—as hallmarks of ideal Filipina femininity." Nevertheless, Cruz and I find common ground in terms of María Clara's ultimately desired excision from what Blanco would call the patrimony of the Philippine republic given that "her status is unsettled by a horrible secret: she is the illegitimate daughter of a friar and tied to the hypocrisy of Spanish rule, and her character is thus haunted by narrative uncertainty." Cruz adds, "For some, she represented everything a Filipina should be: modest and chaste, loyal and servile. For others, she was the epitome of a dying tradition, symbolic of the shackles of Spanish Catholic rule." For Cruz, this indeterminacy and uncertainty confer the fantastical flexibility to María Clara as a pliant signifier to serve a multitude of political ends. Indeed, Cruz brilliantly articulates and confirms my understanding of the contempt with which Rizal wished his readers to hold for María Clara: "Her ignorance, vapid response to the world, naïveté, and desire to follow parental and filial order represent all that Rizal despised about friar rule and its enslavement of his people."[29] Even though, as Cruz's *Transpacific Femininities* has shown, María Clara's meanings have shifted over time particularly vis-à-vis the masculinist anxiety provoked by women's suffrage movements in the 1930s and 1940s in the Philippines, furnishing myriad and often contradictory meanings, such diversity of interpretations does not equal complexity or nuance in Rizal's case. María Clara's reflections on the broken dialogue of knowledge—which, indeed, her silence brings to the anticlerical and anticolonial critiques of Spanish colonialism—paint a far more nuanced portrait of colonial suffering. To be made to serve the nation; to sacrifice well-being, happiness, and freedom for the cause of Philippine sovereignty; and to have that service be met with (at best) exclusion and (at worst) derision is perhaps the true injustice of Spanish ecclesiastical corruption in the archipelago. That María Clara is born from this corruption might be the ultimate allegory of Filipino suffering and can aid us in sketching a robust feminist and queer-of-color theory of justice.

Mestizaje, Queerness, and Compulsory Able-Mindedness

The madness of María Clara marks which kinds of racial knowledge about the colonial social order are knowable or even articulatable. In this instance, I am referring to the provenance of mestizos through the colonial imposition of sexual violence. While many theorists have worked to theorize mestizaje as a form of hybrid subjectivity, it is also a reproductive logic that feeds into national imaginaries about embodiment, heritage, and inheritance, typically furthering the heterosexual couple as the cornerstone of the nation.[30] In this section, I assert that María Clara is a queer figure whose mixed heritage marks a perversity that cannot be encompassed by the Filipino national project—a national identity constructed through a mestizo enlightenment. While it is certainly within some semblance of artistic license that a colonized writer would furnish a narrative that ends in a tragedy whose abject dimensions would make the reader ponder the existentialism of colonialism, I suggest that we pause and think about how the unsuccessful arrangement of the typical heteronormative trope of two hybrid mestizo subjects results in the madness and containment of the mestiza.

María Clara's mother is most certainly the victim of sexual violence at the hands of the Catholic colonial order. The painful discovery of her mother's attempts to unsuccessfully abort her through the use of medications demonstrates the extent to which the mestiza does not belong: the native mother attempts to terminate the mestiza. María Clara, like her mother, goes mad. She isolates herself and is isolated from the nation. An isolation through confinement, then, carries with it the connotation of madness, disability, and institutionalization. I ultimately argue that mestizaje as an intellectual project and reproductive logic in the Philippines translates to a compulsory able-mindedness in which we see the powerful intersection of heterosexuality and normative mental capacity. Colonial able-mindedness is the political and representational node from which anticolonial nationalism emanates. The political exterior of this node is the convent turned asylum. The asylum then might be under the purview of the nation-state, but it does not contain citizens in the conventional sense. And hence, because of her treachery, stupidity, and tragedy, María Clara is excised from the political privileges at the heart of the reproduction of national and anticolonial power embodied in the institution of marriage—an institution that, as we shall see, she herself rejects even as it rejects her.

As to the sexual violence of colonialism, for an analysis of *Noli me tángere*, insight comes with the recognition that María Clara is the product of the prurient coupling of a priest who breaks his vows of celibacy and a native Filipina who is forced to carry the product of that union. Following Foucault's reasoning, certain epistemologies don't even meet the threshold of what is considered scientific because they are not articulated by an expert via channels of legitimate discourse.[31] Therefore, for anticolonial critics like Rizal, knowing the true state of affairs of the Philippines is a dubious prospect that means piecing together, as Foucault put it in his archaeological recovering of the history of madness and civilization, a broken dialogue of stammered speech acts.[32] We see the effect of such brokenness, I suggest, in the silence that accompanies María Clara's revelation of her parentage; she is the product of the sexual violence at the core of Spanish colonialism. The rhetorical effect in Rizal's novel is a secret that is so devastating that its unfiltered revelation would peel back the manifold traumas that structure the colonial social order even as those traumas demonstrate this order's untenability. Thus, the revelation is paradoxically communicated through silence. So pervasive, however, is this arrangement that even in civil cultural situations that would demand equivalent exchange among a community of interlocutors who convene to discuss what is best for the nation we see active silencing. This brings us to the dinner table. Such is the auspicious beginning of the novel as a dinner scene in a chapter titled "Una reunión."

In this scene we are introduced to María Clara's Filipino father "don Santiago de los Santos, conocido popularmente bajo el nombre de capitán Tiago" (don Santiago de los Santos, known popularly by the name of Captain Tiago), who "daba una cena" (was hosting a dinner).[33] In the lines that proceed this propitious introduction is the place setting used by Benedict Anderson in *Imagined Communities* to help bolster his argument about the fungibility of literary representation in constructing the nation through print capitalism. Tiago's home—in which a salon is hosted whose subject is the prospects of a burgeoning nation whose intellectuals quite vociferously agitate for more political autonomy—is meant to be interchangeable with any Filipino home. This is an interchangeability that speaks to the promise of text in unifying a nation through the "limited" project of Filipino literature (as opposed to Asian literature writ large), thus offering a vague yet intimate portrait of the country through written word.[34] While the others at the national dinner table are pastiches or national projections of an underlying Filipino political communion—or, perhaps national allegories, to paraphrase Frederic Jameson[35]—"Sin embargo, fray Dámaso no era misterioso como aquellos; era alegre y si el timbre de su voz era brusco como el de un hombre que jamás se ha mordido la lengua, que cree santo e inmejorable cuanto dice, su risa alegre y franca borraba esta desagradable impresión" (Nevertheless, Friar Dámaso was not mercurial like the others; he was ebullient and if the timbre of his voice was brusque like a man who had never put his foot in his mouth, one that believes himself saintly and infallible, his happy and frank laughter erased that disagreeable impression).[36] A translation for Rizal's inimitable satirical style: the friar never shuts up. Moreover, Rizal would certainly have us believe that the loud-mouth priest overestimates his knowledge of the islands that he shepherds. Gently—and, of course with the utmost courtesy and humility befitting a man of the cloth—the friar antagonist of Rizal's *Noli me tángere* pronounces,

> —Yo, por ejemplo—continuó fray Dámaso levantando más la voz para no dejarle al otro la palabra,—yo que cuento ya veintitrés años de plátano y morisqueta, yo puedo hablar con autoridad sobre ello. No me salga usted con teorías ni retóricas; yo conozco al indio....
> —Conocía á cada habitante como si yo le hubiese parido y amamantado: sabía de qué pie cojeaba éste, donde le apretaba el zapato á aquél, quién le hacía amor á aquella dalaga....
> —¡El indio es tan indolente!

> —I, for instance—continued friar Dámaso, raising his voice to not let others get a word in edgewise,—I who have lived on plantains and *morisqueta* for twenty-three years, I can speak with authority over such things. Present to me neither your theories nor rhetorics, I know the Indian....
> —I knew each habitant as if I'd given birth to and nursed them: I knew which foot was lame on this one, how the shoes fit on the other, which was making love to which (Filipina) woman....
> —The Indian is so indolent!"[37]

The obvious critique is that Dámaso overestimates the knowledge that he has of the Filipino people, creating a false narrative to suit his interests. Assuming authority over a populace certainly does not equate to deep intimate knowledge of the trials and tribulations of "each habitant," especially if such presumed familiarity is filtered through colonialism. This reasonable critique may actually belie the problematic sex and gender ideologies that inflect Dámaso's garish discourse. I suggest that María Clara is a spectral presence underlying Dámaso's racist diatribe. As the true father, the friar's admission that he knew which indolent "indio" was making love with which "dalaga" (young woman) tacitly avows the sexual knowledge that he possesses of the Filipina—a knowledge that María Clara's mother could not bear but had to bear to fruition. This dinner conversation sets the stage for the colonial tension that Rizal wants to explore throughout; it is centered, Blanco suggests, "around a woman whose bastard origins catalyze the hero's unjust persecution and recourse to revolution against the Spanish colonial government."[38] Dámaso's supposed knowledge of the *indio* (or in this case, the *india*) is, on the one hand, a moment of colonial racism we are meant to scorn, and, on the other hand, predicated on a deep-seated sexual knowledge that he extracts and imposes on the "lazy" Indians.

An unintuitive reading of the opening scene of Rizal's novel is that the underlying secret of the dubious heritage of María Clara is introduced *here*, in this opening scene, indexing the ways that the colonial power struggle between Spanish colonialism and a Filipino intellectual class inheres on María Clara's bastard, impure, mestiza body. Dámaso most certainly knows who was "making love" with whom. The vitiation of the mestiza demonstrates the extent to which mestizo enlightenment in the Philippines turns on the regulation and exploitation of Filipina sexuality even as it animates a critique of Spanish colonialism. It is a colonialism articulated through an originary sexual violence against and exploitation of the Filipina (María Clara's mother), which produces the corporeal mestiza evidence that gives impetus to the mestizo as an intellectual and agentive subject.

Thus, agentive politics in the anticolonial sense translates to a rejection of the product of sexual exploitation while also demanding her abiding loyalty. The delegitimization of the mestiza bastard manifests as and through her insanity and eventual confinement. Amazingly, Rizal makes María Clara choose this fate for herself. In an incredible reversal of the conversation in "la reunión" at Capitán Tiago's home is the dialogue Dámaso has with his Filipina daughter, whose life he ruins through the colonial institutions that he himself recognizes for their violence. Dámaso's recognition of this institutional violence is what I mean by *reversal*. As will become apparent in the dialogue, he wishes to protect his daughter from such violence and yet he is the single most powerful architect of the social forces that demean and ultimately derange María Clara. Her self-selected isolation paradoxically serves as a refuge for her even though it is ultimately her demise when she proclaims, "El convento o la muerte" (The convent or death).

Following the ultimately false discovery that her love Ibarra is killed by gunfire when he attempts to flee the Guardia Civil, María Clara rejects an arranged marriage and through this rejection paradoxically complies with the nation through her dutiful self-excision from it. While she defies Dámaso's attempts at marrying her off, her treachery makes it impossible for her to truly be a part of the nation for which her love for Ibarra is an allegory. Rizal's idealized Filipina character is rendered a stupid dupe and is meant to satirize the ways that Catholicism made the Philippines compliant and intellectually wilted. In an intense scene between her and her true father, worth quoting at length, María Clara makes her position clear:

—¿Me ama usted aún?

—¡Niña!

—¡Entonces... proteja usted á mi padre y rompa mi casamiento!

Y la joven le refirió su última entrevista con Ibarra, ocultándole el secreto de su nacimiento.

El padre Dámaso apenas podía creer lo que oía.

—¡Mientras él vivía—continuó la joven,—pensaba luchar, esperaba, confiaba! Quería vivir para oír hablar de él... pero ahora que le han muerto, ahora no hay razón para qué viva y sufra.

Esto lo dijo ella lentamente, en voz baja, con calma, sin lágrimas.

—Pero, tonta, ¿no es Linares mil veces mejor que?...

—Cuando él vivía, podía yo casarme... pensaba huir después... ¡mi padre no quiere más que el parentesco! Ahora que él está muerto, ningún otro me llamará esposa... Cuando él vivía, podía yo envilecerme, quedábame el consuelo de saber que él existía y quizás pensaría en mí; ahora que él está muerto... el convento o la tumba....

¡Ser monja, ser monja!—repitió.—Tú no sabes, hija mía, la vida, el misterio que se oculta detrás de los muros del convento, ¡tú no lo sabes! prefiero mil veces verte infeliz en el mundo que en el claustro... Aquí tus quejas pueden oírse; allá sólo tendrás los muros... ¡Tú eres hermosa; muy hermosa, y no has nacido para él, para esposa de Cristo! Créeme,

hija mía, el tiempo lo borra todo; más tarde te olvidarás, amarás, y amarás a tu marido...á Linares.

—¡O el convento o...la muerte!—repitió María Clara.

—Do you still love me?

—Child!

—Then protect my father and halt my marriage.

The young woman informed him of the last conversation she had
with Ibarra, but hiding from him the secret of her birth.

Father Dámaso could barely believe what he was hearing.

—While he was alive—she continued,—I planned to fight, I hoped
and trusted! I lived to hear news of him... but now that they have killed
him, now there is no reason to live and suffer so.

This last point she made slowly, in a low voice, with calm and without tears.

—But, silly girl, isn't Linares a thousand times better than...?

—When he was alive, I could marry...I thought of fleeing after-
ward...my father wants nothing more than family! Now that he [Ibarra]
has died, no other will call me wife...When he was alive, I could grow
old, I was consoled by the knowledge that he existed and that he might
think of me; now that he has died...it's the convent or the grave."

—A nun! To be a nun!—he repeated.—My child you know not the life
of misery that is hidden behind the walls of the convent, you know it
not! I'd rather see you unhappy in the world than in the cloister...Here
your complaints can be heard; there you'd only have the walls! You are
beautiful, so beautiful, and you were not born for such an existence, to
be the wife of Christ! Believe me, my child, time erases all; later you'll
forget, you'll love, and you'll love your husband...Linares.

—Either the convent or death!—María Clara repeated.[39]

"The convent or death" becomes a rallying cry for María Clara against Padre
Dámaso's protestations and the revelation of the abusive system of the convent. Recall that she knows her true parentage, knowledge that she hides
from Dámaso, and affectively she uses this to her advantage. Naturally, Dámaso is aware that he is her biological father, which is why he fights against
her wishes to be cloistered. What can we make of María Clara's choice to
exile herself to what is effectively an asylum, to institutionalize herself?

As far as the articulation of a crip colonial critique goes, it is my contention that anticolonial culture or counterhegemonic cultural production in
the Philippines constitutes a disability archive. María Clara demonstrates

how her disabilities articulate a queer subject position that rejects the marriage proposal. She highlights a pivotal queercrip archive that allows us to read anticolonial cultural production against itself for its recalcitrant ableism while also understanding the constrained agency of colonialism. Mestizaje is the literary and racial aesthetic through which this archive is articulated and, thus, reproductive and rehabilitative logics intertwine. There is certainly the contestation of incapacity that is central to the imposition of colonial power. It seems to be an intuitive political response that if you live under a system that oppresses you, you should question the terms of that oppression. You affirm that you do, indeed, possess the qualities that are dispossessed from you. In the case of a robust intellectual culture that is articulated against the grain of the colonial order, we can qualitatively measure cognitive capacity as the characteristic that unveils the social injustices of colonialism while also providing tools to diagnose it. Yet mestizo intellectuals' capacity seems to consolidate in a matrix that dispossesses María Clara of sanity and freedom. The project of self-authorship in anticolonial literature comprises a set of disability aesthetics and principles that should be of interest to a transnational turn in the field of disability studies. Some scholars have cataloged a set of political propositions, cultural formations, and artistic sensibilities that make up a disability aesthetic.[40] Petra Kuppers has nominally invoked a "disability culture" to organize the ways that invasive scientific discourses hierarchize bodies in ways that advance medical knowledge.[41] Within a disability framework attentive to anticolonial and postcolonial thought, texts such as *Noli me tángere* take on importance precisely because they assert the intellectual capacities for self-rule that are typically dispossessed by colonial authorities that seek to justify their continued dominance. To be fully a part of the project of authoring the nation, you cannot be institutionalized in the convent—which, as has been established by Rizal, is an asylum for crazy women. The asylum represents the constitutive outside of the nation. It is a space where María Clara simultaneously shows her undying devotion to Ibarra while also abdicating participation in the institution of marriage.

Much scholarship might theorize such exclusions from institutions of heterosexuality as "queer."[42] Even those subjects that we could define as "straight" or heterosexual could occupy queer subject positions if they have uneven access to heterosexual privileges.[43] In the instance of the relationship between the state and marriage, which aligns your life with national heteronormative time, those that do not or cannot subscribe to the life trajectories of state temporality can live lives that are nonheteronormative.[44] While disability does not constitute a sexual orientation per se, it can have similar effects on the ways that people occupy heteronormative temporality marking them as useful or not to the state.[45] Although this is not the only connection between sexuality studies and disability studies, it has certainly been a fruitful intersection for understanding the queerness of disability—partially captured through the analytic of "crip." I imagine María Clara's queerness and cripness via the ways that her racial identifications and bastard genealogy frustrate her ability to participate in the nation as a fully heterosexual subject. As we have covered, the manifestation of this exclusion is marked by her madness. Her racial identity as an impure mestiza indexes her incommensurability with the foundational fiction of heterosexual romance constitutive of Filipino nationalism.[46] In lieu of the romance of the nation, the tragedy of the convent/asylum substantiates that María Clara not only occupies a queer subject position vis à vis the nation but also a crip one. Indeed, not occupying the nationalist time of heteronormative romance results in a crip temporality visible through María Clara's insanity.[47] Disability marks her failures to comply with heteronormative romance. She is "too crip" to be a proper bride for Ibarra, the mestizo intellectual whose liberalism rehabilitates the nation suppressed by colonial rule. María Clara's insanity is an index of the very necessity for said rehabilitation. The intersection of cripness and queerness is where I locate a postcolonial understanding of the representational and political aesthetics of mestizaje in the Philippines.

María Clara is warped and perverted because of her heritage and therefore is unsuitable and excluded from the franchise of heterosexual marriage with the protagonist of Rizal's novel. She is literally an unfit mate not destined to be a companion to the nation that Ibarra sets his sights on bettering. If his is a project to bring the nation into the modern era via the benevolent rehabilitative function of education, she is undeniably uneducable (recall that Ibarra has returned to the Philippines to build schools to educate his compatriots). She is a mind not worthy of cultivation. She is a by-product of the social illness that plagues the Philippines. As she cannot reap the rewards and benefits of heteronormativity, she is "too queer to rehabilitate" and thus excluded—a traitor to the nation that she is meant to dutifully serve.[48] She has been too spoiled by Spanish colonialism; it is better to exclude her from the nation's future than allow her to continue polluting it. While it might be controversial to some, calling attention to the ways that María Clara's queerness and cripness hinge on her exclusion from the political privileges of heterosexuality begs the question of the ways in which her image has been deployed in Filipino popular culture and mythology to solidify heteronormativity as a national and patriotic value.[49] In actuality, it seems that tying Filipino identity and pride to a heteronormative national order belies the dubious nature in which heterosexuality emblematizes a Spanish colonial architecture mired in duplicity, treachery, and corruption—a corruption that is allegorized by the illegitimate child of a Catholic priest. Perhaps an overall redeeming virtue of Rizal's novel is to demonstrate the ways that heterosexuality performs these disruptions on and unto itself, rendering crip colonial critique a relatively straightforward enterprise. Nevertheless, perhaps what *Noli me tángere* demonstrates most effectively is that national membership is predicated on an enmindedness that is not available to the mestiza.

Perhaps unexpectedly, the ostensible heteronormativity that the Filipina bastard literally embodies through compromised mestizaje mirrors a foundational critical move central to crip theory. Many disability scholars, in an effort to clarify the aims of what crip does or performs vis-à-vis disability as a category of analysis, use *queer* as a productive analogue.[50] A seemingly intuitive starting point for establishing a conversation between these fields is in the recognition that homosexuality and disability have a shared history of pathology. Scholars like Robert McRuer have made the less intuitive yet no less foundational claim of the shared regulatory function of heterosexuality and able-bodiedness. He writes,

> I put forward here a theory of what I call "compulsory ablebodiedness" and argue that the system of compulsory able-bodiedness, which in a sense produces disability, is thoroughly interwoven with the system of compulsory heterosexuality that produces queerness: that, in fact, compulsory heterosexuality is contingent on compulsory ablebodiedness, and vice versa. The relatively extended period, however, during which heterosexuality and able-bodiedness were wedded but invisible (and in need of embodied, visible, pathologized, and policed homosexualities and disabilities) eventually gave way to our own period, in which both dominant identities and nonpathological marginal identities are more visible and even at times spectacular. Neoliberalism and the condition of postmodernity, in fact, increasingly need able-bodied, heterosexual subjects who are visible and spectacularly tolerant of queer/disabled existences.[51]

Heterosexuality, as critiqued by queer theorists for decades, gains its disciplinary power through its relative invisibility and neutrality compared to the pathologies that it creates in its wake. Michael Warner has labeled this the proliferation of "regimes of the normal."[52] In the colonial Philippines, an anticolonial nationalist form of heterosexuality is precisely that regime. That is to say, heteronormativity emerges as a power structure precisely by propounding the myth of heterosexuality as a natural and more desirable attribute of humanity. Indeed, it is read as coextensive with the human. While this is elementary information for many, queer analysis is not typically viewed as a germane reading practice for Filipino enlightenment literature. Moreover, a disability analysis seems even more foreign to the late nineteenth-century world of the *ilustrados* and Rizal. Nevertheless, McRuer has insightfully pointed out that able-bodiedness is, perhaps, even more discrete in its masquerade as a nonidentity than is heterosexuality. So strong is his claim that he has actually argued that a necessary condition of inhabiting the political privileges of heterosexuality is able-bodiedness.[53] This argument, at least to my mind, becomes more and more convincing given the preponderance of evidence historically linking homosexuality to mental instability and the physical incapacities attributable to HIV/AIDS. It becomes clear to even-tempered thinkers that homosexuality unjustly implicates disease, dysfunction, and debility.

These are stigma that actively need deconstruction and, less apparent to many, decolonization. While contemporary crip thinking critiques neoliberal capitalism as the dominant ideology through which heterosexuality and able-bodiedness network in their discipling of human difference, I suggest that other historical and colonial contexts see and further substantiate the consolidation of compulsory able-bodied heterosexuality. Mestizaje is a fruitful archive for such analyses in disability studies, for instance. As I will discuss in later chapters, further pressure has been placed on the centrality and overemphasis of the body at the expense of the mind as has been argued in studies of neurodivergence and the racialized histories that subtend cognitive variation.[54] The so-called mad turn in disability reclaims madness as an identity and even a point of pride, resisting the pathologizing dehumanization of medical sciences.

María Clara is evidence—in the national literatures that make up the Philippine Enlightenment and protract Hispanic modernity into the twentieth century—that a "compulsory able-mindedness" was necessary for complete participation in broader anticolonial movements. María Clara is so queer, so excluded from the political structure of Philippine national heterosexuality as sketched by Rizal, that she goes mad. Madness contains her poisoned mestiza heritage. She is, to use McRuer's language, a "cultural sign of queerness and disability"; such signs point to those subjects that are too perverse to rehabilitate and reintegrate into the national political community and are therefore confined from it. This is indisputably the case with María Clara and is consistent with extant histories on the ways that modernity has disciplined madness.[55] Yet instead of being confined to the asylum, as sketched by Foucault, María Clara is sentenced to wail away, a tragic figure, in the convent. This seems like a poetic and inevitable colonial send-up and contextual adaptation of what Foucault calls "the Great Confinement"—that is, a moment in the European classical age, or the Age of Reason (so dubbed by Foucault), in which unreason had to be classified and contained, thus birthing not only the clinic but also the asylum.[56] Rizal links María Clara's depravity and lack of rehabilitation to the corruption of Catholic colonial institutions as emblematized by the convent, which is represented as a feminized "asilo para locas" (madhouse). The cultural sign of her irredeemability is her madness. The convent becomes, especially for Rizal as the mestizo viewed as the harbinger of reason for the Philippine republic, the institutional seat of unreason and derangement of the Philippines—a fitting destination and fate of the bastard María Clara.

The Social Cancer

Centering the mad bastard María Clara, I suggest, gives a different queer and feminist genealogy of the Philippine Enlightenment. I contend that her meanings exceed Rizal's authorial designs and authority. She is the mad underside of anticolonial reason. The elite class of liberal Filipino *ilustrados* as fully modern rational subjects that favored reason and science over the irrational rule of friars drew their power as an anticolonial and masculinist vanguard through the deranged and delimited sanity of the mestiza María Clara. Given this context, Rizal's intervention was the strident anticlericism of his work—a critique that steeped Filipino nationalism in the cerebral and sane logic befitting their class. This anticlerical posture has an underlying mode of production. The consecration of sanity as the locus of Filipino reason required the confinement of the subrational from it. Rizal's work traffics in a gendered asymmetry of power that confines irrationality to the Filipina in the form of María Clara. Mestizaje is the representational and aesthetic matrix through which a division of cognitive capacities is imposed within and as a structuring feature of Filipino thought. Let's pause and think about what mad feminist perspective we can imagine from the mad mestiza María Clara. What sort of mad "mestiza consciousness" can we envision through the hybrid colonial bodymind of a character seemingly so reviled by the architect of Philippine modernity?[57] It seems that the impossibility of heterosexuality signals precisely its disciplining function of tragic figures like María Clara—a discipline that manifests through the technology and allegory of her madness. Might this mad mestiza be at the center of the Filipino national project? Or how might we reevaluate and revisit Filipino thought and nationalism by intentionally centering such a figure?

To conclude this chapter, I'd like to focus attention on the very beginning of Rizal's novel. In the "Dedicatoria" addressed "A Mi Patria" in the 1909 publication of *Noli me tángere*, Rizal describes the "cáncer" that infects the Philippines:

A MI PATRIA

Regístrase en la historia de los padecimientos humanos un cáncer de un carácter tan maligno, que el menor contacto le irrita y despierta en él agudísimos dolores. Pues bien, cuantas veces en medio de las civilizaciones modernas he querido evocarte, ya para acompañarme de tus recuerdos, ya para compararte con otros países, siempre se me presentó tu querida imagen con un cáncer social parecido.

Deseando tu salud que es la nuestra, y buscando el mejor tratamiento, haré contigo lo que con sus enfermos los antiguos: exponíanlos en las gradas del templo, para que cada persona que viniese á invocarte á la Divinidad les propusiera un remedio.

Y á este fin, trataré de reproducir fielmente tu estado sin contemplaciones; levantaré parte del velo que encubre el mal, sacrificando á la verdad todo, hasta el mismo amor proprio, pues, como hijo tuyo, adolezco también de tus defectos y flaquezas.

Europa, 1886.

El Autor

TO MY FATHERLAND

Recorded in the history of human sufferings is a cancer of so malignant a character that the least touch irritates it and awakens in it the sharpest pains. Thus, how many times, when in the midst of modern civilizations I have wished to call thee before me, now to accompany me in memories, now to compare thee with other countries, hath thy dear image presented itself showing a social cancer like to that other.

Desiring thy welfare, which is our own, and seeking the best treatment, I will do with thee what the ancients did with their sick, exposing them on the steps of that temple so that everyone who came to invoke the Divinity might offer them a remedy.

And to this end, I will strive to reproduce thy condition faithfully, without discriminations; I will raise a part of the veil that covers the evil, sacrificing to truth everything, even vanity itself, since, as thy son, I am conscious that I also suffer from thy defects and weaknesses.

Europe, 1886.

The Author[58]

The Philippines is sick. Indeed, what the crazy mestiza María Clara might show is evidence for the sickness that Rizal wishes to diagnose. This sickness certainly did not escape the attention of the translator from whose work the above translation of the original Spanish is sourced. Charles Derbyshire, as many translators do, offered his own thoughts on *Noli me tángere*, commenting on the "peculiar fitness" of the title. Indeed, he reimagined the title as *The Social Cancer*, no doubt inspired by one of the most compelling statements made by the protagonist Ibarra to the *filibustero* Elías. Recall that Elías aided in Ibarra's escape from Spanish authorities, perhaps shifting Ibarra's consciousness from that of a reformer to that of a revolutionary. So pivotal is this dialogue between the outlaw and the lapsed reformist that Blanco also references Ibarra's "diagnosis of . . . colonial society in which a perpetual disavowal of the due process of law effectively forces the colonial subject to resort to the very sedition he or she is presumed to propagate."[59] Ibarra exclaims,

> ¡Ellos me han abierto los ojos, me han hecho ver la *llaga* y me fuerzan á ser criminal! Y pues que lo han querido, seré filibustero, pero verdadero filibustero; llamaré á todos los desgraciados, á todos los que dentro del pecho sienten latir un corazón. . . . Nosotros, durante tres siglos, les tendemos la mano, les pedimos amor, ansiamos llamarlos nuestros hermanos, ¿cómo nos contestan? Con el insulto y la burla, negándonos hasta la cualidad de seres humanos. ¡No hay Dios, no hay esperanzas, no hay humanidad; no hay más que el derecho de la fuerza!

> They have opened my eyes, made me see the cancer, and they force me to be a criminal! And since they want it thus, I *will* be a filibustero, but a true filibustero; I will call on all the disenfranchised, all those who feel within their breasts a beating heart. . . . For three centuries, we have extended our hand, asked from them love, longed to call them our brothers. How do they answer us? With insults and mockery, denying us even the

status of human beings. There is no God, no hope, no humanity; nothing more than the right of force![60]

In Derbyshire's "Translator's Introduction," he reflects strangely on the botanical connection of "a comparison with the common flower of that name"—that is, the touch-me-not. Also note that the translation for "llaga," which means "wound," is translated as "cancer." In line with Ibarra's diagnosis of the ills of colonial society, Derbyshire also reasons that "the term [touch-me-not] is also applied in pathology to a malignant cancer which affects every bone and tissue in the body, and that this latter was in the author's mind would appear from the dedication and from the summing-up of the Philippine situation in the final conversation between Ibarra and Elías."[61] Of course, it is more commonly understood that "noli me tángere" refers to those words that Christ spoke to Mary Magdalene after he resurrected. Derbyshire can be forgiven the exuberant reading emphasizing the "malignant cancer" of colonial society, especially given Rizal's training as a medical doctor. Moreover, the sympathetic reader cannot help but feel Ibarra's frustration after being so degraded due to the machinations of the Catholic colonial order. He realizes that diplomacy and "extend[ing] our hand, ask[ing] from them love, [longing] to call them our brothers" will not work; Ibarra's is a lapsed reformism no doubt reflective of Rizal's own well-known reformist politics. "Nothing more than the right of force" will suffice after being exposed to the "cancer" of colonialism—the excision of a tumor.

This is not, however, the only instance of care that we can attribute to Ibarra. He literally cared for María Clara when she fell ill, sending her the medicines she required for her convalescence. This sets into relief not only the juxtaposition of Ibarra, ardent patriot, with his foil, the ignorant and impressionable María Clara, in terms of who is in the position to come to the epiphanies that are the substance of the rallying cry for the nation ("llamaré a todos los desgraciados, a todos los que dentro del pecho sienten latir un corazón") but also a juxtaposition based on literal physical health. Ibarra's is an agency based on able-bodied vigor. María Clara's character flaws are partly reflected in her predisposition to sickness, which requires the various poultices and medicines conveyed to her by Ibarra's goodwill and love—allegories for the nation, no doubt. And while her body can be healed by Ibarra's benevolence, her mind seems to wane.

So what problem does madness solve for Rizal? The more obvious reading is that the Filipina *loca* (madwoman) takes on the burden of colonial stupidity. The *ilustrado* can transcend this incapacity through his very own representation of it—through his own epistemic capture of a feminized colonial bodymind. A second, less obvious, reading might be that it is an aesthetic commentary on mestizaje. María Clara is white, "tal vez demasiada blanca" (maybe too white), clearly perverted by the colonial theocracy and housed in its institutions to go mad and then becoming some kind of ghost to be exorcised and excoriated. The mestizo novel convokes a colonial bodymind through a psychophysical division of capacity. The *loca* is the political unconscious of Philippine national literature as evoked in its most luminary novel. Hers is a mind that is not unlike Claude Lévi-Strauss's conception of the "savage mind." He writes that this mind is "neither the mind of savages nor that of primitive or archaic humanity, but rather mind in its untamed state as distinct from mind cultivated or domesticated for the purpose of yielding a return."[62] The cultivated mestizo mind needs an undomesticated one. It is not enough to show the corruption of the colonial Catholic order. Rizal's measured anticlericalism needs the presence of an unruly, insane mind as well—a mestizaje that is an "untamed state" resulting from a mixture of colonial imposition, whereas the mestizaje presented by the Philippine erudite "[yields] a return," and a productive one at that.

It has been the aim of this chapter to further destabilize (while not completely dispensing with) the province of Philippine national intellectual achievement as emblematized by the *ilustrados* by recuperating a mad perspective at the scene of anticolonial thought. Much in line with the thinking of Frantz Fanon, who critiqued national intellectuals by demonstrating the incommensurability of on-the-ground politics and the colonized intellectual, I seek to show the mutual constitution of anticolonial enmindedness and proper heterosexuality. This matrix I have called, drawing on Robert McRuer, a colonial "compulsory able-mindedness." The mutually constitutive nature of these frameworks is articulated within the field of Filipinx mestizaje and therefore directly contends with the ways that the racialization of disability is variegated by colonial sex and gender systems. Decolonizing our dependence on narrow conceptions of bodyminds can make decolonial movements more inclusive to all. In chapter 3, I further elaborate on the regime of heterosexuality and its collusion with the feminization of disability. This requires a return to the question of the Orientalism of Philippine Hispanic culture, which links US American benevolent rehabilitation with anti-Chinese animus.

Three

Filipino Itineraries, Orientalizing Impairments

CHINESE FOOT-BINDING AND THE CRIP
COLONIALITY OF TRAVEL LITERATURE

This chapter attempts to locate a salient flashpoint in the homosociality of Filipino *mestizaje* (racial admixture, miscegenation) during the beginning years of US colonial empire in the Philippines. Continuing the critique of previous chapters that insists that Filipinx American critique constitutes an important genealogy of crip analysis, I look toward mestizo Filipino political figures that benefited explicitly from the "benevolent rehabilitation" of colonialism producing an Americanized Asia ready to embrace modern political liberalism and capitalist development. Toward this end, I focus on a particularly significant travel narrative written by Teodoro Kalaw, *Hacia la tierra del zar* (*Toward the land of the czar*, 1908), which narrates the travel of an entourage of Filipino mestizo statesmen throughout an Asia that the author characterizes as savage compared to the American-colonized Philippines. There is some variability to this characterization in which Japan is coded as developed whereas China is not. Kalaw details his travels, accompanied by a retinue of other Filipino statesmen, intellectuals, and politicians, to an international congress held in St. Petersburg. Notably among his Filipino compatriots was the mestizo and eventual first president of the Philippines, Manuel Quezon. Quezon and Kalaw were then the First Philippine Assembly's representation at the congress to be held in Russia. While St. Petersburg was their main destination, their travels took them through Tokyo, Hong Kong, Shanghai, Formosa (Taiwan), Moscow, Paris, and Port Said, Egypt. Through Kalaw's narrative what is apparent is the ways in which they fashion themselves as the very rehabilitated subjects assimilated into US colonial regimes. They are the beneficiaries turned well-traveled agents of benevolent rehabilitation. And yet, the ways they distinguish their Asianness within "el oriente" also draws tactically on their citation of and within a Spanish humanist tradition. They furnish a mode of Asian mestizaje that is differentiated from an Orient that is perverse and disabled. Such assimilation demonstrates the ways that emanations of the Spanish colonial refract within and as part of a US imperial racial order.

I argue that, under US occupation, Filipino intellectuals sublimated the colonial debilities orchestrated under imperial benevolence to an Asian female body symbolically and literally disabled by the practice of foot-binding. A critique of the representation of the foot-bound woman is where the homosociality of enlightenment enters as an instructive analytic. I reinterpret the conversation "between men" to understand how postcolonial autonomy for Filipino intellectuals materializes through the conduit of a disabled Asian female body engulfed by the particularity and savagery of her bound feet, her "pies aprisionados" (literally, "imprisoned feet").[1] While it is not explicitly "Indianness" that is analyzed in this chapter, I suggest that is important to understand how Filipino mestizaje also contended with problematic renditions of the Orient in order to understand the ways that the Indianness from whence Filipino mestizos emancipated themselves, on the one hand, and Orientalism, on the other, collude in the propulsion of colonial ableism. Particularly in an age of Chinese exclusion, Filipino Hispanic humanist writing furnishes evidence as to the depravity of the Orient that must be kept out while self-fashioning a modern Filipino subject that can be let in. Such a framing evidences a key foreshadowing of anti-Asian animus present in José Vasconcelos's *La raza cósmica* (The cosmic race, 1925), productively demonstrating an earlier iteration of the coconstitutive nature of Orientalism and ableism.[2] I suggest that the modern Filipino that benefits from the Orientalization of ableism serves as evidence of the "success" of US rehabilitation, thus ramifying exclusivist ideologies, while Asia itself is open for liberal travel and penetration of its borders. At the crossroads of US imperialism, Chinese exclusion, and the colonial logics of Hispanism, Filipinos become the agents of the colonization of an Orient that sorely needs intervention by presenting it as a container for cultural and physical impairments that the Philippines has overcome. Presentation of racialized disability partly demonstrates how some of these colonial logics of benevolent rehabilitation infiltrate the minds of "enlightened" Filipino intellectuals as they literally and metaphorically navigate the vast expanse of the "Orient" structured by a Westernized imaginary. Such tensions are bound up in the symbolic deficiencies of the Asian female body—at once an object of abjection and scorn as well as one of care and a site potentiating reform.

Because of the atavist stasis that foot-binding comes to represent in Philippine enlightened resignifications of Asia, the corpus I privilege is the often-studied colonial genre of travel literature. I privilege this writing because it is predicated on the literal physical capacity to travel and the cognitive capacity to represent the locales that are traversed. The kinds of "tourism" of which travel writing is a product point to the ways that capitalism and ableism subtend ideologies of movement through a developmentalism that is consonant with the literal physical ability to move.[3] These Filipino "Orientals" are endowed with the ability to move through an Orient that meanwhile is kept out of the United States after 1882. This makes historical sense given the contradictory impulse of US imperialism to incorporate and assimilate the Philippines, along with Cuba, Guam, Hawaii, and Puerto Rico, while its immigration policy excluded entire groups of people by race. Filipino "little brown brothers" are "let in" because of their capacity to be brought up in the social mores of civilization while marking out, much in the same spirit of a *raza cósmica* that has upbraided the deficiencies of an Indigenous past, those that are unassimilable by contrast. Orientalism and Oriental imagery emblematized by the potent and problematic figure of the foot-bound woman is a gendered and ableist trope whose deployment explicitly connects disability with colonial development.

Philippine intellectual histories and archives offer an important vista into the ways that disability and colonialism interlock.[4] Typically, such intellectual histories with respect to the Philippines are historically concentrated on the late nineteenth century.[5] This is for good reason, as this period is one of a nationalist awakening for many in the Philippines. As I stated in the introduction, some historians have denoted this epoch as one of "national consciousness." While there does exist work that focuses on political developments in the twentieth century, the presence of works in Spanish by Filipinos is complicated by their contextualization within the US colonial period. For me, Filipino Hispanic writing navigating US imperialism is a productive archive to enhance a Filipinx American approach, which itself potentiates a vital "crip colonial critique" in its critical entanglements with US benevolent rehabilitation, as I explored in chapter 1. Such an approach of reading a Filipinx American cultural archive in a more intentionally transnational and multilingual arena also aids us in reconceiving the global context in which queer and crip analysis operate. Some of these authors are marked by a Spanish intellectual tradition (evidenced by their writing in Spanish) and thus considered more "enlightened" than other Filipinos who, as I have attempted to establish in this book's case studies, need uplift and rehabilitation. In this chapter, this Philippine Enlightenment is one that I would characterize as a long homosocial conversation among men reflecting on the tensions between civilization and barbarism in ways that are not too dissimilar from those of the Americas. One explicit difference, however, is that the "Orient" serves as a discursive marker for the barbarism from which Filipinos' own "Orientalness" is differentiated. In the space of this chapter, I essentially explore the ways that Filipino mestizos projected an image of the Orient as barbaric in order to differentiate Philippine Asian identity as immanently more modern, tactically drawing on a tradition of Hispanic humanism, on the one hand, and a rehabilitated liberal American subjectivity (what we could call a liberal Filipino Americanism, despite its "Hispanic" elements), on the other.

Since the political prospects of intellectual Filipino men are tied to their caricaturizing of a Chinese woman endowed with neither the same physical nor cognitive capacities of movement, I explicitly align the critique of this chapter with interventions made in the field of what crip theorists Sami Schalk and Jina Kim have productively called "feminist-of-color disability studies."[6] I consider my book project a contribution to a feminist of color disability framework and this chapter in particular as an example of the ways that women of color, in this case an "Oriental" woman, serve as intermediary figures of racial disabled savagery that intermediary figures like male mestizos can use to galvanize their mobile bodies as evidence of the success of colonial rehabilitation. I further the crip feminist critique crucial to *Crip Colony*'s interventions that I elaborated on explicitly in chapter 2 on María Clara as the paratextual fulcrum around which *ilustrados* (intellectuals) like José Rizal anchored their rational criticisms of Spanish colonial decadence and abandonment. In this chapter the racialized gendered figure of an Asian woman becomes the index through which enlightened mestizos performed and enacted their sovereignty. The chapter also takes a cue from postcolonial criticism that has thematized the enlightened subject at the center of travel/touristic narration. I align such insights with crip theory's formidable critiques of the constellation of assumptions around the mental and physical capacities that serve as the underlying yet often unspoken mode of production for the transparency of the subject.[7] That is, in order to ascend as a universal subject of movement and travel whose agency is unfettered, a sublime object of pity that constitutes the antithesis of universality must be represented: she is the absence of movement, emblematic of an extreme provincialism contradicting cosmopolitanism, and antithetical to modernity. While she is not uniformly the "Indian" savage that finds iterative representation in many of the case studies throughout this book, she foreshadows an equally savage unredeemable subject in Vasconcelos's meditations on mestizaje in *La raza cósmica* as a corporealized vista of the Orient where disability is positioned—meditations that I critiqued in the introduction.[8] In order to understand movement and stasis's relationship to coloniality and ableism, some context for Kalaw's life and meaning to Filipino studies is required.

Teodoro Manguiat Kalaw (1884–1940) was one of an emergent class of new Filipino intellectuals who came of age in the years just following the Philippine wars for independence. Kalaw represents a "new" Filipino intellectual, or *ilustrado*, in the sense that his prolific work in Spanish proceeds and is epistemologically indebted to late nineteenth-century anticolonial writings produced through the Propaganda Movement. He would be classified as one of those who contributed to the proliferation of Hispano-Filipino literature and culture during the US colonial period noted by historians and literary critics in Filipino Hispanic studies as a "golden age."[9] Despite following in the intellectual patrimony of Rizal, Kalaw differed. I suggest that Kalaw was partially the product of the US colonial enterprise of benevolent rehabilitation rather than the Filipino anticlerical discourse of the late Spanish colonial period. That is, the colonial enlightenment discourse that once agitated for Philippine autonomy was reformulated to navigate—and, in some cases, accommodate—US empire. Kalaw was a product and agent of imperial reform. Yet rather than claim that Filipino *ilustrados* were universally American apologists, instead we must understand their intellectual production as being articulated within the constrained field of agency of imperialism—what Irene Villaescusa Illán has described as treading the "split between the spiritual dimension of Hispanic heritage (idealistic and honorable) and the material aspects of American liberalism (materialistic and mundane)."[10] For my purposes, I analyze Kalaw's reinscription of anticolonial enlightenment under US occupation as part of articulating a genealogy of colonial disability integral to studies of global imperial histories more broadly.

Kalaw's historical positioning brings us irrevocably into an American-occupied Philippines. *Hacia la tierra del zar* could be viewed as part of an underexamined "tradition" of "American" Hispano-Philippine writing in the twentieth century. Kalaw might constitute an archive unto himself; for this reason I feel motivated to give him a deep and singular treatment in this chapter. In fact, Kalaw's writing was so prolific that Philippine historian Teodoro Agoncillo would forgive students of Philippine historiography for calling the American colonial period the Age of Kalaw—a period of writing roughly encompassing 1900–1940.[11] Apropos of political logics of debilitation, Kalaw's book actually ponders the position of the Philippines and Filipinos as what he calls a "race that is destined for death"—a discourse of colonial debility that he focalizes through the prism of post-Boxer Rebellion Manchuria and czarist Russia (part of the namesake of his travel narrative).[12] More specifically, this chapter engages in a crip colonial critique of Kalaw's navigation of American and Japanese imperialisms as he travels throughout Asia, ultimately ending up in Russia. Such a reading draws explicit connections to the politics of gender in empire. As we'll see, gendered tropes of colonial masculinity and rescue inform the movements and ability of *ilustrados*. I thus align this critique as a furtherance of what Nirmala Erevelles denotes as a "transnational feminist disability perspective."[13] Citing Erevelles in their conception of a feminist of color disability studies, Schalk and Kim write on the noticeable absence of engagement with disability politics in third world feminist analysis "despite the disabling legacies of colonialism and the ableism of the patriarchal state."[14]

By establishing Kalaw's travel writing as a map of the circulation of transnational capital in American transpacific expansion, Japanese militarized economic imperialism, and the failed imperial decadence of czarist Russia, I show how the able-bodied/able-minded itinerant *ilustrado* projects the debilities of imperialism and Orientalism onto the body of a Chinese woman to (1) rehabilitate her as an able-bodied laborer, (2) position the *ilustrado* as the enlightened steward of an Asia with cognitive and physical capacity, and (3) reinscribe the enterprise of benevolent rehabilitation as a racialized gendered discourse on colonial cognitive capacity and debility. Such a reading takes us from the colonially occupied Philippines, to the Japanese sugar plantations of Formosa (Taiwan), to the immiseration of a war-torn Chinese Manchuria after the Boxer Rebellion (1899–1901). It should not surprise us that the "pies aprisionados" of the Chinese woman would appear alongside travels into an immiserated China; the stasis of China serves to orient the movement of the *ilustrado* as a participant in colonial travel narration and therefore the modern progress of development. He is active and in motion; she is not. He is able to move and able to represent that movement; she is silence personified with the physical inability to move.

In what follows I offer close readings of Kalaw's travel narrative to understand how he frames the intellectual freedom of the mestizo *ilustrado* who moves through a static Asia. A static Orient sets off liberal Filipino itineraries navigating toward modernity. Kalaw is, ironically, an Asian mestizo subject with unprecedented mobility surveying a landscape that is undeveloped and in stasis. In the next section, I analyze the terms and conditions of his movements inspired by capitalistic and imperial developments in Asia by Western colonial powers. Following that I analyze the ways that such movement is in contradistinction to the "Chinese Woman" who is disabled—and whom Kalaw disables—in order to frame her as an object of pity, rescue, and rehabilitation.[15]

Cripping Colonial Travel

The colonial travel narrative has been theorized as a space where intellectuals have gained access to the sovereign tools of enlightenment. Of interest to disability studies, perhaps, is the contention that such access is predicated on disembodiment—what Mary Louise Pratt has called the "erasure of the human" from the landscape that is observed.[16] Put simply, the observer is erased as an active participant in the "nature" that they shape and document. Pratt has argued that this erasure both invisibilizes the debilitating effects of colonialism in travel literature under the guise of scientific objective "truth," thereby absolving the colonial traveler from ethical responsibility for imperialism. Pratt denotes this erasure of self—and therefore abdication of moral concern for the environment represented—as the "imperial eyes" of colonial representation: eyes attached to and that accumulate, through observation, political authority for an "imperial I." Imperialism is an important context for colonial travel literatures because it is what enables and shapes the desire for travel to far-flung sites in the first place. In this formulation of travel writing, the "totalizing project lives in the text, orchestrated by the infinitely expansive mind and soul of the speaker."[17] I suggest that we can productively theorize colonial travel writing as another of the ableist and debilitating architectures of representation that produce the "normate" (the able-bodied and able-minded subject).[18] Disability theorist Ato Quayson, writing in the realm of postcolonial literary aesthetics, addresses the normate as a colonial aesthetic produced from "the cluster of attitudes that govern the nondisabled's perception of themselves and their relations to the various 'others' of corporeal normativity.... There are complex processes by which forms of corporeal diversity acquire cultural meanings that in their turn undergird a perceived hierarchy of bodily traits determining the distribution of privilege, status, and power. . . . Corporeal difference is part of a structure of power, and its meanings are governed by the unmarked regularities of the normate."[19] I suggest that we might extend our understanding of physical descriptions of nature and the disembodiment of the natural observer as a colonial aesthetic that attends to the cognitive. By capturing the intersection between the critiques of the "expansive mind and soul" of the colonial traveler and the normate aesthetics of colonial literature, I aim to present a crip colonial analytic particular to colonial renderings of travel as a normate imperial eye/I.

The normate imperial eye/I positions the travel narrative as space in which the postcolonial Filipino *ilustrados* access the transparent status of sovereign subject—an able-bodied and itinerant eye/I physically able to cross borders and cognitively capable of representing what it sees, in Spanish, the language of the Philippine Enlightenment. Spanish and the humanist tradition that it represents are a crucial factor differentiating a modern rehabilitated Asian from a depraved Orient—an existential container of impairment, perversity, and bodily abjection. The appearance of the "Chinese Woman" operates as symbol engulfed by the spectacle of her savage impairment:

> Pero estas chinas, estas pobres chinas, con sus pies aprisionados, muy diminutos, ¿en qué piensan, qué hacen, por qué están tristes? Nunca una sonrisa amable asomó a sus caras pintadas de rosa, nunca. Y si alguna vez lo hicieron fue porque, queriendo dar señales de alegría, no tuvieron más remedio que abrir sus bocas pequeñas y hacer brillar sus dientes marfileños.

> But these Chinese girls, these poor Chinese girls, with their imprisoned feet, so diminutive; what are they thinking, what do they do, why are they sad? Never does a smile appear on their rose-colored faces, never. And if they do occasionally smile, wanting to give signs of happiness, they have no remedy but to open their small mouths and let their ivory teeth shine.[20]

While it is a brief mention, I suggest that this spectacle of racialized gendered impairment adumbrates not only the *ilustrado*'s travel itinerary as unbound savant but also emphasizes a boundless cognitive interiority mapped through Spanish. Similar to other disabled cultural figures, the representation of bound feet here highlights how the "Chinese Women's" "cultural visibility as deviant obscures and neutralizes the normative figure that they legitimate." Writing more generally about US culture, Garland-Thomson argues that "disabled literary characters . . . operate as spectacles. . . . Indeed, main characters almost never have physical disabilities."[21] I suggest that the foot-bound woman represented by Kalaw fulfills a similar representational function as a spectacle that neutralizes the normative figure of the *ilustrado*.

Readers should note that the logics of visibility and erasure in literary representation coincide with those logics germane to travel narrative. Again, what Pratt names the "erasure of the human" from the nature that they document is functionalized as the colonial traces of ability left in the wake of colonial travel narration and the impairments produced by the movements of imperialism. In Kalaw's journey toward the "land of the czar," it is curious that such a grand tour is made possible in the wake of the colonial devastation of the Spanish-American and Philippine-American Wars. "Nature," or what Kalaw homosocially comes to call "cuadros de miseria" (portraits of misery), becomes the raw material that is made flexible for disposal. This exploitation is the logic of capitalist colonialism. Such transparency, however, is traversed by a US colonial gaze both by virtue of the American absent presence throughout *Hacia la tierra del zar* and the political support offered by American colonial embassies.

What Kalaw's book allows is a reexamination of the genre of the colonial travel narrative for this genre's ableist investments. Such a reading compels our attention to the epistemological function of travel and its narration as constitutive of an able-bodied subject capable of movement not only across physical space but also through the representational logics predicated on others' relative developmental stasis. This process evokes the mind/body split necessary for the masculinist discourse of colonial enlightenment to materialize. The *ilustrado*'s erasure from the Asia that they represent is the very departure point for their emergence as sovereign agent of rehabilitation. The departures and arrivals represented in *Hacia la tierra del zar*—the literal and figurative border crossing between different Asias—narrate the colonial bodymind through a racial materialist division of labor evocative of the movement of global capital. That is, the enlightened gesture to transcend and rehabilitate the body is mediated by and mediates the global diffusion of capital that extracts surplus value from human labor. If the Philippine Enlightenment protracts through a homosocial continuum of *ilustrados* navigating American imperialism's investment in Asia, then Filipino homosociality concretizes through and as a globalizing discourse of disability. The literal ability of *ilustrados* to traverse borders across multiple empires

(American, Japanese, Russian, and Spanish) is enabled by an epistemic sovereignty in which the travel narrative is situated as a colonial medium of representation. Yet the cognitive capacity that this ineluctably implies is a product of transnational capital and a racialized gendered division of labor. Therefore, the centralization of the body ("pies aprisionados" and mestizo travelers) and embodiment is crucial in this analysis. The physical embodiment of the *ilustrado*, with the bourgeois capitalist capacity to move across borders as colonial observer, is made transparent or "erased from nature" through the physical overembodiment of the Asian female body—it is a severely disabled figure meant to shock even horrify the Westernized reader: the "Chinese Woman" evacuated of interiority whose deformed body epitomizes a disabled Asia—immobile, literally bound, and figuratively stuck in time. I thus argue that the epistemic fissure of cognition from embodiment is the very mechanism that enacts the representation of a desire for an international division of labor whereby global capital penetrates Asia. Kalaw demonstrates that his travels coincide with the movements of capital that he documents coevally. The question of the restructuring of epistemology in the Philippine Enlightenment during the early twentieth century is not disentangled from economic restructurings occurring in Asia writ large.

It is difficult to understand the evocative representation of the Chinese "pies aprisionados" without coming to terms with the broader context of racial capital. In Kalaw's travels, the spectrally infinite cognitive capacity of the imperial eye/I is abstracted from both the material landscape it purports to document and the materialist conditions that precipitate travel in the first place.[22] This normate imperial eye/I endows itself with an infinite cognitive capacity to assiduously and scientifically document what it sees. Yet the disembodiment and the erasure constitutive of this cognitive ability to represent is intimately tied to a colonial body that can travel, cross borders, and traverse landscapes. For Pratt, we observe how the representation of nature actually produces desire for the objects observed by the eye/I and articulates colonial bodies as temporally static.

Kalaw's normate eye/I documents the "pies aprisionados" of the "Chinese Woman" to posit an atavist Asia as a racialized gendered discourse on female impairment. Significantly, this body is one that is at odds with transnational capitalist designs on a perfectible laboring Asian body. That is, this colonial genre is a materialist cartography opening up entry points for the penetration of capital through the representations of bodies, vast material wealth, and natural resources and the extension of American benevolent assimilation rehabilitating the Filipino intellectual as civilized colonial subject. We can observe that nature becomes the raw material for the flexibility of a normate body for whom such natural resources, native peoples, and land unfold naturally and apolitically.

Nevertheless, before the estrangements enacted on and through the "Chinese Woman" as the symbol of a debilitated Asia can properly orient a postcolonial crip reading of the *ilustrado* as a cognitive figure, I establish *Hacia la tierra del zar* as protracting the Philippine Enlightenment through a homosocial continuum between an American empire and a Filipino nation. It is through this continuum that we can understand this Filipino travel narrative as a racial materialist survey of the economic developments in and around Asia at the turn of the twentieth century—an Asia that the Philippines as colonial satellite and sovereign national project gets to reform and subsequently deform. In the following section, I will explicate the broader colonial dynamics involving China, Japan, Russia, and the United States and the ways these shape the ableist ideologies of the travel narratives of and from the crip colony.

The "Milagro Japonés"

Accompanying Kalaw were various future and then current Filipino statesmen that would play a pivotal role in the shaping of the Philippine government and nation during US occupation.[23] Significantly, one of Kalaw's closest friends and confidants accompanied him on this Filipino grand tour—perhaps, the most famous Filipino politician in the history of the country in the figure of Manuel Quezon. Significantly, Quezon is one of the central figures of Kalaw's touristic impressions as evidenced by his homosocial dedication to

> el que ha sido testigo personal de estas impresiones de viaje; el que ha visto, a lo largo de las estepas rusas, cuadros de miseria; el que ha sentido simultáneamente, en su paso breve por pueblos, el ambiente de la libertad y el ambiente de la opresión; el que sabrá recoger, en una palabra, — porque es inteligente y porque es joven, — de las ciudades populosas, enseñanzas para su pueblo sometido, dedica cariñosamente este libro. . . .
> Manila, 10 de septiembre de 1908

> the one who has been a personal witness to these travel impressions; the one who has seen, through the Russian steppes, portraits of misery; the one who has simultaneously felt, in his brief passage through villages, the feelings of liberty and oppression; the one who will know how to

apprehend, in one word - - because he is intelligent and because he is young - - from these populous cities, teachings for his own subdued nation, I dedicate this book affectionately. . . .

Manila, 10 September 1908.[24]

Kalaw and Quezon are the "personal witness[es]" to the "cuadros de miseria" represented in the book. These "cuadros" are, most notably, Chinese Manchuria after the Boxer Rebellion and bucolic subproletariat Russia. The dedication speaks fascinatingly to the historical positioning of *Hacia la tierra del zar*, most notably to a homosocial relationship between men as this kinship extended across "other Asias," to borrow a phrase from Gayatri Spivak.[25]

"Asias" come to be othered by Kalaw as the sovereign *ilustrado* representing, redrawing, and critiquing borders that muddle the transparent referent that we might call *Asia*. Kalaw leverages the description of a flexible Asia where "enlightened" Filipino writers negotiate a complex domain of intersecting imperial projects. Indeed, *Hacia la tierra del zar* indexes major literal and imaginative shifts in the geopolitical arena of Asia as the United States acquired its first Asian colony. In a section of Kalaw's travelogue titled "La Mandchuria sangrienta" (Bloody Manchuria) in which I will anchor this part of my analysis, we find a productive yet tense historical ambiguity: Which conflict precisely left Manchuria in bloody shambles? That is, it is unclear on a cursory read of this part of the journey toward czarist Russia which martial conflict has led Manchuria to become so war-torn and destitute. The reason I bring in Manchuria here is that it is impossible to historicize Kalaw's book without it. We can assume that the time and place of the narrative that sees Manchuria "bloody" is the Boxer Rebellion, which witnessed an eight-nation alliance of Western states (including Russia, the United States, and a rapidly industrializing Japan) against the nationalist movement of Chinese Manchurians. Japan becomes a sign of Asian economic success and, by proxy, scaffolds the Philippines, as recipient of American imperial largesse and as a civilization worthy of racial uplift. In this formulation, however, Kalaw notes that Japan has its own colonial goal of uplifting an economically potent Asia. In Formosa (what today is known as Taiwan), "toda la atención se puso entonces preferentemente en el azúcar . . . crearon un sub-departemento del azúcar" (all attention and preference was placed on sugar . . . they created a subdepartment of sugar).[26]

Japanese-occupied Taiwan is transformed into a sugar plantation. The transformation is so complete that, indeed, "they created a subdepartment" dedicated entirely to the cultivation and exportation of sugar. Kalaw's description of Japanese economic agricolonialism admires the shrewd and efficacious uptick represented in the "milagro japonés" (Japanese miracle). He writes,

> La primera medida es ayudar a los capitales particulares: a los que adquirían máquinas modernas para el beneficio del azúcar el gobierno ayudaba con una donación de un 20 por ciento del capital invertido. Ya, con este emolumento, muchos se sintieron con deseos de emprender el negocio. Actualmente la isla cuenta con 10 máquinas modernas como las que se encuentran en Cuba y Hawaii.

> The first step is to aid in particular capital developments: to those that would acquire modern machines for the benefit of sugar production the government provided a donation of 20 percent of the total capital invested. So, with this stipend, many felt motivated to pursue this business venture. Today the island [Taiwan] possesses 10 modern machines like those found in Cuba and Hawaii.[27]

Significantly, this economic "miracle" is measured in US terms: agricolonial development of Cuba and Hawaii. These parallel imperial projects are interesting read in the historical context of the period after the Russo-Japanese War. Japan triumphed over the nation, characterized by Kalaw as a "medieval" violent empire given its martial exploits in Manchuria that left the latter "bloody" beyond recognition. The transformation of Taiwan into an economic hub that helps to fund Japanese imperial expansion cannot, then, be separated from the very visible militarization marked by Kalaw as he travels through the miraculous modern renovation effected by the Asian empire, where "fortificaciones y obras de defensa que se construen desde Ki-lung (hasta Tai-pé)" (fortifications and defenses are being constructed from Ki-Lung [to Taipei]).[28]

The connections of the sugar economies of Japan are not distanced from similar economic militarism undertaken by the United States "like [that] found in Cuba and Hawaii." US sugar plantations have been documented to have prompted and benefited from a massive migration of Filipino laborers.[29] One might wonder that since the United States is sponsoring and providing interpretive support for this trip, what is it that it wants these *ilustrados* to see? How do the sites of US imperialism shape the sight of the normate eye/I? The fact that this implicit triangle between a Japanese occupied territory and the US-occupied territories of Hawaii and the Philippines is deemed by Kalaw to be a political success perhaps suggests mainly that the "consul americano" succeeded in convincing some *ilustrados* of the benefits of their own assimilation. Indeed, según los datos que nos facilita el consul americano, antes de la ocupación japonesa, la isla sólo producía 10 mil toneladas de azúcar al año. Hoy, bajo el dominio de los nipones, produce 70 mil. Y tan grande es la esperanza para el porvenir, que los severos y sabios directores del sub departamento, en un momento de legítima fe en su obra, han dicho que dentro de 5 años ellos esperan una producción de 250 mil toneladas

according to the information provided by the American consul, before the Japanese occupation, the island only produced 10 thousand tons of sugar per year. Today, under the dominion of the Japanese, it produces 70 thousand tons. So large is the hope for the future that the strict and wise directions of the subdepartment [of sugar], in a moment of supreme faith in their work, have stated that within 5 years they expect an output of 250 thousand tons.[30]

The assiduous attention given to the governmental organization of sugar economies in Formosa transpires in the name of maximizing the latter's production. This suggests that the pattern of coloniality characterized by imperial agricolonial development represents a possibly pivotal step in eventual postcolonial sovereignty for the Philippines. Within this literal and symbolic economy, Kalaw's travelogue can be read as an important historical index of the material economic transformations that transpired at the turn of the twentieth century in Asia. Additionally, the positioning of the text among multiple imperial projects (in Japan, Russia, and the United States) speaks to the ways in which the Philippine Enlightenment is scoped in the crosshairs of these competing imperialisms—all of this before Kalaw's critique of imperialism inches closer and closer to Russia by way of Manchuria. It is important to note that in addition to the Boxer Rebellion and the Russo-Japanese War, there is another conflict that adds to Kalaw's materialist critique, however.

Despite the historical convulsions of the Boxer Rebellion, and the Russo-Japanese War's effects on Asian-European relations, another "minor" conflict in US imperial history articulated a substrate that we might understand as yet another ghost that haunted Philippine Enlightenment discourse: the Philippine-American War. The collision of a Filipino writer and a "Bloody Manchuria" speaks to the temporal coincidence of the Boxer Rebellion as an anti-imperialist Asian movement with that of the Philippine-American War (1899–1902). The "insurrection" technically ended at the time of Kalaw's writing, but it continued in the rebellions of the Muslim south of Mindanao until approximately 1911. What can be gleaned from the coincidence of an insurrection that had not yet ended in the Philippines and the representation of post–Boxer Rebellion China? I suggest that Manchuria stands as a bloody allegory of a hotly contested Asia—a mutable and shifting geopolitical zone between an American-occupied Philippines and Russian imperial China. We are left to ponder: Which Asia are we seeing as we read *Hacia la tierra del zar*? Which Asia does the *ilustrado* want us to see? What are the representational strategies of the normate eye/I as an active shaper of debilitated and capacitated Asias?

One of the tactics that Kalaw employed in his adaptation to American imperial rule was the deployment of Orientalist imagery. To demonstrate the shifts, translations, and mutations that the Philippine Enlightenment experienced (and by extension Asia itself), I turn to a scene from Kalaw's travel diary in which multiple Orients converge with and on US empire, which constitutes a rather stunning "Filipino American" moment:

> A la hora de la cena, instintivamente, por impulso "racial," los cinco Filipinos quisieron encontrarse en una sola mesa y dialogar sobre las tristezas de la Patria. Considero a Rogers, con criterio liberalmente cosmopólita, un Filipino. Somos: Salvador Roxas, Narciso Alegre, Quezon, Rogers y el que escribe estas cuartillas. Los americanos que, al principio, se sentaban con nosotros, viendo nuestro amable intimismo y nuestros alegres corazones nos dejaron, por completo, el control de la mesa. Es pues, en medio del exótico ambiente, una mesa Filipina.

> During dinner, instinctively, due to a "racial" impulse, the five Filipinos decided to meet at a single table and discuss the tragedies of the Homeland. I consider [Theo] Rogers, with liberally cosmopolitan criteria, a Filipino. We are: Salvador Roxas, Narciso Alegre, [Manuel] Quezon, Rogers, and the one that writes these very lines. The Americans who, at first, sat with us, seeing our friendly intimacy and our happy hearts, left us total control of the table. Hence, in the middle of this exotic environment, [there was] a Filipino table.[31]

In this scene, the *ilustrado* becomes the benevolent subject extending Philippine citizenship to the American. This "Filipino American" intersection should not be considered outside the overarching framework of Orientalism. The "mesa Filipina" is where "unos chinos sacerdotales, con sus amplias túnicas blancas, misteriosos dentro de su orientalismo, nos sirven ceremoniosamente, con parsimonia mandarinesca" (some priestly Chinese, with their ample white robes, mysterious in their orientalism, serve us ceremoniously, with Mandarin parsimony).[32] The table is oriented within the modern scene of the Japanese gunboat, "el *Hong Kong Maru*," representative of an economic and martial change for the Philippines as it finds articulation within a shifting frame of reference that is "Asia." Whose Asia is being represented—and, who's Asia—in such an imperial patchwork become increasingly important questions as Kalaw continues. While these travel diaries begin in Asia, the reader is confronted with the instability of such a geopolitical referent. Various "Orients" converge at "una mesa Filipina," unraveling any monolithic image of Asia that we might entertain reading Southeast Asian literature. This scene resonates with a similar convergence of multiple Orients in the 1899 *Puck* magazine cartoon "School Begins" (which I analyze in chapter 1), in which the Chinese "coolie" and the Filipino *indio* appear in the same imperial scene, frustrating clear geographic or racial delineations.

These "chinos sacerdotales" are represented as vicars of an oriental essence that comes to circumscribe their "parsimonious" service to the future Philippine heads of state that consort momentarily with their American diplomatic attachés before conversing alone. Yet even as this essential "parsimonia mandarinesca" is held up as fulfilling an austere Orientalist stereotype undoubtedly assumed to be circulating in the mind of Kalaw's imagined reader, the *ilustrado* at the center of the production of Asianness in this sentence (indeed, served by it: "nos sirven ceremoniosamente") subverts, while also dining on and furthering, the "mystery" of Orientalism. This subversion is articulated through the crossroads of the Orient that is represented vis-à-vis (cultural) capital and its attendant privileges, enjoyed by Kalaw as an Asian author with the powers to perform such a representation. Such subversion, I argue, transpires through the transparency of enlightenment—the ability to represent as a threshold subject within and without Asia as a Filipino through the medium of Spanish.

Such threshold subjectivity mirrors the intermediary nature of mestizaje as a nodal point between various racial projects. It is this threshold "Asian" sovereign that cannot only exploit Chinese labor through an Orientalist racialization but can also invite Americans to the table, as it were, by redefining the term *Filipino* with "criterio liberalmente cosmopólita." I suggest that the *ilustrado* profits from the erasure of US imperialism via the surprising assimilation of white Americans into the Philippines seated at the same table as, ostensibly, equals. Indeed, it is the invitation of "America" to the table that elaborates one re-formation of who composes Asia. As we see in the passage above, in the midst of a presumably rousing discussion about the "tristezas de la Patria," Kalaw makes a stunning observation—the

American, Rogers, is an American that is a Filipino. Here the Philippines is symbolically made part of the United States.

It is unproductive to assume that this "new" brand of twentieth-century Filipino *ilustrados* represented a monolithic American apology. While it is certainly the case that the overall effect of this text is as American accommodationism, it is also certainly the case that there is a very limited window of agentive possibilities within a political landscape largely structured by a United States imperial apparatus.[33] I have argued thus far that the United States' absent presence in Kalaw's travel impressions does not signify the displacement of it from the sovereignty of the Philippine intellectual discourse. Indeed, the scene I quoted from above is one of the only instances in which Americans actually appear in the text. The deployment of Orientalist imagery and affirmation of exploitative imperial economic developments by Japan (and tacitly by the United States) fashions a flexibly defined "Asia" that Kalaw can suffuse with new political meanings as a mestizo interlocutor. The pliancy of Asia as an unstable referent, simultaneously connoting Orientalist savage and savant, demonstrates that Kalaw's *Hacia la tierra del zar* evokes the colonial travel narrative as the racial materialist representation of the movement of global capital. For instance, the colonial subject (yet emancipated intellectual) of the *ilustrado* repeats a postcolonial Enlightenment project as the very mechanism through which American imperial and economic interests ramify through the flexibly redefined Asia that Kalaw himself maps out. Stated more simply, the Filipino mestizo is the product-cum-agent of US benevolent reform and rehabilitation. This cartographic imperative transpires through the homosocial continuum (the table conversation among intellectual men discussing "las tristezas de la Patria") of the Philippine Enlightenment. Yet there are several episodic interventions that Kalaw stages in his narration that shift the homosociality of the Enlightenment to allow a consideration of the genre of the travel narrative itself through a postcolonial disability studies lens of imperial benevolence and "white love."

Cripping the Philippine Enlightenment: The Ilustrado Ideology of Ability and White Love

The representation of Manchurian dissent in opposition to the presence of Russian military force serves as the literary mechanism through which Kalaw politically reimagines Asia. Such reimagination endows Asia with a sense of pliancy that can be understood in the context of the itinerancy of the *ilustrado* traveler and the power to represent such a space through Spanish under the beneficent tutelage of American empire. The ruination of Manchuria after the Boxer Rebellion and the subsequent Russian occupation of China are understood through the framework of the failed Philippine insurrection against the United States in the Philippine-American War. Surprisingly, the destination that makes sense of these intersecting colonial conflicts is the bucolic Russian countryside; Kalaw presents the material effects of poverty that the Russian state has all but ensured for its citizens. Paying due attention to the ways that whiteness and the love for it are represented through the Filipino framework of mestizaje demonstrates the productive effects of US benevolent rehabilitation of the Philippines. Mestizaje is elevated above—and indeed becomes a rehabilitative force toward—Russian whiteness. The impoverished Russian hinterlands is where the thread of the Filipino homosocial brotherhood between Kalaw and Chinese mestizo, or *sangley*, Manuel Quezon is substantiated further:

> Ayer, en uno de esos villorrios obscuros en donde los trenes hacen paradas momentáneas, mi compañero, Quezon se acercó a un grupo de emigrantes que acababan de llegar al pueblo, queriendo contemplar de cerca a aquellas pobres víctimas del hambre. Indudablemente, serían miembros de una familia. El compañero llamó a un mugriento niño de 5 años, enclenque y tímido, figura del hambre y del esclavo, con un abriguito que era un trapo, le dió una monedita rusa. La madre que lo vió, no pudiendo ocultar su satisfacción y su gratitud, ordenó al hijo, en lengua moscovita, que besara la mano del buen extranjero.
>
> Y el niño, educado en la sumisión de todo un pueblo, se acercó con mucho miedo al dadivoso compañero y le besó la mano generosa.
>
> Ese cuadro simbólico representa la educación social de una raza.

> Yesterday, in one of those obscure hamlets where trains make but fleeting stops, my friend, Quezon, approached a group of emigrants that was just arriving to the village, with the desire to inspect these poor victims of famine. Undoubtedly, they were members of one family. My friend called to a filthy boy of 5 years, sickly and shy, the figure of hunger and poverty, with a rag for a coat, [and] he [Quezon] gave him a Russian coin. The mother saw it; unable to hide her satisfaction and her gratitude, she ordered her son, in Russian, to kiss the hand of the kind foreigner.
>
> And the boy, brought up in the submission of an entire people, fearfully approached my generous friend and kissed his benevolent hand.
>
> This symbolic portrait represents the social education of a race.[34]

In this scene Quezon, the future first president of the Commonwealth of the Philippines, is represented as a "kind foreigner" extending his "benevolent hand" to a poverty-stricken Russian boy. Quezon charitably gifts him a Russian coin. In the context of the benevolent assimilation of American imperialism in the Philippines, this encounter between the white, impoverished, Russian boy and the Filipino intellectual takes on a special meaning. One can observe in the passage one of the "cuadros de miseria" that Kalaw alludes to in his dedicatory remarks to Quezon, the star of this particular scene. The future head of state is depicted as a "príncipe filipino" (a Filipino prince), a monarchical reference meant to temper the oppression of the subproletariat Russian boy (under the Russian monarchy) with the benevolent hopefulness that is afforded the charity of the *ilustrado*. The benevolence in this scene should not shock those familiar with the discursive arrangements that organized the affect of American imperialism in the Philippines as one of "white love," as theorized by historians like Vicente Rafael.[35] Indeed, couched in the affect of love for the Americans' "little brown brother" was the white man's burden to educate the Filipino in the ways of the civilized world. The polarity between civilized American and barbaric Filipino is upended in this representation of *ilustrado* charity to the white boy, ruined by the imperial despotism of Russia—a decadence only amplified by the Manchuria "ensangrentada" (bloodied Manchuria) preceding such descriptions of white poverty.

A whiteness ruined by imperialism is saved by the *ilustrado*. The political reversal here is that of the erudite *ilustrado* benevolently extending his "mano generosa" to the "mugriento niño." This scene of "white love"—or, rather, love for the white boy—speaks to and reverses the racialized, gendered, and sexualized encounter between the white man and the native boy; indeed, it is the pivotal frame through which I suggest we should understand the reversal that Kalaw stages for his reader. It is through such a reversal that we can note the strategy through which Kalaw represents Asia as a site for reclamation, reimagination, and rehabilitation vis-à-vis the civilizing discourse of enlightenment.

The reclamation of Asia is the keystone of an intersectional paradigm in which discourses of race, gender, sexuality, and class innervate the twentieth-century Philippine Enlightenment. The repetition of such a paradigm through the medium of travel narration gains its iterative power through the staging and restaging of the colonial encounter—encounters in which the *ilustrado* performatively gains power as agentive subject. The stage in which these colonial encounters between self and other reside can be theorized as a *contact zone.* Contact zones describe the highly syncretic space where "disparate cultures meet, clash, and grapple with each other, often in highly asymmetrical relations of domination and subordination."[36] Queer-of-color theorist Eng Beng Lim has similarly examined how such encounters are steeped in various gendered and sexualized histories of colonial relations refracted through the paradigm of the white man and the native boy.[37] The repetition of coloniality in Filipino intellectual discourses demonstrates both the constrained agency of the *ilustrado* and the problematic limitations of sovereign cognition.[38] The benevolent assimilationist protocols of US imperialism in the Philippines similarly gain traction as an intellectual project of colonial benevolence in Kalaw's staging of Quezon and the white Russian boy. In much the same way that Filipino *ilustrados* reformulated and iterated the Philippine Enlightenment when confronted with American empire, scholars like Lim understand the dyad of the white man and the native boy as a repetition of an "unhomely" trope that always, already reads racialized gender and sexuality in colonialism.[39] Such a paradigm consolidates for analysis the ways in which racialized gendered relations are constitutive of a Filipino (anti)colonial intellectual project at the turn of the twentieth century.

In one sense we can read as already a factual state of affairs that the very production of this travel narrative is a repetition of the colonial white man / native boy dyad that Lim gets at. The mestizo author is the rehabilitated evidence of the benevolent outcome of such a dyad—a dyadic power arrangement that he gets to invert through his relation to the white Russian boy. The historiographical precedent in Filipino studies analyses of "white love" has concluded as much. A crucial difference is the subtle and overt ways in which Asia is itself a fertile and shifting ground of contested meanings that is resignified depending on the colonial project described in the journey toward the Kremlin. Cultural productions such as these leverage themselves on a polysemous "transnational and sometimes unruly itinerary . . . meant to trouble the ascribed unidirectionality of critical and complicit energies and logics that often accompany the provenance of 'Asia' as a stable and static category in [the] twentieth century."[40] Lim takes to task the "classic colonial/native encounter of post-Enlightenment modernity" wherein the product of structural colonial seduction is a rational colonial white subject that is fully formed and agentive and thus "inspires a biography" while the native, Brown "bottom" is infantilized, bounded and fetishized by and as tradition, thus "disappear[ing] into a mob."[41] I add to this dyadic paradigm by considering the contributions of postcolonial enlightenment movements in a supposedly "post-Enlightenment modernity" that Lim's homosocial/homoerotic encounter takes as its historical and temporal assumption. *Hacia la tierra del zar* is, in this sense, a crucial text detailing the beginning of US imperial power's relationship with a "post-Enlightenment," post–(Spanish) colonial, Filipino *ilustrado* that repeats the dyadic white man / native boy colonial encounter with a difference: it is the biography of enlightened "postcolonial" Brown boys that we consider as they simultaneously center and disappear their white men (both Spanish and "American"). To be clear, I'm not suggesting that there is an erotic component to the representation of the relation between Quezon and the Russian white boy. Rather, there is an erotics to tutelage that structurally, rather than individually, informs the prospect and continued viability of custodial benevolence. Victor Román Mendoza has denoted this erotic colonialism as a form of racial-sexual power endemic to US imperialism.[42] What is significant in Kalaw's "cuadro" of Quezon is that he is inverting the paradigm in which the Philippines takes on the role of benevolent assimilator of a ruined Russian whiteness—or, more accurately, a successfully rehabilitated Filipino subject of benevolent assimilation who can advance US "benevolent" interests throughout Asia.

The presence of rehabilitative logics might offer us perceptual evidence of what this journey toward the czar has to do with disability. The "white boy" recipient of *ilustrado* benevolence is actually part of the debilitated landscape uplifted by *ilustrado* enlightenment—a "cuadro de miseria." The white man / native Brown boy dyad (what in Filipino American critiques of US empire is read as a fraternal, if tacitly sexualized, relation of the white male (anti)imperialist to the "little brown brother") helps us to understand not only the gendered and racialized components of American empire in the Philippines but also the ways in which problematic gender and sexual politics come to underwrite the Philippine Enlightenment. As we see in the colonial encounter between Quezon and the Russian boy, there is a powerful political reversal of the trope that Lim offers us: it is instead the *ilustrado* extending his benevolent colonial hand to the white child ruined by a failed antimodern Russian empire. Yet the failures of another Asian imperialism in this scene are a foil for the success of the benevolent assimilation of these Filipinos into a US imperial imaginary of racial uplift for the Philippines. That is to say, the success of the *ilustrado* only makes sense given his receipt of American imperial largesse—the little Brown boy grown up. Therefore, the cursory liberating potential of the dyadic Brown *ilustrado* man / off-white child gains traction in its underlying mode of production: manhood and masculinity attained through the tutelage of a "disappeared" white daddy. The reversal that Chinese mestizo Manuel Quezon displays demonstrates the success of US assimilation. Given the appearance of US American diplomatic attachés (such as Theo Rogers) who are "liberally" considered Filipino by Kalaw, it seems equally valid to consider the Filipino Quezon as an Americanized subject that can and has inverted the Orientalizing constraints of his personhood. Despite being the clear agent of US colonial rehabilitation, the Orient still serves as a container for depravity and disability. Quezon overcomes his debilities through his approach to the white child, in much the same way the "little brown brother" is infantilized in spite of his Orientalness. If the representation of the Orient wasn't an impaired one, then Quezon's (and likewise Kalaw's) narrative of upward mobility overcoming it wouldn't make sense. In a sense, Filipinos uplifted by an American progressivism and fluent in a Hispanic humanist tradition overcome the entrapment of a disabled Oriental body through a liberal contract of intellectual elitism secured through the freedom of travel. In the next section, I will connect the projection of a rehabilitated Filipino mind made possible partly by its juxtaposition with a disabled Asian body.

The Coloniality of Able-Mindedness

Taking Lim's productive queer-of-color framing of the erotics of colonialism, there is one other such staging of colonial encounter that is enabled by the homosocial enlightenment logics proliferated by Kalaw that implicates the logics of disability. While the image of the foot-bound girl is certainly halting, it is a representation that is similarly ensconced in a wider web of ableist imagery in which the Orient not only connotes savagery but also incapacities that set off the capacities of the *ilustrado* mestizo. The disappearance of the white daddy and the retooling of mestizaje as a racial discourse of uplift for *white people* are complicated and propped up by the conjuring of a symbolically iterated impaired figure of the Asian woman as articulated and temporally bound by the social practice of foot-binding. This figure is disabled through the discursive exclusion from enlightened cognition that characterizes the masculinist domain of enlightenment proper, as well as its postcolonial rearticulations. Additionally, the representation of the figure of "Woman" as literally physically impaired provides another angle through which to view the discourse of the Yellow Peril that characterizes Kalaw's appraisal of China as a "mancha negra, sucia, ululante" (black, dirty, wailing stain) and "ensangrentada" (bloodied). The "black bloody stain" emerges, I suggest, through the misshapen feet of the "Chinese Woman."

The emergence of this figure, which precipitates the colonial encounter of *ilustrado* / disabled girl, returns our vista to Manchuria, where Kalaw poses the question, "¿Hay razas destinadas a morir?"

"Are there races that are destined to die?" Kalaw asks in a section titled "La Mandchuria sangrienta" (Bloody Manchuria), highlighting the high costs of imperial war.[43] Erevelles argues that "disability and war" should be a crucial framework through which "feminist disability studies and third world feminism" understand the production of disability through the machine of imperialism.[44] I suggest that the exploitative dynamic of imperial capitalism intersects with the propagation of global disabilities. A "bloody Manchuria" exists in an asymmetrically cripped relationship to Russia, Japan, and the United States. Such a bloody state of affairs leads the enlightened Filipino subject to ponder whether some "races" exist on the "horizon of death."[45] Nevertheless, within the same breath we can observe that the bloody state of Manchuria coincides with the racialized colonial uplift of Formosa as a sugar plantation under Japanese imperialism. Erevelles pushes for a materialist understanding of disability as a condition, response, and sign of the proliferation of war since imperial conflicts historically are "one of the largest producers of disability."[46] With disability, then—whether it takes the form of economic debility, bodily harm, environmental devastation, "slow death," or the colonial presumption of incompetence—Kalaw testifies to the widespread precarity orchestrated in colonial relations.[47] The Philippines is a vital site to understanding the propagation of global impairments through the circulation of transnational capital; the Hispanized imposition of the Philippine Enlightenment on other kinds of Asias (imperial Japanese, colonized Taiwan, bloody Manchuria) exists alongside the persistent discourse of benevolent assimilation that has come to historically mark American-Philippine colonial relations.

The existence of Kalaw's travel narrative during the time of transition from Spanish to American colonialism contradicts presumptions of racialized incompetence that US colonial discourse relied on. Kalaw and Quezon cannot reasonably be said to universally be products of US tutelary influence given the protraction of Hispanic modernity and the Spanish language that serve as the media through which the Philippine Enlightenment extends its geopolitical sphere of influence. The travel narrative is an important genre here, as it wholly relies on the able-bodied and able-minded itinerancy of the colonial traveler to cross borders and represent them. Disability, I suggest, systematically defines the *asymmetry* in power relations constitutive of the contact zone in which travel narrative representations circulate. The process of racialization in which imperialism is thoroughly embedded utilizes disability tautologically as a major technology for justifying its own existence. Erevelles's intervention, alongside Pratt and Lim's formulations of the colonial encounter, allow us to see colonialism as a systematic imposition of mass disablement and postcolonialism as a theoretical worldview dealing with the aftermath of historically produced physical impairments and perceived, ostensibly putative, cognitive disability.

While physical debility and impairment are certainly aspects of a critique of martial imperial conflict that disability studies should explore, the examination of such debilitating effects of empire should be done alongside the colonizing assumptions around intelligence and cognitive capacity that often justify imperialism as a benevolent enterprise. Put bluntly, the Brown mind is deemed so stupid that imperial war waged against the Brown body does not ethically count as violence. In fact, imperialism gains moral traction insofar as it articulates itself as a project that restores the battered Brown body to approximate the normate white (imperial) body. Violence against the Brown body doesn't meet the threshold of ethical harm if the Brown mind is recipient of the rehabilitative civilizing influence of American imperialism. Kalaw takes up the presumption that such benevolence is a constitutive aspect of any successful empire. More specifically, his rhetorical question about the horizon of death that colonial conflict inevitably inaugurates is posed as part of an ongoing reflection on the presence of Russia in Manchuria as testament to what failed imperialism looks like—an "Imperio moscovita," "despótica" and "paneslavista," succumbing to a base "idolatría" and "ortodoxa" that proves that "en la Santa Rusia hay más ignorancia que religión."[48] Indeed, when in Russia, Kalaw exclaims "Esto no es Europa: esto es Asia" (This is not Europe: this is Asia).[49] The representation of Russia as a Europe that is really Asia is difficult to read outside the devastation of China wrought after the Boxer Rebellion. While Russia as a European nation is rendered barbaric given both its proximity to and imperialism of Asia, the Philippines attains cultural capital as an enlightened Asia given its rehabilitation as a domain of American empire.

Such stunning swirling critiques of a superstitious antimodern Russia juxtaposed with the contradiction of a devout, enlightened Philippines leads Kalaw to come to the remarkable conclusion that Russia is actually Asian.[50] One possible but rather improbable reading of this statement is invested in an anticolonial politics that would see the liberation of Manchuria from Russian imperial control in a post–Boxer Rebellion historical moment. Such an anticolonial sentiment connects a twentieth-century repetition of Filipino enlightenment to a broader Asian anti-imperialism that would rewrite the necropolitical destiny of Asia as a "race" that is "destined to die." In reality, though, the declaration of "Asia/Europe" as an oppositional binary in all likelihood did not signal a utopian political reversal. That is, Kalaw did not write these words about Manchuria or in direct reference to Russian imperialism in China. While a "bloody Manchuria" is certainly not part of the political worldview that Kalaw would like to impart to his reader, he does not claim Manchuria for Asia; rather, he disclaims Russia as European, Slavism as Euromodernity. Russia is Asia and therefore *less than*. Kalaw writes,

> ¿En qué consiste ese paneslavismo? ¿Cuál es su finalidad? ¿De qué tiempo data? No es posible tratar en estas breves impresiones de asuntos de capital importancia para el desenvolvimiento actual del Imperio moscovita. Cuando los europeos llegan a las puertas de Moscow, desde donde se abre ante la curiosidad natural de los turistas un mundo sepultado en la Edad Media, con sus viejas Iglesias y sus íconos pálidos y todopoderosos, no pueden menos exclamar:—Esto no es Europa: esto es Asia.

> What does this Slavism consist of? What is its objective? From what time does it originate? In these brief impressions, it's not possible to engage such important issues for the current development of the Muscovite Empire. When European tourists arrive at the portals of Moscow in which a world stuck in the Middle Ages is opened before their natural curiosity, with its old churches and its pale omnipotent icons, they won't be able but to exclaim: "This is not Europe: this is Asia."[51]

The European touristic subject (a subjectivity that Kalaw tacitly claims for himself) is at the "portals of Moscow." Yet we cannot disentangle Moscow from Manchuria in the narrative progression that Kalaw choreographs. His reflection on the despotic decadence of the superstitious empire, with its "pale" medieval icons, is connected to the cruelty of the imperial project of its neighbor China. In an oblique way, Kalaw does call for the decolonization of Chinese Manchuria. But he does so through a narrative and epistemological reliance on an Orientalist project that equally attests to the savagery and premodernity of Asia—not *his* Asia, though; ironically enough, *Russia's* Asia. Russia's Asia (in both the possessive form and as a contraction) has three convergent yet distinct meanings here: (1) Russia is barbaric in its imperialism of Asia; (2) additionally, Russia's savagery and backward superstition is measured through its qualitative similarity to and its subsumption into "Asia" as it is exclaimed by a European (read: Filipino) touristic gaze;

and (3) the very object of Russia's imperial possession is China. China is scripted into the savior complex constitutive of the *ilustrado*'s redefinition of Asia; China is discursively "saved" through a critique of a Russian imperial project. Yet the critique of Russia as antimodern depends on an Orientalist vision of China, which is cast as an object of pity, scorn, and care by a travelistic ethos that is rehabilitative in nature—a rehabilitation that is imbricated with and accumulates power partly through US benevolent assimilation. My point here is that *ilustrado* mestizo subjectivity in this instance is itself a continuation of US benevolent rehabilitation. Mestizaje is the vehicle through which such progressivist ideologies of reform and uplift piggyback on and find narrative diffusion via a Filipino subject with powerful and persuasive mobility and movement.

China becomes the Orientalist and barbaric substrate on which the Philippine Enlightenment relies. In an earlier reflection on Kalaw's voyage through Hong Kong he observes that "desde el primer hasta el último momento, la única nota sensacional que hiere y que cautiva son esas manchas negras, sucias, ululantes, que se llaman 'chinos'... lo primero que huele es un chino" (from the first to the last moment, the only sensational observation that injures and captivates are those black, dirty, wailing stains that are called "the Chinese"... the first thing one smells is Chinese).[52] Significantly, the description of a Chinese essence as a "black, dirty, wailing stain" precedes a section titled "Peligro amarillo" (Yellow Peril). As we will see, however, it is not simply the national space of China that serves as the atavist catalyst of a new, better-enlightened Asian subject. Rather, what's more interesting here is China's corporal and material representation as the racialized gendered disabled figure vis-à-vis its practices of foot-binding. Hence, the question that began this section—"Are there races that are destined to die?"—can refer to the supposed slow death of the racialized gendered figure of the "Chinese Woman" whose feet are bound in space and time contrasted suspiciously with a mobile Filipino subject unfettered, unbound in space, progressively moving forward in time toward a modernity teleologically ensured by US rehabilitation.[53] Again, "these poor Chinese girls, with their imprisoned feet, so diminutive; what are they thinking, what do they do, why are they sad?"[54]

A discourse of foot-binding and the construction of Chinese femininity represented through the trope of "pies aprisionados" is a crucial moment in Kalaw's writing. Kalaw deploys the iconic image of bound feet to mark the Chinese's antimodernity vis-à-vis a Western definition of civilization. Dorothy Ko has comprehensively studied the cultural and historical underpinnings around the social practice of foot-binding and argues that there exist many foot-bindings, not just one.[55] That is, it is impossible to understand such a geographically and temporally pervasive cultural practice through one framework; instead, we must be historically specific in any analysis or supposedly "moral" claim about gender asymmetries in Chinese society. Indeed, it is controversial to universally argue that the practice of foot-binding and the "Chinese Woman" subjected to it are tantamount to debilitation and disability. It was a practice of the elite and a marker of class privilege that represented social mobility, refinement, beauty, and the apex of genteel femininity. Nevertheless, Ko situates herself "outside the anti-footbinding enlightenment discourse" that only ever ensures Western modernity as the arbiter of gender parity.[56] That is, for the Western eyes that observe the scene of foot-binding, despite its unique and specific cultural milieu it obtains as a disability for cultural processes that prize ablebodiedness. The gendered dynamic between Chinese woman and Filipino man likewise shapes a liberal discourse of reform that is reliant on the developmentalist distance between a Hispanic American Philippines and an Orientalized China. Like Spivak, Ko objects to the paradigm of "white men saving brown women from brown men."[57] Yet, what is to be made of Brown men saving Brown women from Brown men?

Like the dichotomous representation of *sangley* mestizo Quezon and the impoverished Russian child, a similar dichotomy between the mobile Filipino intellectual body and the bound feminized Chinese body frames Kalaw's travel narrative—indeed, it is indispensably the arc of his journey to the heart of (Russian) "darkness." This colonial encounter, I argue, is foundational to the normate eye's/I's perception of reality. A connection exists between Kalaw's depiction of the material division of international labor and the cognitive division of intellectual capacities intrinsic to postcolonial enlightenments. The *ilustrados*' touristic itinerary as portrayed in *Hacia la tierra del zar* mirrors and relies on the movement of capital; indeed, the *ilustrado* crosses the border as a liberal subject of enlightenment due to the liberalizing of borders to facilitate the movements of transnational capital at the turn of the twentieth century. This movement, however, ironically relies on the stasis of "Asia," flexibly reinterpreted—an Asia literally and figuratively bound. The static image that constrains and enables the duality of the Asia that Kalaw articulates is the racialized, gendered (and inevitably sexualized) image of Chinese foot-binding. It is through the disabled Asian female body that a cognitively judicious and able-minded Filipino *ilustrado* can critique failed imperial projects in and around Asia (namely,

Russia) while simultaneously, albeit ambivalently, manipulating American imperial interests to advance Filipino sovereignty. But, following Ko, what kind of foot-binding in particular does Kalaw describe?

What I claim via this illustration of "pies aprisionados" is that the social construction of disability is rooted in enlightened cognition. The interiority of the "Chinese Woman" debilitated by the erotic gaze of Chinese men (and alternatively aestheticized by the enlightened gaze of the *ilustrado*) is never really considered. The "Chinese Woman" is only operative as a symbol evacuated of interiority. To borrow language from cultural theorist Anne Anlin Cheng, the "Chinese Woman" *ornaments* Kalaw's travel narrative through the spectacle of her impairment.[58] Here the colonial gaze of the Philippine Enlightenment maneuvers through and functions as the "stare" that dehumanizes the disabled body that is foundational to Western modernity's constitution of normate bodies.[59] "Saving" such a hapless disabled girl does not involve a robust consideration of her interior life, her subjective experience, or the material conditions in which foot-binding operates. Instead we receive a line of questioning from Kalaw: "What are they thinking, what do they do, why are they sad?" Robust answers to these questions never materialize in Kalaw's Orientalist impressions. Instead a remark on their smile of "ivory teeth" from a moment of provisional happiness is rendered, repeating the ornamental image-conscious discourse that could be said to have imprisoned their feet in the first place. "Chinese Women's" experiences are never truly elaborated on in order to buttress Western rationality as the most desirable human and gender rights model. Kalaw subscribes to a Western model of gender parity and the normative body in order to become the master of subjectivity in this instance. In the same vein, the "Chinese Woman's" entire corporeal (and cognitive) existence, impossible insofar as she remains a symbol, is subsumed by the fetishization of her impairment. The female body is functionalized as a machine whose purity is not to be disturbed by the earthly barbaric practices of a backward culture. This reading corroborates Ko's excavation of the historical roots of the anti-foot-binding movement in British missionary culture. According to Ko, the "body as machine" as a theological concept cannot be fully explained through a supposedly divine law that could never really secure the gender equality upheld on the theoretical level by Western societies; the language of parity is a convenient cloak for Orientalist discourse that also masks British imperial projects in China.[60] The real "sin" of the practice of foot-binding is that it hinders the productivity of the body. The disabled body hinders full incorporation into capitalist systems of labor exploitation.

It takes a cognitive "enlightenment discourse," such as that exemplified by anti-foot-binding societies and what I have been calling the Philippine Enlightenment, to secure the liberal humanist discourse that ensures the proper "democratic" protection of bodies from debilities and impairments that would halt the movement of transnational capital. Kalaw's racial materialist grand tour affirms cognitive capacity through the impaired ornamentalization of these "pobres chinas aprisionadas" (poor, imprisoned Chinese women). I agree with Ko's gesture that enlightenment discourses can be seen as trafficking in "a loathing for the stagnant female body,"[61] one whose impairment is at odds with the sovereign cognition that serves capitalist penetration into Asia—a capitalist penetration that was venerated earlier in Japanese-occupied Taiwan and tacitly in the US-occupied Philippines.

Filipino Itineraries of Crip Colonial Critique

I have argued that a mestizo Filipino homosocial continuum gains traction through variously staged colonial encounters in which the *ilustrado* "inspires a biography"—a representational impulse that allows for a materialist redefinition of Asia—while disability frames the Orient as an object of pity in need of rehabilitation that bolsters such a biography. This representational tactic is one that coheres with other renditions of mestizaje in the Americas—notably, in José Vasconcelos's *La raza cósmica*, with which I engaged in the introduction. In Kalaw's Filipino itineraries of mestizaje we see that one Asian subject is allowed full representational authority and all the cognitive capacities that are implied by said authority. Contradictorily, this authority is achieved through a pervasive Orientalism that frames Asia as disabled, feminized, and in need of rescue. Like Vasconcelos would two decades later, Kalaw renders the Orient a container of depravity, perversity, and disability. I suggest that such Filipino Orientalist ableism iterates US benevolent rehabilitation as an ideology into which Filipino Hispanism cathects. Initially, I established the Philippine Enlightenment as a homosocial continuum that traverses from the United States through the Philippines, thus ramifying American imperial power through the Asia that Kalaw pliantly redefines. Homosociality is concretized through the colonial reversal of "white love" performed in Quezon's patronizing uplift of the Russian white boy in the depressed countryside rendered as "cuadro de miseria." Indeed, mestizaje functions here much like whiteness in that it can rehabilitate Russian whiteness so dispossessed by Russian monarchical exploitation and abandonment. The underlying substrate on which these resignifications and disidentifications with white imperial paternalism occur is the colonial encounter between the cognitively able-minded *ilustrado* and the disabled Chinese girl—herself evacuated of agency and voice. This girl is wholly embodied by and subsumed into the fetish of her impairment— the symbol of the "Chinese Woman" and her bound feet. Her appearance in the travel narrative is crucial to reinterpreting this colonial genre as one that relies tacitly and explicitly on disability tropes.

The cognitive itinerancy and literal border crossing of the *ilustrado* are secured through the stasis and literal binding of the impaired Asian female body. Since the movements of the *ilustrado* reflect the movement of transnational capital in Asia, disability (and the cognitive capacity that is immanent in disability's transcendence) becomes the node through which capital can burrow into the body, to paraphrase Neferti Tadiar.[62] While this argument certainly mimics the itinerant subjectivity constantly in flux and moving in *Hacia la tierra del zar*, I formulate it as part of a broader critique in this chapter to further establish the contours of crip colonial critique—furthering the project of cripping the colony as a mode of analysis that reads against the ableist grain of colonial genres of representation that postulate sovereignty in narrow terms that reify disability rather than questioning its logics.

While the broader context of imperial statecraft in Asia and the Pacific certainly speaks to the asymmetrical power dynamics in which we must contextualize representations of disability, I elect to study those disabled by such a context, who in turn entrench colonial ableism, in the construction of their political subjectivity. The mestizo writer Kalaw is one such figure that casts a gendered, feminized image of Asia as an object of rescue and rehabilitation, thus liberating himself from the disabling strictures of Orientalism by unfortunately reifying them. In the postcolonial context, ableism and the normative colonial subjects that advance its assumptions can refer to several abelist constructions: the liberal human, the abstract citizen-subject, the autonomous (androcentric) able body, and, in my analysis, the able-minded mestizo *ilustrado*. Philippine-US imperial relations, as well as the Philippine Enlightenment that struggled to navigate its way through American colonialism's grasp, represents a fascinating historical convergence of the ideas of a minority politics and its uneasy relationship with the "normal."[63]

In the political landscape of the Western industrialized nation-state, some of disability critique's priorities (whether in the form of political organizing or intellectual intervention) can be construed as a reformist critique of the state. I suggest this because the state apparatus about which domestic formulations of disability theory engage can be treated as if it does not have a colonial history.[64] The state in this instance should not be theorized as a disembodied entity outside colonial history but rather as the product of multiple colonial projects whose tactics of control are reliant on a global diffusion of "race" as an architecture of disablement. Such a deployment of race is the constitutive feature of Western imperial statecraft, which historically erupts as genocidal white supremacist violence subjecting the colonial body to manifold incapacitations—a reality from which Western disabled bodies potentially abscond in the formation of their request of accommodation from a colonial state apparatus.

A minority identity of disability, however radical and however necessary to ensure a quality of life for those that experience impairment in Western industrialized societies, relies on a liberal domestic framing that unconsciously leverages the traumas of a mutilating colonial violence in order to articulate disability's lived traumas to the state—an articulation that generally results in colonialism's obfuscation as politically vital knowledge for a robust theory of global disability. That is to say, US disability theory—no matter how crip, queer, or feminist—can run the risk of propounding colonial disability when engaging imperialism is not a theoretical priority. We should be attentive to the ways in which such intellectual or political moves repeat patterns of compulsive omission that characterize imperialism's historical justification and invisibilization. Given this context, I suggest that the material histories of transnational capital as mapped by the movements of *ilustrado* travel writing make two main interventions I'd like to highlight here for US domestic framings of disability and crip theory, on the one hand, and Filipinx studies, on the other: (1) challenging the rather obscurantist trajectory of a Filipino American cultural studies that privileges Anglophone and largely US-based renderings of "Filipino experience," and (2) how US disability studies' deconstructive moves problematizing the primacy of the able-body (in its liberal humanist or biomedical configurations) can abstract such critiques from colonial history.

The point that I would like to make here is that postcolonial enlightenment projects should be arenas where both crip theory's critique of the Western Enlightenment and Filipinx American studies can ponder the extent to which ability and disability should become part of our theoretical strategies. I would go as far as to say that all postcolonial enlightenment projects following in the "tradition" of the Haitian Revolution are anticolonial disability critiques. Such gestures toward the emancipatory protocols of enlightened cognition are a means of discursively articulating a notion of citizenship that results from "disputes regarding the best way to discern the field of not-disability."⁶⁵ That is, anticolonial revolutionary struggle demonstrates that Black and Brown bodies can also become fluent in the political language of sovereignty as it is tied to the nation-state. Such moves toward the epistemic sovereignty of enlightenment, however problematic or ableist such a move by the *ilustrado* may be, cannot be disarticulated from the screen of colonial violence, which constitutes manifold projects of mass disablement through war, poverty, and categorical exclusion from the "human"; indeed, such *ilustrado* discourse is itself a dispute of the systematic mass disablement that Spanish and US colonial projects have enacted. Postcolonial enlightenment, then, is an insistent corroboration of capacity under the duress of genocidal imperial violence.⁶⁶ Yet it also problematically inheres and reifies ability is the main currency of development and autonomy.

I gesture toward the complications entailed in the "situated" critiques of disability as proffered by a project toward postcolonial disability studies. What constitutes ability and disability radically shifts depending on context, language, and historical circumstance. We might critique the so-called Philippine Enlightenment for subscribing to the very technologies and ideologies of ableism that excluded Filipinos from humanity in the first place. In that critique, however, I would be hesitant to begrudge or efface the revolutionary movements that such epistemic sovereignty inspired and the revolutionary potential incumbent in such anticolonial histories. But my project here is not to fully redeem the Philippine Enlightenment, ironically through a disability studies optic; such a project has major limitations. One such limitation is that it renders opaque various kinds of feminized labors that ensure the construction of masculinist cognition as the underwriting protocol of the postcolonial Filipino nation. In this analysis, the site of both cognitive extraction and generation of surplus value is the symbolic "Chinese Woman" and her deformed body. This was similarly the case in chapter 2, where José Rizal's anticlericism hinged on the madness of María Clara as a victim of the sexual violences of Spanish colonialism. My aim in this particular chapter has partly been to foreground a postcolonial critique of disability or a move to "disable postcolonialism" as urged by theorists like Clare Barker and Stuart Murray, and Nirmala Erevelles, in order to more fully interrogate the intersections of postcoloniality and disability.

Four

A Colonial Model of Disability

RUNNING AMOK IN THE MAD COLONIAL
ARCHIVE OF THE PHILIPPINES

In short, the history of amok is a history of colonial discourse. The violence of the
Malay running amok functions as a smokescreen for the violence of colonialist capitalist
voracity. . . . "Amok" became the psychological and legal basis for the criminalization of
entire peoples and the justification for the subjugation of colonized populations. The
word "amok" in the English language thus ricochets between British and American
imperialisms and between Malay and Filipinx forms of resistance.
                —SARITA SEE, "Language Run Amok"

A report from Jolo, an island in the Philippines, dated August 20, 1934, and
addressed to the US director of education in Manila described the local
situation concerning the "Amoks of Sulu." K. W. Chapman, the acting educational division superintendent of Sulu, detailed the tragic and harrowing
case of the "violent deaths of teachers Felipe Collante and Ruperto Rosos
by a Moro amuck" in the city of Laum Tabawan at "about 9:00 A.M. on
August 11, 1934."[1] Accompanied by a Philippine Constabulary patrol, Chapman went to investigate.[2] He noted that a "Moro[,] Ansol of Licud," went
mad and ran amok, hacking teachers to death with a "bolo," or machete.
Evidently, in accordance with other similar instances of amoks among the
Moro communities of the southern Philippines, they sought "honorable"
deaths in combat against a deserving enemy—they "ran amok" (or "amuck")
in an acute, grave, and even lustful loss of reason particular to their race,

destroying all in their path. The presence of colonial forces in the Philippines meant there may have been ample targets for such a bellicose practice emblematic of racialized madness. Yet it wasn't American colonial officials that were targeted. Rather, Ansol targeted Filipino teachers working in a US-instituted schoolhouse whose function was to instruct in civics, literacy, and English. Ansol was eventually killed by a retired teacher, Ignacio Aguilar, using Rosos's own shotgun, which he procured from his home during the attack. Aguilar showed a "rare presence of mind and by his action probably saved the lives of other persons. The teachers acted valiantly in defense of the schoolchildren sacrificing their lives." This "rare presence of mind" is juxtaposed with the frenzied mental state and murderous intent of Ansol. Indeed, "Collante was fatally wounded while assisting a small boy to escape"; Chapman suggests that Collante showed a unique level of empathy and self-sacrifice, further damning the barbaric practice of Filipino "Mohammedans." Collante died at the scene. Rosos died later from gruesome injuries he sustained from the attack. Chapman makes clear the bravery of both, stating that "it is very evident that had Rosos and Collante concerned themselves only with saving their own lives both would have escaped."[3]

For those familiar with such instances, the term *Moro juramentado* would also be apt for describing the perpetrator of the incident detailed by Chapman. For instance, in a brief report in the periodical, the *Bulletin*, dated October 2, 1934, a "moro juramentado" case is described in which people were killed by a "maddened man." This case was less a premeditated attack, as was most likely the case with Ansol, and more a case of a crime of passion in which the juramentado "went mad" in the moment. The disturbing report is as follows: "Lucio Rosanable returned home at noon for lunch, and finding that no food was prepared for him by his wife, pulled his bolo and thrust it into the abdomen of the woman, who was at the time nursing a four month old baby. The other children of Rosanable witnessed the tragedy. After killing his wife Lucio Rosanable went to his neighbors' yards bent on killing whomever he happened to meet." As will become notable in such cases as this chapter develops, the amoks often found their end executed by a Philippine police response rather than a US military one. In the case of another "berserk" juramentado simply referred to as "Moro Tominabao," he ran amok on September 17, 1934, on a commercial steamship, the *Manok*, where he "hacked four persons with a 'barong'" and then jumped into the waters to escape. In the same report detailing the Rosanable case, the "juramentado [Tominabao] was shot by Miguel Libre, a policeman in the municipality of Oroquieta," where the *Manok* was anchored—a typical end to these events.[4]

Amoks appeared in spaces of relative tranquility disrupting civil order with a warlike ravenousness that normally would be seen on the battlefield. Significantly, these cases of juramentados and amoks transpired decades after the Philippine-American War (1899–1902), many in the same year of Philippine conditional independence conferred with the US congressional Tydings-McDuffie Act (passed on March 24, 1934). In the case of Ansol, a classroom might at first glance be an unlikely background for such occurrences.[5] Nevertheless, the context of the imperial classroom of US empire—aestheticized so effectively for us in *Puck* magazine's cartoon "School Begins" (1899), which I analyzed in chapter 1 concerning the "benevolent rehabilitation" of colonialism—finds archival resonance in the case of Filipinos that took up the rehabilitated mantle of educators or students, on the one hand, and the seemingly murderous intransigence of tribal Moros running amok and afoul of such rehabilitative efforts, on the other. Here we can locate a provocative resistance to US benevolent rehabilitation concretizing the scene of the imperial classroom as one of colonial violence. In this book, I have established a visual and discursive pattern wherein the feasibility of uplift of the Indigenous subject of empire sees Asianness, Blackness, Indigeneity, and whiteness as coconstructive of a racial hierarchy organized via differing levels of mental capacity. In this chapter, US settler colonialism becomes a filter through which Filipino amoks are racialized and disabled.

The Indigenous Moro amok is transformed into the colonial bodymind in which the violence of colonial disablement is anchored and thus rendered the benchmark attesting to Filipino success or failure under US benevolent rehabilitation. In the case of the amoks of Sulu, colonial agents made meaning of the relative uncivilization of Moro Filipinos vis-à-vis the successfully capacitated Filipinos that acted as their educational agents precisely through speculation on their propensity to inhabit mental states of madness, frenzy, and fury. The madness of the *indio* became a way to differentiate between the relative capacities among subjects under US tutelage, thus calcifying racialized nontribal versus tribal and Christian versus non-Christian differentiations for adjudicating capacity for self-government. Naturally, there are racist inconsistencies in the application of such mental evaluations. The reason for the attack was enigmatic. In conjunction with the constabulary investigation, Chapman could not discern "that there was any motive behind the killing." Yet there are signs that this was a premeditated attack with a precise target, to which (or toward whom) Ansol traveled on foot, and not a random act of violence that might conventionally describe a momentary loss of sanity. This contradicts other accounts of the Moro amoks and juramentados of the time:

> A real juramentado is carefully prepared for the ordeal. He must first secure permission from his parents, his chief, and the Sultan. After this he goes to the Imam for purification. He bathes, cleans his nails, has his eyebrows shaved and a string wound around his testicles. He now dresses in a white sarong and is ready for the ordeal of killing until he is killed. Apparently his first victim is picked with care in order that he may receive the reward promised to those who exterminate an infidel. After this he kills men, women, and children without distinction of race or creed until he is killed.[6]

So was there no motive, and thus it was the action of a madman. Or was it a preplanned attack consistent with a religious practice and carefully cultivated spiritual worldview? From Chapman's perspective, the logical adherence to a religious worldview that results in such pathological and antisocial behavior cannot obtain as a rational motive in a colonial society that ought to be marked by law and order. While violent in its own right, Ansol's "amokness" is singled out as particularly spectacular and exceptionally violent. Nevertheless, the surrounding context of colonial violence is normalized and acceptable particularly in the southern Philippines.[7] Americans have a discursive monopoly on what counts as contraventions to cooperation; such contraventions are tactically disabled and labeled "amok." The attack seemed random as the teachers, Chapman attested, neither knew nor had seen Ansol before. Buried here is a long history of anticolonial revolt against encroaching Philippine and US colonial interests in the Muslim South deemed variously as seditious, an insurrection, outlaw, and, as I will elaborate further, *crazy*.[8] Advancing a crip colonial critique, what can the examination of the coformation of race and madness illuminate for the fields of disability studies, US empire studies, and Filipinx American studies?

The term *Moro* itself puts pressure on these fields given its roots in Spanish colonialism. In Spanish, it is sometimes an epithetical term used to refer derisively to those of the Muslim faith. It highlights a historical and epochal split in the Iberian Peninsula when the Reyes Católicos (Catholic Monarchs), Queen Isabella of Castille and King Ferdinand II of Aragon, unified the country into what today is known as Spain. Following the conquest (also known as the Reconquista) of the Muslim Kingdom of Granada in 1492, those of the Jewish and Muslim faiths were expelled from the peninsula or, using newfound inquisitorial powers endowed to them by Pope Sixtus IV, were forced to convert. For the observant reader, the year 1492 also coincides with the Catholic Monarchs' financial investment in a Genoese explorer by the name of Christopher Columbus—an investment that inarguably changed world events. These histories are certainly far more complex than can be covered in the space of this chapter. Nevertheless, the Reconquista of Spain and the conquest of the New World intersect in furthering a global racial world order shaped by European exploration. This racial order later turned on and produced the conditions of possibility for the cultural and political discourse of *mestizaje* (racial admixture, miscegenation) that has been so central to this book's interventions and archives. Mestizaje replicated and ramified colonial hierarchies of racial difference along chauvinist ideals of savagery and civilization endemic to Christian colonial power. To wit, the term *Moro* in the Philippine context draws implicitly on a difference between Filipinos that converted to Catholicism and those intransigent Muslims in the south that vehemently resisted colonial rule. This split based in religion accrued additional anthropological and racial meanings with the institution of University of Michigan professor Dean Conant Worcester's Bureau for Non-Christian Tribes as an apparatus of colonial control during the US colonial period in the early twentieth century—a context in which we observe a landscape plagued by mad "non-Christian tribes" populated by juramentados and Moros run amok.

Despite the tragedy and "sordid tale of two teachers brutally murdered by a Moro amuck," Chapman affirmed that he would return with two new teachers. He declared defiantly, "The work must of course go on."[9] What might "the work" refer to in this context? Naturally, the work of civilization through the institution of colonial education. It is not insignificant that a school created and administered through the US colonial bureaucracy would be targeted by Ansol. While it is impossible to tell from the archival evidence that is available to us, the appearance of amoks is not attributable to a sudden emergence of psychosocial disorders particular to Indigenous Filipinos. Instead the appearance of this kind of racialized madness might offer us another lens through which to understand an Indigenous complaint to colonial domination. To be clear, it is not my intent to engage in a diagnostic evaluation of the "actual" psychology of the amok. It is through the juxtaposition of sane and insane that we can identify how US administrative colonialism thought through the particularities of the mental states of colonial subjects they were attempting to rehabilitate through Western education. This mental state is clear from the archival record: the racialized madness of the "Indian amok." This is a madness that is *racially* ascribed to Indigenous Filipino Moros. This chapter will not speculate as to the clinical psychological state of people like Ansol; whether or not he was actually mad is beside the point. Instead it is the structure and environment of colonial ableist racism, in which his presumed psychological state is classified as (supposedly) empirically "mad," that interest me more. This is part of a broader project in disability studies to not locate disability in the individual, who may or may not possess physical and cognitive variation from those in their community. Rather, disability is located in the social environment that engineers such psychophysical variations as impairments that are disabling.

I extend these insights on the social model of disability to consider the context of US imperialism to elaborate on what we could call a colonial model of disability. The politics of madness in this mad colonial archive, as I'll call it, is a product of racial stratification and coloniality. As I'll elaborate further, the racial ascription of what we could call the ethnological mental disorder of "running amok" is articulated through a colonial and normative sex and gender system. Racial and tribal madness curiously appear as a causal outcome of the perversion of the institution of heterosexual marriage particularly evident in the practice of polygamy. Before we can get to this reading, it is important to gain clarity on what "running amok" is, exactly.

The Mad Colonial Archive: "A Frenzied Malay"

In order to apprehend the archival traces of Filipino "amoks," it becomes important to attain some level of certainty around the very definition of the term. The *Oxford English Dictionary* (OED) furnishes for us a useful start in its entry on "amok."[10] The second listed definition gives us perhaps the standard generally understood definition: "a murderous frenzy; the act of running amok." Running amok went afoul of a stable colonial society marked by order and progress. This is relevant to the administrative coloniality of the US occupation of the Philippines in the early twentieth century because of the implementation of bureaucracies that determined productive and nonproductive labor of the citizen-subject and, notably, which behaviors were deemed constructive or destructive for the smooth functioning of political life. Disturbing the edifying institution of education that is meant to better and uplift the native Filipinos perturbs a colonial social order whose violence is normalized; ironically, it is the backdrop of this colonial violence that serves as the matrix through which the madness of the Filipino is determined to be pathological and thus contradicting the work of civilization. Adapting a historical materialist reading, it becomes a plausible undertaking to understand the ways that mental health, its management and classification, work alongside the abstraction of human labor. If there are any power asymmetries in this system, it may become evident why fury and rage seem like inevitable outcomes. What are deemed antisocial or uncooperative behaviors, largely understood through discourse around mental capacity and fitness, accrue a diagnostic language around them in the service of optimizing human life in the service of productivity and social order.[11] For the present analysis on the "amoks" of the Philippines, race is an unavoidable historical force in apprehending the biopolitical metrics brought to bear on the racialized mad. Moreover, the global imposition of colonialism, an imposition within which the Philippines is obviously only one historical case study, may be an unavoidable variable to consider when approaching what mad studies scholars like Tanja Aho, Liat Ben-Moshe, and Leon J. Hilton, as well as Geoffrey Reaume and Michael Rembis, have denoted as the "mad turn" in disability studies.[12] This "mad turn"—that is, the activism and scholarly centering of mental disability in an effort to point out the overemphasis on physical disability—must contend with colonial and racial histories in which rationality and irrationality are defined.

My overall claim is this: The mind becomes abstracted through the racialization of the body. And yet while the white American mind may exist as a disembodied artifice, the racial discourse of US colonialism anchors the mind to a racialized body whose actions, behaviors, and interiority signify a madness to be managed or expunged from political life. If this is the case, the fury and savagery that madness might connote reveal something deeper and more complex about social relations—a complexity that is passed over in favor of stultifying diagnostic discourses attributing insanity to personal demons that the individual must overcome or something that must be violently eliminated.[13] In any event, rather than treat such events of seeming mental disorder as epiphenomenal to a political order of things and bodies, I'd like to ask the question of what such mental states reveal about prevailing political hierarchies. What might Ansol of Licud be responding to, exactly? Could a "mad colonial archive" be a realm in which analysts could tease out the relationships between mind, body, and social structure in more productive ways? Following Nirmala Erevelles's and Anna Mollow's work, I agree that we have yet to give a nuanced cultural and historical account of the ways that our social shorthand (indexed by the use of the expression "he ran amok") and commonsense notions of madness are, at times, deeply imbedded in racial power dynamics.[14] They are not only racial. In the case of the Philippines, they are *colonial* in nature. The lens of the historical material might need the addition of the philological to make sense of this constellation of phenomena. It is the very first entry in the OED that gives us a linguistic etymology of the amok wherein racialization and disability cohere in the colonial archive. It defines *amok* as "a name for: a frenzied Malay."[15]

The English term *amok* entered the language from its original usage in the Portuguese *amouco* or *amuco*. The first instance of its use in Portuguese was in 1516 in reference to a group of *amuco* in Java that "would go out into the streets, and kill as many persons as they meet." The term then serves as a colonial conduit through which the expansive reach of the Portuguese Empire in Southeast Asia from the sixteenth century onward can be understood. Portugal's presence in Malaysia, the Indonesian archipelago, the island of Java, and New Guinea demonstrate the ways that, even in the early colonial period, imperial designs contended with how to understand the violent seemingly mad reactiveness of the "frenzied Malay." Ironically, however, an apt definition for conquerors and conquistadores might be "those that would go out on global voyages, and kill as many persons as they meet." What is mad, indeed?

It appears that the term finds its first usage in the written English language in John Dryden's allegory *The Hind and the Panther: A Poem in Three Parts* (1687). Dryden was a prominent poet during the Restoration of the British monarchy in the seventeenth century. *The Hind and the Panther* describes Dryden's conversion to Catholicism, much to the chagrin of Protestant authorities at the time. Church and state are unified in Dryden's work against dissident sects of Protestantism that did not conform to British monarchical rule. The poem describes a churl who sloughs off the redundancy of the seven sacraments, since "he knows Confession stands for one / Where Sins to sacred silence are convey'd." The churl, "Frontless, and Satyr-proof [satire-proof] . . . scow'rs the streets / And runs an *Indian* muck at all he meets." Dryden seems to describe a lowborn peasant immune to satire—indeed, without a "front," as it were. Outside the bounds of civilized discourse, "He thrusts about . . . / So fond of loud Report."[16] He becomes and runs an "*Indian* muck"—a racial body attached to the very substance and root of the word. The Indian, "Frontless" and "loud," is found to be affixed within the very etymology of "amok." The subject of Dryden's poem is assumed to be white. Madness attaches to the white body through its racialization of a mad "Indian."

Amok can help us track the ways that the racialization of madness was integrally a part of the justification of the colonial project. As we can see, this is a centuries-old word whose circulation cannot be understood outside European and US colonization of South and Southeast Asia. Significantly, in the Philippines its circulation in English via US bureaucracy inculcates the term with a problematic substrate of Indigenous tribality, accruing additional meanings within the racial-colonial landscape of Southeast Asia where we might not expect to find "Indians." This justification draws on the contractuality endowed to Euro-American colonizers from the European Enlightenment, wherein the relevant tools of universal reason and "presence of mind" were forged. The frenzy of the amoks, whether from China, India, Java, or the Philippines, demonstrates an Indigenous antisociality so grave that only the highly regimented institutions of colonialism are the answer in rehabilitating or even just managing these mad Indians.

Not simply a historical oddity in the colonial archive, "amok" or "amok syndrome" has appeared in the American Psychiatric Association's *Diagnostic and Statistical Manual of Mental Disorders* (DSM), though its categorization has shifted over time. In the fourth edition of the manual (DSM-IV), "amok" appears within an entry detailing "culture-bound" symptoms or disorders. In an article titled "Running Amok: A Modern Perspective on a Culture-Bound Syndrome," Manuel Saint Martin clarifies that while the general public is aware of the notion of "running amok," the "psychiatric literature classifies amok as . . . culture-bound based on its discovery 2 centuries ago in remote primitive island tribes where culture was considered a predominant factor in pathogenesis." Relevant to the colonial understandings of this phenomenon in the Philippines particularly with regard to "moros juramentados," Martin clarifies that, historically, it was understood that "the primitive groups' geographic isolation and spiritual beliefs were thought to produce a mental illness not observed elsewhere in the world." In a useful historical contextualization from a clinical perspective, he continues in a passage worth consideration at length:

> *Amok*, or *running amok*, is derived from the Malay word *mengamok*, which means to make a furious and desperate charge. Captain Cook is credited with making the first outside observations and recordings of amok in the Malay tribesmen in 1770 during his around-the-world voyage. He described the affected individuals as behaving violently without apparent cause and indiscriminately killing or maiming villagers and animals in a frenzied attack. Amok attacks involved an average of 10 victims and ended when the individual was subdued or "put down" by his fellow tribesmen, and frequently killed in the process. According to Malay mythology, running amok was an involuntary behavior caused by the "hantu belian," or evil tiger spirit entering a person's body and compelling him or her to behave violently without conscious awareness.

Because of their spiritual beliefs, those in the Malay culture tolerated running amok despite its devastating effects on the tribe.

Shortly after Captain Cook's report, anthropologic and psychiatric researchers observed amok in primitive tribes located in the Philippines, Laos, Papua New Guinea, and Puerto Rico. These observers reinforced the belief that cultural factors unique to the primitive tribes caused amok, making culture the accepted explanation for its pathogenesis in these geographically isolated and culturally diverse people. Over the next 2 centuries, occurrences of amok and interest in it as a psychiatric condition waned. The decreasing incidence of amok was attributed to Western civilization's influence on the primitive tribes, thereby eliminating the cultural factors thought to cause the violent behavior. Modern occurrences of amok in the remaining tribes are almost unheard of, and reports in the psychiatric literature ceased around the mid-20th century. Inexplicably, while the frequency of and interest in amok among primitive tribes were decreasing, similar occurrences of violence in industrial societies were increasing. However, since the belief that amok is culturally induced had become deeply entrenched, its connection with modern day episodes of mass violence went unnoticed.[17]

The presence of conquerors and settler terrorists like Captain Cook demonstrate a clear racial and colonial hierarchy that is central to configurations of amok and the explanatory power it holds in describing the mental states of the colonized. The term *amok* first entered into historical clinical literature in 1849, and it was usually mentioned on the basis of anecdotal colonial reportage. The DSM-IV describes the ways that amok syndrome and the surge of multiple homicides that accompanied it generally proceeded moments of extreme personal loss and grief anteceded by a prolonged period of brooding and pensiveness. It was thus classified in more modern clinical terminology as being "plausibly linked to a depressive mood disorder … psychosis, personality disorders, or a delusional disorder."[18]

The colonial meanings inscribed in the word *amok* also limn the ways that psychosocial sciences have attempted to understand and apprehend it. Further investigation reveals that given the prevalence of Malay amoks in the colonial archive, it makes sense that we would find corresponding diagnostic discourses making sense of such behaviors. Because of its appearance in the DSM, it is evident that the genealogy of the term *amok* shows that criminal conduct and its evaluations for antisociality have colonial origins in explicitly racial understandings of the mind. This is significant, as it lends credence to the argument that our commonsense understand-ings of antisocial or criminal conduct reveal a window into the ways that colonial histories—particularly in Southeast Asia, encroached on by several colonial powers—continue to shape how we think through race, its classifi-cation of different human bodies, and the ways that we think about sound minds—all these in the service of, in Foucauldian terms, a functional and productive society.

While Michel Foucault is best known for his work on the history of sexuality, his critical work on madness was an intervention that preceded his theory of biopolitics. The ways that he describes how modern society confined the mad away from the reasoned (i.e., those endowed with reason) presage the institutional forces that conspire to hold power over life and its various mechanisms (for additional discussion of this, see chapter 2). The distinction between reason and unreason (what we might call the sane and insane) is perhaps one of the most significant historical transformations shaping modern political life since the European Middle Ages. Arguably, this distinction based on mental faculties is at the root of the incitement to discourse that describes the ways that sexuality becomes a sustained object of study for the "expert" and a social force modifying aberrant behavior. In Foucault's own "archaeological" method, he argues that psychopathology cannot write a complete history of the relationship of madness to civiliza-tion, for the split between the mad and everyone else happens in ways that are not containable to only scientific conceptions of insanity. A satisfactory analogy would be the medical diagnosis of the pathology of homosexuality and other sexual "abnormalities" that elicited manifold speculation on the mental stability of the patient.[19] While different kinds of sexual expression and identity are common instances in the history of various civilizations, the denomination of such antinormative expressions as deviant to a par-ticular social order is rather new. "Hysteria" as an ungovernable emotional excess in women comes to mind as another such diagnosis in which gen-der was implicated in and constituted mental fitness and wellness.[20] Such diagnoses, of course, have been disproven by the scientific community in the contemporary moment; nevertheless, they demonstrate the ways that dimensions of difference like sexuality, which would not normally involve disability, do indeed have a subtended disability genealogy.

The relationship of sexuality to disability is a productive node to think through given that in Foucault's own work, the genealogical development of these threads of analysis draw on one another. Pathology is the diagnosis that many sexologists and psychoanalysts in the twentieth century ascribe to homosexuality. Queer studies and activists have historically attempted to depathologize this condition as one of "benign sexual variation," as anthropologist Gayle Rubin has put it.[21] In essence, effectively making homosexuality not a disability perhaps demonstrates an important distinction between pathological discourses and disability. Nevertheless, for both sexuality and disability, the appearance of the expert who determines scientific fact, the repression of such behaviors from the public eye, the confinement and categorization of individuals exhibiting such behaviors, and the explosion of discourses to explain and rationalize such oppression all conspire in a well-oiled machine to consolidate state apparatuses of sovereign power. While absolutely insightful are Foucault's archaeological finds, much like the mad that are confined in the Age of Reason (so called by Foucault), he confines his own archive to the geographic environs of the European continent. Many scholars have questioned this confinement (another "Great Confinement," to use Foucault's term), in which the abstract properties of reason are similarly abstracted from the material (read: colonial) circumstances of their production.[22] For sovereignty is not only a question of the personal autonomy of the individualized citizen-subject; it is also a geopolitical question where a huge swath of the globe must be captured (literally and metaphysically) as subrational.

Black theorists and scholars like La Marr Jurelle Bruce have attempted to elaborate how Black modernity is shaped by captivity. This becomes an inescapable reality to understanding constructions of the mind. The very perception of Black mental capacity is shaped by the existentialism of captivity. The question is fundamentally one of diaspora. Black people are "estranged from concrete 'truth' or a stable 'homeland'" due to the transatlantic slave trade. In a move that resonates with the peculiar frenzied state of the Malay, Bruce goes as far as to claim that the "African [is] categorically mad." That is, they are "wild, perverse, subrational, pathological, mentally unsound." Consistent with other philosophy-of-race thinkers, the presence of Africa and other colonial territories was an undeniable factor in shaping the proliferation of rationality as a property inherent to European modernity—the age of colonialism *is* the Age of Reason as it is defined by Foucault. Indeed, Bruce notes, "by the height of the Euro-Enlightenment, preeminent philosophers like G. W. F. Hegel, David Hume, and Thomas Jefferson posited Africans as ontological foils for the modern, rational, European subject" and thus "the black-cum-mad as antithetical embodiment of *un*freedom and *un*reason" became a foundational disability logic propounded throughout the world.[23] Reason does *not* exist, then, in an ontology outside the political economy of slavery and colonialism. Black mad scholarship makes productive moves in complicating the relationship between race and disability. For those unmoored from their homeland and thus made to live a diasporic existence under the cruelties of chattel slavery, even their desire for freedom away from such a system is medically diagnosed; Black freedom becomes the domain of unreason. To show that this is the case, scholars like Bruce, as well as Therí Alyce Pickens, remind us that Samuel Cartwright coined the medical term *drapetomania* in 1851 (coinciding with the time period in which the term *amok* entered diagnostic language, in 1848) to describe "the purported mental illness compelling slaves to flee bondage."[24] Following Bruce's ruminations on "mad diasporas" of transatlantic Blackness, I think we can reasonably point out significant gaps in what Foucault calls his archaeology of silence, which I initially contended with in my analysis of María Clara in chapter 2—the "evidence of a broken dialogue . . . [that] thrusts into oblivion all those stammered, imperfect words without fixed syntax in which the exchange between madness and reason was made."[25] Rather than excavate and translate the "stammered, imperfect words" of the mad, Foucault is more curious about the historical forces that engineered their silence. Another such "broken dialogue" as it pertains to histories of madness, as well as disability writ large, is the coloniality of such forces of human difference. The advent of colonialism and the invention of race in the late Middle Ages are other significant historical milestones that ushered in the early modern Age of Reason—what Foucault refers to as the Classical Age and what many would understand as the Renaissance.[26]

Other scholars have similarly pointed to the ways that Foucault's archaeology might have limitations for the ways that we understand the construction of reason. Bruce, for instance, complicates the Foucauldian genealogy of madness neatly traced from the Middle Ages to Foucault's so-called Classical Age to the modern political era. Bruce situates a racial genealogy of madness tied irrevocably to the transatlantic slave trade. In a similar move critiquing the Enlightenment philosophies of Europe that bound reason to the geopolitical environs of the continent, as we see in work by Susan Buck-Morss or Denise Ferreira da Silva, Bruce gestures to how the dispossession of reason—what in Foucault's terms might be the "derangement" of an entire population—facilitated the very process of enslavement.[27] While Foucault helpfully gives us the tools to locate this derangement within particular institutional networks that led to the confinement of the mad, other scholars also situate the differentiation of reason from unreason in the Cartesian dualism that cleaves mind from body. For this reason, this book has invested in the critical elaboration of the colonial bodymind as a way to suture the split of Cartesianism.[28] Centering the political economy of transatlantic slavery as a foundational moment exceeds the limited framing of the Parisian asylum as the only relevant place that the insane are to be found. The Black body(mind) of chattel slaves was dominated through a process of abstraction that endowed Europeans with universal and abstract reason.[29] In line with the thinking of scholars like Bruce, Erevelles, and Pickens, whose work has reoriented our understanding of Hortense Spillers's reading of the injuries of the enslaved Black body through the lens of disability, we can posit the slave ship and not just the asylum as foundational instantiations and purveyors of a global disability.[30]

Thus, the passage of Europe from the medieval period to the Renaissance is difficult to fully apprehend outside the age of maritime exploration and conquest. Mad Black studies scholars help us to see that Foucault makes unavoidable nautical gestures with his send-up of the "ship of fools"—a quasi-mythical phenomenon in which medieval European towns expelled their mad, confining them to ships at sea (which is portrayed in art by painter Hieronymus Bosch and others). For Foucault, this practice is different from the ordered administrative confinement of the mad in institutions—a practice that describes a shift in monarchial power in seventeenth- and eighteenth-century France. What we could call the mad colonial archive catalogs for us instances of what Bruce calls "phenomenal madness": "severe unwieldiness or chaos of mind producing radical crises of perception, emotion, meaning, and selfhood." While Bruce's understanding is irrevocably and notably tied to articulations of Blackness in a global frame wherein the economic system of slavery was actually the province of reason and thus sanity was conceptually bound to slavocracy, the categorical imperatives of Western reason held undeniable influence in transpacific networks of empire building as they shaped Philippine historical experiences of race and disability.[31] While this Black and disability diasporic frame does not completely apply to internal colonial dynamics in the Philippines, it does elucidate the ways that domestic racial formations in the United States shaped transpacific colonialism. Such work reframing the travel of colonial discourse from metropole to colony as a dialectical relationship rather than a unidirectional one is foundational to Filipinx American studies.[32] Additionally, the "mad diasporas" of Black people result from a foundational displacement traced to the transatlantic slave trade. The colonial project in the Philippines revolves around similar questions of displacement and dispossession. For this reason, I find the framework of diasporic madness to be a compelling one in grappling with the question of the Indigenous madness of the Filipinx subject.

The Philippines' acquisition and entrance into European imperial networks demonstrates the global reach of Foucault's Age of Reason. The Age of Reason, marked by the Great Confinement, converges with the age of discovery. The initial expansion of reason is perhaps enabled by an initial colonial expanse. While Foucault's critical apparatus is exceedingly powerful and not one to be dismissed out of hand, I am aligned with the "mad turn" in disability studies that would attempt to tell the story of madness from the perspective (or at least as closely aligned and attenuated to the perspectives) of the mad as is archivally possible.[33] In the case of the amoks, it is difficult to find sources that would comprehensively tell this perspective. In a way, the colonial archive serves as a mechanism through which the derangement of the Indigenous of the Philippines is further realized. Our work as analysts, especially those of us that are ancestors of those dispossessed, is to read against the grain of the colonial archive as an apparatus of unreason. Indigenous and colonial madness certainly produces manifold "epistemic uncertainties," to borrow from historian Ann Stoler in her work on archival technologies in Dutch Indonesia—another site where we would be likely to find amoks.[34] Recall one of the etymological threads of the Portuguese, *amouco*, as describing a group of Javanese that would run into the street and murder all that they happened to see.[35] A vast colonial network of reason and unreason appears ingrained in our own contemporary colonial common sense to such an extent that we unthinkingly utilize the phrase "to run amok" in quotidian speech. What might be the "phenomenal madness" of the amoks of Sulu?[36] Might an examination of their material social conditions produce for the colonial archive a "radical crisis of perception"?[37] Much like the "drapetomaniacs" of the nineteenth century, for the amoks in the Philippines madness emerges as a colonial construct to compel compliance with an unjust system of exploitation wherein the desire to not be exploited and the desire to reject benevolent rehabilitation can be categorized as mental instability.

The Deviant Sexuality of Madness

I began this chapter with the disturbing report of colonial education superintendent of Sulu, K. W. Chapman, detailing the deaths of two Filipino teachers at the hands of Ansol of Licud. The case of Ansol is notable in that we see an implicit connection wherein we can observe the sexuality of disability. We might also note Carl Moore's description of the Moro juramentado tightly winding string around their testicles as part of a concerted effort to link pathological sexuality to mental incapacity.[38] That is, colonial officials contended with the prevalence of Indigenous madness precisely through an understanding of how Filipino Moros deviated from civilized sex-gender relations. When there was an instance of an amok, it was often explicitly connected to and explained through the framework of heterosexual union; this union and bond were often perverted. The racial meanings that attach to the Filipino Moro body denote deviant sexuality. In terms of analytical method, it becomes necessary to think about how the racialization of madness transpires as a parallel formation to the racialization of sexuality. Given the etymological development of the word *amok*, it might be productive to speculate that the biopolitics of disability variegated by sexuality would obtain in other colonial contexts besides the Philippines. In the colonial context, to administer and manage one of these (namely, sexuality) was to administer and manage the other (namely, disability). For this reason, I have noted the genealogy of thought on colonial disability in which we can trace a relationship between the confinement and control of madness and the proliferation of biopolitical apparatuses to discipline human sexuality. While Foucault does not explicitly think about race or the ways that colonialism influenced the European cultures of discipline that he so painstakingly analyzes, the genealogical links between his work on madness and the biopolitics of sexuality are absolutely indispensable. I suggest that it is not surprising that we see within the development of Foucault's own line of thinking a turn from the disciplining of the mad in Europe to later thinking through the incitement to discourse around sexual abnormality in his *History of Sexuality*.[39] This resonates with the ways that, in the colonial Philippines, sexuality and disability intersect and animate the machinations of US empire. Indigeneity, sexuality, and madness all converge in the colonial context of US-Philippine administration of Filipino Moros, in particular. Ostensible Moro madness gives us a vista through which marriage, one of the cornerstones of Western culture and perennial benchmarks for normative behavior and optimal political life, is perverted by what colonial officials would deem to be a bizarre and primitive religious worldview.

Chapman highlights for us that when Ansol ran amok to murder the teachers, it was to honor his dead wife, who succumbed to complications related to childbirth. As is the custom of Ansol's people, according to Chapman, "Mohammedan" husbands join their wives in death but cannot die by suicide. Instead they must "die in combat," in an honorable death. This is confirmed in a Philippine Constabulary report authored by First Lieutenant

Joaquin Espiritu, who speculates that "the only possible motive behind the amuck's bloody act was that his wife on August 10, two days after her delivery, died." Espiritu was the lead officer praised by Chapman in his report on the incident. Espiritu's report in his capacity as a Philippine Constabulary officer intrigues me, as it potentially indicates the extent to which different bureaucratic and institutional apparatuses were at play attempting to make sense of the gruesome "murderous frenzy."[40] The first lieutenant mirrors the diagnostic language of Chapman in categorizing the event in terms of "frenzy" and Ansol as an "amok." US colonial officials like Chapman were not alone; the Philippine state, empowered by US colonial bureaucracy, was activated to respond to the crisis brought about by the maddened state of a Moro Filipino. While it is difficult to surmise from where Espiritu himself hailed in the archipelago or what his ethnic or religious background may have been, it is not controversial to speculate that the social disorder of amoks fits within a structure differentiating Moro Muslim Filipinos from Christian ones. These religious differences clarify hierarchies of civilizations among Filipinos depending on which side of the US colonial bureaucracy they might stand. I additionally suggest that Filipino madness is captured within a web of ethnological meaning making that circulated in the Philippines for decades at the historical moment of Ansol's grief-stricken attack. Consider the following image (produced almost thirty years before Chapman and Espiritu went to investigate Laum Tabawan), in which the Philippine Constabulary makes one of its first photographic entries into the Filipinx American colonial imaginary.

The image, captured by Dean Conant Worcester, is a triptych of three photographs depicting what is presumed to be the same man, a "Bontoc Igorot," in profile, in various stages of "civilization."[41] In the left-hand photograph he is shirtless, with long dark hair; he appears to be more "native." In the middle panel he is somewhat more civilized, dressed in a white coat, with shorter hair—vaguely Orientalist in appearance. The right panel depicts him in a Philippine Constabulary uniform, clean-shaven and decidedly Westernized. His long hair has been done away with in favor of a more practical haircut.

What is evident in this rather iconic image for Filipinx American studies and US empire studies is that the rehabilitation of the native Filipino transpires through the martial masculinity of the Philippine Constabulary. The fact that we can find the archival trace of Philippine officers managing the Ansol incident furnishes us a noteworthy case study in which the ethnological telos of civilization circulated in the Philippines. This circulation is particularly relevant in thinking through the relationship between Manila,

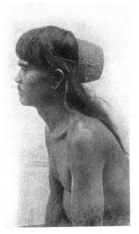

EDUCATIONAL VALUE OF THE CONSTABULARY.
1. Bontoc Igorot on entering the service, 1901.   2. After a year's service, 1902.
3. After two years' service, 1903.

FIG. 4.1. *Educational Value of the Constabulary*, a triptych of photographs taken by ethnologist Dean C. Worcester in the early 1900s. The photos depict what is presumably the same "Bontoc Igorot" man in various states of dress and hairstyle, meant to highlight his development and progress to modernity via the Philippine Constabulary. Chamberlin, Frederick. *The Philippine Problem 1898–1913*. Boston: Little, Brown, and Company, 1913, 160–61.

as the seat of a colonially rehabilitated government, and the Muslim South in the Philippines. A respectable masculinity shaped by US values becomes the likely node of social order to manage the unruly savage masculinity of the Moro amok. Lieutenant Espiritu, as Chapman's liaison, is the dividend of Worcester's investment, exhibiting the "value" of the constabulary in rehabilitated Philippine manhood. Looking at the intersection of disability and colonialism demonstrates the extent to which US American masculinity, as evoked in the figure of the militia officer, is one of the mechanisms through which Filipino assimilation of the sociopolitical norms of elevated society can materialize. Indeed, it is not just in the actual physical space of the classroom in which teachers Collante and Rosos met their untimely ends where colonial education takes place. The constabulary itself, the police arm of the US-Philippine colonial state, articulates the rehabilitative logics of coloniality and benevolence.

While sartorially and physically there are clear changes in the masculine performativity staged in the photograph of Worcester's "Bontoc Igorot," given that the emphasis of the photograph is on these changes' "educational value" it is not unfair to speculate on the imagined transformations of the non-Christian Filipino mind. That is to say, those Filipinos, having embodied and internalized the educational values of martial imperial masculinity, are better able to keep their wits and resist the racial urge to descend into the frenzy of running amok. The illegitimate violence of racial madness is exchanged for the legitimate violence of agents of colonial social order as functionalized by a police state populated by US-rehabilitated Filipino officers. Those that do not inhabit the colonial logics of US masculinity, may, indeed, go mad. Nevertheless, the true test of civilization is the extent to which these rehabilitated natives can control and manage those bodyminds that do not conform to the telos of what historian Gail Bederman has aptly called the logic of "manliness and civilization."[42] The extent to which colonial officers duplicated the diagnostic language of racialized frenzy reveals the ways that racial and colonial power propagated as much through a hierarchy of minds as of bodies. Worcester's "Bontoc Igorot" is sane; Ansol the amok is a delinquent ethnologically inhabiting a state of unreason. The racialized frenzy of the amok, the attempt to discipline the propensity to madness emblematized by the imperial classroom (the scene of the crime), and the propagation of US styles of police governmentality ineluctably shaped by the martial masculinity of the Philippine Constabulary all point to the ways that sexuality, gender, colonialism, and disability interweave.

There can be little doubt that Ansol's attack was a premeditated assault consistent with a religious practice or rite. This is significant because Ansol's mental state cannot be completely understood as an acute racialized and pathological disorder. The accuracy of the description and information available to Chapman notwithstanding, what is clear is that the unit of the heterosexual marriage (described by Chapman as comprising a "husband" and "wife") emerges as a meaningful factor for the albeit shallow attempts at understanding the social disorder that amoks presented for colonial law and order. With some rage and frustration of his own, Chapman describes how this situation ended on satisfactory terms for the couple (Ansol and his wife) and for the people of Laum Tabawan, Ansol's place of origin:

> From the standpoint of the natives of Tabawan and the relatives of the Moro Ansol this man has covered himself with honor and glory. His grave occupies a prominent place in the village cemetery where he lies beside the wife he has honored by his death. The grave is decorated and at the present time is a gathering place for the people of his village. From

the standpoint of the people of the village the affair has ended highly satisfactorily. Two government employees [the teachers] have been killed and Moro Ansol has gone to heaven on a white horse. The way that this case has been treated cannot but encourage other Moros to follow the same practice.[43]

Chapman paints the scene of a floridly decorated gravesite where the honored couple has been laid to rest. Ansol has, supposedly, achieved a spiritual afterlife of honor consistent with a religious practice of his people's framework of marriage and all that it stipulates. His frenzy and extreme violence were a way to honor that marriage contract, which then claimed "two government employees" that worked for the Philippine and US educational apparatus. As far as this case is concerned, the amok might not draw on conventional pathological discourses regarding sexual abnormality, but the phenomenon of the amok does present a challenge to respectable heteronormativity. If heterosexual marriage represents a union that is one of social order, a religious worldview that furnishes an understanding that to honor such a contract must result in death by combat flies in the face of Western understandings of marriage. Here marriage does not function as an institution that inaugurates state order. Instead its perversion is how we are to understand the relative primitivity of the Moros. To not conform to "proper" heterosexuality sets into relief the madness of the amok. This is consistent with the discernible pattern of amoks that demonstrated an inability to calmly adhere to stable and respectable family relationships.

However spectacular the attack may have been, this was not an isolated incident, as at the time of Chapman's report in August 1934, Ansol was the "third outlaw killed by teachers in Sulu since June."[44] As a matter of fact, archival records in several periodicals and bureaucratic reports confirm a notable pattern of exclusively Muslim "tribal" men that would become or "run" amok, which for officials and "civilized" Filipinos was an antisocial and pathological state inconsistent with the colonial order of things. Another instance, also in Jolo, is detailed in a report to the provincial governor dated January 24, 1935, in which on January 17 teacher Sofronio Aquino "in the Dalo school on the island of Mantabuan was killed by Alihasan, about 18 to 20 years of age, a neighbor and friend who went amuck." The author of the report, F. G. Roth, details that "Milaham, the father of Alihasan, had recently lost money [and] goods intended for his son's dowry [sic] in a gambling game with a Chinese trader; and without the money for the dowry, Alihasan's betrothed would not marry him." Roth further explains that Alihasan intended to "revenge himself" against the trader who got away with his bride-price. For some reason that is unexplained in Roth's report, the school became the target for Alihasan's "grief and disappointment." Following Aquino's murder, Milaham, feeling responsible for his son's actions, evidently went amok himself. An additional man named Hadjarat apparently joined the men, forming a band of amoks for reasons not completely clear in the report. To respond to the social kerfuffle, constabulary officers were sent to reestablish order. Ironically, "the presence of the constabulary and other strangers possibly made the little difference which turned Hadjarat amuck." That is to say, the presence of Philippine police activated some deep-seated animus that aggravated the very problem that they were sent to rectify. Roth details the disturbing hunt for these amoks by Philippine Constabulary soldiers. At the end of the ordeal, the three amoks lay dead along with three Filipino soldiers. With a surprising attentiveness to local politics and animosities, it was clear to Roth that the presence of a police force in Mantabuan laid bare the conflict between the locals and Philippine authorities. In fact, Roth admits that the violent conflict ending in six deaths and several injuries could have been avoided: "Without local police the only possible way to avoid the encounter would have been to withdraw the constabulary completely; but in that case, the amoks would undoubtedly have secured a boat and escaped elsewhere to kill promiscuously."[45]

This connection between "promiscuous" murder and other savage pagan practices like slavery are consciously linked to the practice of running amok and the perversity of Indigenous sexuality; indeed, "Mohammedanism sanctioned the pagan practices of polygamy and slavery, put iron into their veins and eliminated the fear of death."[46] The deviant sexuality of the Moros, clarified in practices like plural marriage, created the mental conditions for madness. Moreover, it seems that their iron veins and lack of fear of death are undoubtedly linked to the "pagan" institutions of enslavement and the deviant practice of plural marriage. This is an important point wherein we can speculate how the links between sexual perversion, the illiberal and antiprogressive practice of slavery, and pagan religion all constitute the matrix through which the racial madness of running amok obtains. They are both symptoms of racial madness and the cause of it. A student of Hayden's, Thomas Solomon, gives an anthropological analysis of what he calls the "Malayan Mohammedans." Solomon's report, "Public Order among the Moros of the Philippines and the Work of the United States Army," indicates the ways in which disability and heterosexuality intersect in the Philippines. Solomon makes these links rather explicit. Citing the "Annual Report of the Governor of the Moro Province" authored by Brigadier General John J. Pershing from Zamboanga during the extended conflicts of the Philippine-American War in the southern Philippines on June 30, 1913, Solomon reflects on the pagan system of slavery and Malay madness:

> The result of the system is that many a man, unable to bid against wealthy datos for the hand of a woman of his choice, is denied the privilege and the natural right of having a wife. It is from this class of Moros that usually come the "amucks" and "juramentados"; nine out of ten determine upon this course because of disappointment or frustrated purpose in obtaining a mate.
>
> The practice of labor indenture for the family of the girl that a Moro might want to marry in exchange for her hand might still go unhonored by the family. Thus the man does not get the girl that he is promised. Thus [the] Moro often runs "amuck" against his enemies as an act of war, but the principal cause is as above stated. The relation of "amuck" and "juramentado" to polygamy is fully established.[47]

This is a stunning observation that there exists an explicit relationship between amok madness and polygamy. It seems that polygamy, and the sexual deviance that it entails, is inseparable from labor indenture. These factors, indeed, cause the Moro to run amok, to go mad. Deviant sexuality is not abstractly constructed as disability; it, indeed, *is* racialized disability.

Again, the fact that these instances affected the efficacy with which the Philippines and the United States could collaboratively educate the population was of significant concern. These were educational institutions meant to free Moros from such perversities that caused racialized disability. Notably, the rampage of these amoks was in direct contravention to the "noble and edifying" cause of the education of the Filipino people. Typically, classrooms and schoolhouses were targeted in these attacks. And, notably, it was typically schoolteachers that were killed, with very few injuries and no documented deaths of schoolchildren. Part of the project of strengthening educational initiatives, particularly in remote regions of Sulu, seems to coincide with explanations of the contentious marital and family dynamics that seemingly led to the cases of mental instability of becoming or running amok. While the cases of Ansol and Alihasan are only two of a larger trend of Moro amoks, they are neither exceptional nor do they deviate largely from the pattern of some intense family dynamic leading to these transient and acute states of madness and violence. The fact that they are also products of seemingly strange mourning rituals for a recently departed spouse or the problematic marriage negotiations involving the undoubtedly strange and unfamiliar practice of securing a wife through the exchange of a bride-price do not go unremarked by those tasked with reporting on these tragedies. These spasmodic psychological disorders—which are due to a state of madness that, as we have already seen, is particular to those of the "Malay race" and which results in the deaths of family members, neighbors, soldiers, and, significantly teachers—demonstrates the powerful colonial need for educational intervention even as it also shows its untenability. Yet it is not untenable because of a lack of civilization. Rather, as Roth's report implicates, there are other social and political grievances of many of the people inhabiting the southern Philippines that get brushed aside in the name of the more laudable goal of those peoples' colonial rehabilitation.

Madness in this colonial archive helps us to understand the intersection of a biopolitics of sexuality and disability. Normative and productive heterosexuality are markers of a kind of civilization that can attest to a sound and valid society structured by orderliness, a respect for law, and a robust political life befitting modern society. This society must be sane. Marriage is a contract between those of sound mind.[48] The demonstration of these kinds of modern behaviors becomes crucial for a country that is on the verge of independence following their tutelary colonial period under a foreign power; these reports were made on the historical precipice of Philippine independence via the Tydings-McDuffie Act. Madness and the racialized violence of the amoks of Sulu illuminate a tenuous social order that seems to always be on the verge of collapse. If this is the case, are the Filipinos really ready to administer and govern as a sovereign entity? Such tenuousness requires the implementation of colonial social controls to align society with the modern requirements of bourgeois social norms that shape the colonial understanding of the appropriateness of and readiness for independence. The mad and savage Indian serves as a sign of disorder that must be brought into check.

The Transpacific Settler Coloniality of Madness

I suggest that the intersection of imperial education, racialized disability, and the Indigeneity of the Filipino represents an extension of the logic of settler empire shaping the administrative life of coloniality in the Philippines. In this section, I argue that the North American Indians, and the eliminatory logics that manage them, became a rhetorical litmus test for the potential sovereignty of Filipinos: If Filipinos (particularly in the form of the constabulary) cannot manage, control, and rehabilitate their mad

Indians like the United States did, then they are not ready to be fully sovereign political actors. The specter of the North American Indians and their elimination at the hands of US settler empire inform the ways that madness figures within the phenomenon of the amok. The amok was understood at least partially through this settler framing, even though the Philippines itself is not a settler colony in the more established and conventional definition of the term. The Philippines was, of course, not just an object of military interest for the expanding US empire; it was also a case study and object of academic inquiry. Many academics–cum–colonial officials in the Philippines followed in the footsteps of Joseph Beal-Steere and his more famous student, Dean Conant Worcester, in their ethnological surveys of the various Indigenous peoples of the archipelago. Naturally, the kinds of anthropological science that was brought to bear on the United States' new colonial acquisition did not come from a vacuum; instead it drew on race sciences that were developing domestically in the United States in a scientific frame of reference in which the specters of slavery and Indigenous elimination grew to transpacific proportions.[49] This frame temporally extended to the late 1920s and 1930s, shaping the ways that US officials came to understand growing concerns around Philippine independence. Many of the reports on the Moro amoks of Sulu were meticulously cataloged by Joseph Ralston Hayden, a University of Michigan professor and, in the 1930s, vice governor of the Philippines. As Hayden was a professor of political science, the case of the mad Indians of Sulu must have been particularly intriguing to him as an ethnological study on the capabilities of the Filipino for autonomous rule. Indeed, several of his students took up this topic. Trained by Hayden, who himself followed in the footsteps of Worcester, they demonstrated the ways that Philippine anthropology and political studies were also settler disciplines. For instance, political science student Karl Karsian gravitated toward the question of how Filipinos themselves would govern a bunch of amoks. In a sociological thesis titled "Governing the Moros," Karsian writes, "Just as the Founding Fathers looked upon the territory west of the Alleghenies to the Mississippi and beyond as the rightful heritage of a new growing nation, so the Filipinos look upon the fertile lands and trackless forests of Mindanao and Sulu with all their possibilities as the rightful heritage of a people who, they hope, will someday take its place along the side of the nations of the world."[50] Karsian's statement is a testament to the ongoing structure of settler coloniality in the Philippines. As I have been suggesting, US settler colonial precedents informed the ways in which colonial officials and students of empire like Karsian appraised Filipino progress toward independence. This gives further preponderance of evidence that, for many intents and purposes, the Filipinos were viewed at least partially as another group of Indians consonant with the prevailing ethnological tropes of the time.[51] This settler ideology interacted with the benevolent assimilation of US empire in a fascinating way: it split the Philippine people from their Indigenous population, and disability—namely, madness—manages this split. In the split, the reigns of control and management of the Indians fell to civilized and "rehabilitated" Filipinos themselves. This seems accurate given the extent to which both US American colonial officials and Philippine Constabulary officers responded to instances of the amoks. Karsian writes that "after 30 years of struggle in the Philippines Islands, America is again faced by the problem as to what shall we do with the Filipinos." This question collides with the Moro problem—a seemingly intractable people that will not bow down to colonial power, whether it emanates from Manila or Washington, DC. The Moro Indians become the litmus test of Philippine ability in self-government. Karsian cites in his appendix a petition dated June 9, 1921, and addressed to President Warren Harding, that was included in a text titled "Philippine Islands" and penned by Governor General William Cameron Forbes. The petition declared "their [Filipinos'] opposition to the incorporation of the Moro country with the rest of the Islands in the event of the granting of independence." Notably, there is a critique of the Filipinos' mishandling of the Moro problem: "Discounting one-half or even two-thirds of the charges of misdeed and corruption listed against the Filipino rulers, we still have a significant and telling list of arguments showing the inefficiency, corruption, and lack of sympathy on the part of the Filipinos in governing the Moros."[52] The irony is quite stark that it is the Filipinos that are criticized for their corrupt settler governance. Given the settler frame of reference, however, this critique seems to suggest that if the Filipinos can't manage their own *indios* like the US historically managed its Indians, then perhaps the enterprise of Philippine sovereignty is a bankrupt one.

What I suggest is that an extension of settler ideology in the far-flung Philippines shows that settler colonial theorist Patrick Wolfe was correct in his argument on Indigenous dispossession and elimination in more ways than he might have initially surmised. Truly, settler colonial studies is a global theory with implications for the ways that we understanding US imperialism in the Philippines and around the world. The initial dispossession of Indigenous peoples of their lands in North America influenced the policy, education, and rehabilitation of the Philippines during US colonial rule there. Might the "logic of elimination," as defined by Wolfe, refract through the administrative colonialism of the Philippines?[53] The evidence seems to suggest that it does and that disability played a significant role. What might it mean to think of the ways that US empire propagates its logics transpacifically through previously established structures of settler colonialism? The logic of elimination and genocidal destruction of First Nation peoples in North America was a logic that extended through imperial foreign policy, making it apt to call the United States not only a settler colony but also a transpacific settler empire. Settler imperialism describes the ways that the transpacific empire building of the United States consolidated a colonial administrative apparatus to compel compliance through the disability logic of benevolent assimilation and the eliminatory logic of settler colonialism. Settler colonialism echoes in the administrative structures of US empire in the Philippines, which dispossess the native of capacity for self-rule in the service of the false promise of benevolent rehabilitation. We cannot adequately or completely understand the ways that Philippine and US colonialism governed places like Mindanao and Sulu absent their genealogy in North American settler empire.

I suggest that Philippine postcoloniality cannot be understood completely outside the historical and discursive realm of US settler colonialism. This gets at the heart of the problem in many ways and offers a different line of critique for disability studies. Foucauldian mad studies describes how the insane were put on spectacular display in the Middle Ages: "madness [was] elevated to spectacle above the silence of the asylums."[54] How does the confinement of the mad reconcile with the eliminatory logics of settler imperialism? The amoks of the Philippines present a problem for the efficacy of US benevolent rehabilitation. Rather than point to the failures in adequately reforming through tutelary colonialism US custodial subjects, the blame is placed on Filipinos' inability to internalize their rehabilitative ideologies. And yet the solution to this problem of native madness is to shape a Philippine settler colonial apparatus—that is, endowing and shaping Filipino governmentality through the ongoing structure of settler colonialism. The extent to which Filipinos would be successful avatars of this settler colonial governmentality would thus prove to the United States that they were ready for the stage of postcolonial self-rule.

Given the prevalence of the "amoks," the colonial official Chapman brings doubt to the whole prospect of an independent Philippines. His judgment draws precedent from other colonial powers and the United States' own development via its westward expansion in the nineteenth century. Chapman was a veteran of the First World War. Drawing on this experience, he notes that he "knows what it means to see men badly wounded but for brutality and ferocity there is nothing which can compare to a Moro amuck." Indeed, "they never stop chopping their victims so long as a spark of life remains and even then the bodies are terribly mutilated before they are satisfied." As has been noted, this was not an isolated tragedy. Four months prior to his report there were apparently only "four or five 'wanted' men in all of Sulu," but at the time of his report, drawing on other constabulary reports, Chapman states that more than sixty "amoks" were at large in the southern Philippines.[55]

Since this is a recurring issue, Chapman wants to suggest ways that the authorities can prevent the killings. His observations pull in the experience of other imperial powers that administer and control "Mohammedans." Drawing on such colonial common sense, he writes,

> There is a general opinion that nothing can be done to stop Moros from running amuck. Such however is not the case. Moros can be prevented from running amuck if authorities are willing to take stern measures in all such cases. There is no need to experiment to find the solution to this problem. Both the British and the Dutch have large Mohammedan populations in Borneo. Cases of amuck are unknown in Borneo. The solution is very simple.
>
> When a man in Borneo runs amuck the whole village is held responsible. The British promptly burn the whole village. The Dutch cut off the head of the offender and place it on a pole in the market. In no case are relatives allowed to repossess the body of the amuck. These are brutal measures but the Moros do not understand kindness unless it is tempered with the kind of justice they understand. It is impossible for a man to run amuck without the relatives knowing of his intentions in advance. Usually the whole village knows of the intentions of the men and it is for that reason that an amuck seldom kills anybody in his own village.[56]

This extreme measure seemingly matches the frenzy with which Moro amoks wreak havoc—equally violent acts are required, as "the Moros do not understand kindness." It is clear that the work of education, US occupation of the Philippines, and the particular destabilizing presence of the United States in the southern Philippines are seen as acts of benevolence rather than aggravating any reasonable anticolonial sentiment. So benevolent an empire is the United States that Chapman feels he needs to rhetorically justify such brutality as if the project of imperialism has been too accommodating. Moreover, Chapman's statement is striking in that US colonial rule drew consciously from other empires that made their fortunes in Southeast Asia—namely, in the present-day countries of Indonesia and Malaysia. Chapman's colonial vision encapsulates a "contact zone" of asymmetrical power relations within Southeast Asia that are resonant with the etymological genealogy of the term *amok*, as I have noted.[57] While I would be hesitant to claim that there aren't other well-documented instances of colonized subjects that are deemed pathologically violent, the phenomenon of the amok and the kind of racialized madness that it connotes are particular to the area of Southeast Asia; its meanings rippling across populations, empires, and communities that could be characterized as sharing a common though multivalent Malay heritage. In the Philippines, this Malay racialization conspires with North American settler colonial discourses vis-à-vis Indigeneity wherein it is equally apt to describe the phenomenon as, as the British poet Dryden so forcefully puts it, running an "*Indian*-muck."[58] It is absolutely crucial to point out that in the Philippines the ways in which Indigeneity accretes its meanings is through the ascription of tribal savagery that accompanies US cultural understandings of what Chapman called "Mohammedanism." This factor, perhaps more than any other, demonstrates for many colonial agents a cultural poverty, pathological lack of empathy, and blunted understanding of "justice" of those Philippine Indians that practice the Muslim faith. In an unexpected twist, however, it seems that the United States' own history of liberal abolitionism alongside its dedication to heteronormative logics of respectability conspire in shaping an understanding of Moro sexual deviancy.

Returning to Thomas Solomon's analysis of the "Malayan Mohammedans" in "Public Order among the Moros of the Philippines and the Work of the United States Army," sheds light on the extent to which settler colonial ideology shaped ideas of Philippine civilization. Dating all the way back to the discovery of the Philippines by Ferdinand Magellan, Solomon insinuates the United States in a chain of colonial powers set to the task of civilizing the Filipinos. He writes, "The army fulfilled its mission, the predatory civilization of the Moros was reduced to a position of safety; there had been a general disarmament, slavery (catching and selling persons) was abolished, piracy suppressed, robbery, brigandage, and pillage were stopped and cedula taxes were being paid. The public school system was gradually gaining favor because it did not interfere with religion as the Spanish system did." Corroborating that it was, indeed, a joint effort between the Philippines and the United States, Solomon affirms that in the years following official Philippine independence "the era of civilization was dawning on Mindanao and Sulu, the task of furthering the cause of civilization was turned over to the civil authorities with the police work of the Philippine Constabulary to suppress violence and maintain law and order."[59] It is fascinating to ponder how the United States' own development as a democracy and current world power at the time of Solomon's authorship seems to be cited here in evaluating the "predatory civilization of the Moros." That the suppression of piracy and the abolition of slavery are mentioned in the same thought as the establishment of the school system seems to link the question of the rehabilitation of the native of his madness and a progressive ideology whose impetus was partially given by the historical reach of US slavery. This may confirm Bruce's contention that the properties of reason and sanity are, indeed, products of slavocracy even if they are arguments for its abolition.

Archives of Unreason

Using the provocative case of the amoks of Sulu, I have attempted to read against the archival grain of sanity to tease out the interesting inconsistency in the logic of colonial officials in diagnosing the Filipinos as a population of the racialized frenzied.[60] The officials argued that "running amok" was a vengeful state resulting in a crime of passion and meticulously planned attacks consistent with a perverse, sexually deviant religious worldview. Polygamy seemed to cause madness while also being a symptom of a culture defined by ethnological disorder. "Running amok" was a state of racialized frenzy that attested to the need of US civilizing influence—a calm, dispassionate, and reasoned colonial governmentality that endowed Filipinos with police powers defining mad violence as illegitimate while state police violence as legitimate.

Madness became the index through which to justify both the need of continued US presence and Indigenous Moro frenzy, furnishing for us an archival trace for the ways that madness as itself an ethnopathological category usefully drew intraracial distinctions among Filipinos. I have argued that this is productively understood as an extension of US settler colonial ideology whether or not the Philippines is understood in the traditional sense as a settler colony. Instead settler analogues were drawn that turned on racial definitions of madness. A comparative developmentalist reading is apparent: the United States, the new empire, was able to handle its own Indian problem. If the Filipinos could not, then were they truly ready for civilization and self-government? "Amokness" then became a diagnostic category that ethnologically engulfed the Filipino—the Filipino was too mad, too frenzied, to be autonomous. And yet the Filipino was also expected to—and viewed as needing to—contain the madness of their less civilized compatriots: this is the mad and frenzied rehabilitating the mad. This puts a complication into the wider argument of this book: in the colonial situation, if you are a colonized subject that can identify another that is more deranged than you are and that you can in turn rehabilitate, then you cease to be disabled and are thus deserving of the political privileges of sovereignty and self-rule. Put more simply, if you can rehabilitate, then you are not disabled. In this archival record we see that the Filipino is simultaneously marked by this "Malay" strain of madness *and* must transcend the racialized enclosures of this madness to access universal colonial reason in order to prove not only that they are not mad but that they can rehabilitate or cure it. This is not a winning proposition for the Philippines.

For the field of disability studies, it seems more and more important to ask certain questions: What might it mean to apprehend the coloniality of madness?[61] What is the colonial afterlife of madness? What might madness, here, be responding to? Is there an anticoloniality to madness? Certain historical forces are at play that affect how these agents are reading race and debilitated mental states of frenzy. Philippine ability for self-government was at the forefront of people's minds, as 1934 was the year in which the Tydings-McDuffie Act was to be passed by the US Congress. (In fact, the act was passed in March 1934.) The attack on the school in Laum Tabawan occurred in August of that same year. This historical moment of provisional independence for the Philippines was measured through the historical background of the US colonial domination of North American Indians. Rather than it being a failure on the part of the United States for ultimately civilizing the Moros that "ran amok," the failure was instead passed off on the Filipinos that vied for independence. Since the United States was able to control its Indian populations, this became the settler colonial benchmark for determining the viability and ultimate success of Philippine independence outside direct US colonial administration.

The fact that the United States had been present in the archipelago for more than thirty years, having established a far-reaching colonial education network that failed to address or respect the intraracial dynamics of different Philippine groups, was not worth mentioning for colonial officials. The Moros, instead, became a fetishized, mad object that shows that some are far beyond help and civilization, a convenient scapegoat and proving ground for the experiment of Philippine independence. Given these historical factors, can Philippine postcoloniality be adequately understood without contending with the ways that settler coloniality migrated transpacifically to the archipelago? What the presence of the "amok" attacks does is demonstrate the extent to which the presence of colonial educational institutions administered by the United States exacerbated conflict between Catholic, Muslim, and other "non-Christian" Filipino groups—augmented conflict which then became a red herring for Filipino incapacity. Never in question was the bankrupt colonial measurement of an externally verifiable Filipino unity, despite meaningful and deeply ingrained religious, territorial, and identitarian differences. Indeed, racial unity among Anglo-Saxons and North American Indians was never a meaningful measurement gauging the viability of US identity and sovereignty. And yet, in the Philippines, on the precipice of a long-delayed independence, the conflict between Christian and non-Christian Filipinos was a sticking point. White domination of the Indian in the United States became a powerful analogue, framing the unease with which colonial administrators approached what was for them the dubious prospect of a completely sovereign Philippines. Were the Filipinos ready? The figure of the mad Indian would suggest that they were not. Naturally, there would not have been a recognition of the ways that US ethnological categories aggravated Spanish colonial differentiation of Catholic Filipinos from their Moro counterparts. Yet the presence of madness in this archive would suggest that Indigenous peoples in the Philippines were deeply engaged in a critique of colonial politics and domination that exceed the regimes of visibility that structure ableist colonial rule and thought.

A Song from Subic

RACIAL DISPOSABILITY AND THE INTIMACY
OF CULTURAL TRANSLATION

In this book I have tried to demonstrate the ways that colonialism and ableism converge through a logic of racial rehabilitation and capacitation. I have strived to put myself in good intellectual company with scholars that have similarly remarked on the paradox of the "curative" being instantiated within the threat of violence or the promise of democratic freedom similarly produced through the violent movements of colonial statecraft.[1] The political justification for colonialism, while not always explicitly about disability in the medicalized sense, functions by way of hierarchizing humanity through valuations of psychophysical capacity. I have attempted to enhance our focus on this *crip colonial* encounter through the vistas of the Philippines and its multilingual mestizo archive across various genres of cultural, literary, and visual production. And while the Philippines might be a narrow case study for such an all-encompassing force as colonial ableism, I have suggested that the discourse of *mestizaje* (racial admixture, miscegenation) as it manifested differentially in the archipelago provides avenues of comparative analysis that connect Asia to Latin America even if through broad theoretical remonstrances against global colonial debilitation. Personally, as someone whose life has been mapped and produced by colonialism, there is great power in advancing the project of critical theory. I admit that it is an intellectual coping mechanism to subvert the bonds of incapacitation that I suggest characterize the colonialism that dispossessed me and people who look like me.

While it is certainly my deep hope that this book's arguments will be of use in scholarship and activism in some way, its utility has afforded me a kind of self-authorship and actualization that has surprised me. The sophistication and density of theory sometimes feels like an invitation to not be vulnerable. That is, embracing the fetish of classification, theoretical neologisms, and finding the underlying structure that animates colonial oppression are certainly potent ways that those that were once subjected to processes of colonial objectification can become instead subjects of knowledge production in their own right. But it also has the effect of erasure of the emotional terrain in which such a subject navigates in favor of the false promise of dispassionate inquiry. In some small way, I want to rectify that in the space of this conclusion: to take a snapshot of the truly momentous historical period that has characterized world events since the beginning of 2020. But beyond the current moment, I feel more drawn toward contextualizing the life of the person that lives through the vanishing present. We must all, I think, take stock and account for a life (and the lives that subtend it) whose historical geographies exceed the seductive impulse to fetishize contemporary violences as if they were somehow exceptional. In some ways this project is a roundabout way to give a sociopolitical history of my own family and to shed light on aspects of my own personal history that themselves summon multiple geographies of human movement that inform a history of the present.

I have a lived a life that has been completely enervated by US militarism in ways that mirror the compulsive omission of such violence. The origin story is simple enough: my white American father met my Filipina mother on the Subic Bay Naval Base in the 1980s. So many Filipinos with more recent migrations to the United States can tell a similar story of mixed heritage. Complicating the narrative is that this unlikely meeting was during the waning years of the dictatorship of President Ferdinand Marcos, prompting my family's migration to more stable political pastures. I see this moment of my life through grainy news coverage of Epifanio de los Santos Avenue swelling with thousands of Filipinos during the People Power Revolution of 1986. I hear the voice-over of an American journalist proudly proclaiming, and I paraphrase, "And now the Filipinos are teaching the world the meaning of democracy." He sounded like a parent, beaming with pride as his children crossed the finish line of democratic principle. It even seemed sincere. Though, looking back, it was a pride one felt for another that was rooted in self-importance. Within the framing of this book, we could say that it was a contemporary extension of a historical pattern of US beneficence: Philippine democratic practice becoming robust as an effect of US largesse. Or, perhaps, democratic capacity accumulated not through collective moves toward independence but through colonial dispossession. Imagine the logic of the argument that the toppling of a dictatorship through popular nonviolent direct action is an *effect* of historical colonial military occupation—as if durable peace could ever be an effect of violence. The affect of this revolution is palpable even though I did not directly experience it. It offers a lesson for any Filipinx American scholar or theorist thinking through the contradictions of the democratic project. And the self-aggrandizing pride I noted in US journalistic representations of this moment furnishes another contradictory affect—one that I harbor for my actual parents, whose own encounter, love for each other, and love for me were conditioned by the violence of imperialism. Could love be an effect of violence? I write this as the product of that violence—the coming together and even unravelling of sedimented and multilayered geographies. These geographies emerge significantly in the topography of race and also my literal skin as the mixed-race, mestizo, outcome of suppressed revolutions, curtailed sovereignty, and annexation.

Cosmological physicists like Carl Sagan have often shared that we are the stuff of stars. Supernovas allowed the creation of heavier elements that would then order themselves in such a way as to make life possible. Order and beauty from the chaos of violent, radioactive superexplosions: the elegant outcome of random chance. In a poetic way, we then are the universe, given consciousness able to reflect on and think about itself. Imperialism to my mind does not deviate from this cosmic order. It makes a poetic kind of sense that I, like many Filipinx Americans, would be the mixed product of a violence about which we could then reflect and question. As a scholar and professor, I'm in a position to enable new generations of thinkers to sharpen our understanding even further. And yet this capacity for thought, as well as the material conditions and structures necessary to enable thought to be translated into meaningful action, are not without their own craven realities that uphold those very same systems of dispossession.

I write this in an intensified moment (though part of a larger historical pattern) of violence against Asian Americans, which has targeted mostly women and the elderly. I want the reader to appreciate that I write these words in macabre expectation that my mother or my sisters could be a victim of this violence—not to mention myself. I want my reader to know that via the rules of assimilation that we have done everything "right"—learned unaccented English; went to the right schools; became professionals, social workers, and academics; had families and bought homes; ascended into the middle class from more humble origins; are part of a long line of patriotic servicemen and -women who have served in multiple wars. And still the violence comes. How could it not, when a condition for inclusion and the etiology of human migration to this place are rooted in violent displacements? Amid this violence and the hashtag #StopAsianHate is the recognition that these attacks are not siloed from other historical traumas. These violences happen on the streets of the settler colonies where white nationalist ideologies have become even more radicalized and mainstream.

I write these words on the heels of the supremely tragic discovery of the remains of 215 children buried in unmarked graves on the grounds of the Kamloops Indian Residential School in British Columbia, Canada. It should be made clear that it was First Nations peoples that found the remains via use of ground-penetrating radar, and not because of any investigative effort or help from the Canadian state, which operated the school in conjunction with the Catholic Church between 1890 and 1978. It was Canada's largest residential school, and it "educated" thousands of Indigenous children, ripping them away from their families, their native languages, their communities, their customs, and their beliefs, all while subjecting them to physical and sexual assault, disease, and death. Many Indigenous community leaders have cited the traumas of these schools as a main reason for epidemic rates of alcoholism and drug addiction on Indian reservations. Over 150,000 Indian children passed through Canada's residential schools. The schools returned children who were scarred and traumatized, or did not return them at all. Some estimates suggest that six thousand or more children were killed.[2] Read on the screen of this historical settler violence, it does not strike me as coincidental that Vancouver, British Columbia, is the site of the highest incidence of anti-Asian violence in North America.[3]

I remark on both of these examples given the central role that the educative function of colonialism plays out for the "students" of empire. As the colonial classroom has been a site of discursive and material violence in *Crip Colony*, it seems important to highlight that it is through these systematized debilitations and injuries that we can comparatively understand the ways that the Asian American subject has been produced—a subject whose inclusion has been conditioned through an assimilation narrative whose effigy is the model minority, the good student. Such structural conditions have produced two divergent paths of two different subjects of colonial education, and yet both are rendered disposable. One is a model for intellectual virtue and unpolemical assimilation into Western capitalist values, brimming with cognitive ability, and being a good citizen of the classroom—the model minority. The other is those who disappeared from their communities, with the classroom as a scene of violence and tragedy. Given this context, I am beginning to understand where the "amoks" in chapter 4 were coming from and why they targeted US colonial schools in particular. It is no accident that my book has focused rather assiduously on the context of the colonial classroom that allegorized US imperial intervention as an act of benevolence, a site of struggle in the Philippines, a site up uplift for the model minority, and a site of unthinkable cruelty and tragedy giving impetus to the vicious logics of settler colonialism.

It is in this historical colonial context that the model minority, so good at school, is a subject that is strategically capacitated in ways that occlude the politics of racial disposability. In discursive strategies that deny Asian American subjects a radical history, the model minority has historically been endowed with, at times, even threatening amounts of cognitive capacity; so much so that it compensates for, or even *causes*, the physical debilitations associated with the feminized and effeminate, contagious, unhealthy, and dangerous Asian American. A disability analysis of the ways that the discursive construction of the cognition of Asian Americans colludes with and is enabled by the violence of racial disposability that we now see in the streets every day demonstrates the political necessity of cross-racial alliance—that is, to reject the terms of inclusion that foreground colonial pedagogies rooted in settler frameworks of cognitive citizenship.

For me, thinking about alternative capacities necessitates a radical empathy that is cultivated through the underestimated value in American studies of the role of rigorous language study, multilingual comparative scholarship, and the diverse archival encounters across difference that these can generate. Frankly, it is stunning to me that American studies and ethnic studies scholars wouldn't, as a general priority in our field, give great attention to the ways in which "American" ideas are articulated in different languages. The ways that the American archive would be expanded were this the case are difficult to quantify. Given that the violence of the settler colonial residential schooling systems in Canada and the United States was predicated partly on eliminating the active use of Indigenous languages, *and* given calls from Asian American communities to literally pronounce the names of the victims in the Atlanta spa shootings of 2021 correctly in an effort to respect their humanity, it seems to me the politics and ethics of language learning ought to be a much more central aspect of our intellectual and activist pursuits.[4] In academia, language competence is often viewed as a methodological chore rather than a politics of radical and ethical encounter with another that is unlike you and yet with whom you share a common humanity. I confront this constantly in disability studies scholarship that often prioritizes Canada, Europe, or the United States and works principally in Anglophone archives and texts.

Postcolonial comparatist Gayatri Spivak, I think, put it better than most when writing on the meanings of solidarity among third world and Western women through an alterity that ideally respects what she calls the "rhetoricity" of the original text. She implores:

> If your interest is in learning there *is* women's solidarity, how about stepping forth from this assumption, appropriate as a means to an end like local or global social work, and trying a second step? Rather than imagining that women automatically have something identifiable in common, why not say, humbly and practically, my first obligation in understanding solidarity is to learn her mother-tongue. You will see immediately what the differences are. *You will also feel the solidarity every day as you make the attempt to learn the language in which the other woman learned to recognize reality at her mother's knee.* This is preparation for the *intimacy of cultural translation.* If you are going to bludgeon someone else by insisting on your version of solidarity, you have the obligation to try out this experiment and see how far your solidarity goes.[5]

While Spivak views the task of the feminist translator through perhaps a more romantic lens than I, the ways that she conceives of the cultivation of intimacy across difference through the cognitive and physical labor of learning another's mother tongue has the potential of placing oneself in a different ethical orientation toward social realities that are constructed in languages other than one's own. This frame partially explicates my personal and political reasons for learning Spanish as a way to forge affinities across Filipinx American and Latinx identities while recognizing shared colonial histories as denizens of both Spanish and US empire. "You look like the language you speak," is one refrain that seemingly marks a common frame of Brownness and how it signifies in the Americas. It is a refrain that has been stated to me in a number of ways, as mine is a Brown face that speaks Spanish. And this is a reality that renders Spanish, for me, unlikely to be claimed as a cultural commodity attesting to some cosmopolitan identity. A fancy Spanish party where invitees enjoy tapas, flamenco, and *jamón ibérico* is just going to hit differently for someone like me.

"You look like the language you speak" is rooted in a misrecognition that is factually a part of the cultural archive of Filipinx and Latinx comparative racialization. I remember painstakingly conversing with myself in Spanish for countless hours in my university dorm room, closing the blinds and hearing echoes of myself. I did this because I thought I would explore this misrecognition as a gesture of solidarity and responsible "global citizenship" rather than disidentify with it—a disidentification I find supremely problematic given the politics of immigration in the United States. That is, resisting the notion that Filipinos aren't like "those other immigrants" at the border. The granular, corporeal work of learning Spanish, and learning it well rather than just as a methodological instrument, did feel like an intimate act of love and goodwill in the ethical ways that Spivak describes. I've written about this elsewhere with other Filipino Hispanophones where I reflected on "el español filipino-americano como ética de solidaridad"— that is, Filipinx American Spanish as an ethics of solidarity.[6] As I set to the work of learning Spanish, I imagined that I was a different person sonically bouncing from one corner of my room to another as I assiduously—and with great, intimate, even loving effort—adjusted the positioning of my tongue. I remember vividly attempting to remove that abhorrent American "ugh"— evacuating it from the vowels, as it were. One feels it in the throat, mouth, and tongue muscles—even the gums, somehow: they become more lithe matching the prosody of Spanish. Something about it felt more consistent, safe, and even familiar. They weren't just words. Even though it wasn't my language at first (or ever?), I felt that I was aligning my Brownness with Spanish like a planet. Looking back at myself, I can understand what Allan Punzalan Isaac meant when he pondered "if and how 7,100 [Philippine] islands may have floated away from Latin American shores."[7] More important, I felt that this act of learning and solidarity in conjunction with the knowledge of shared colonial histories enabled a particular kind of ethics of being able to see oneself as caring about another collectivity to which you do not intuitively belong.

I view my version of Filipinx American Spanish as a mode of thinking about and culturally translating solidarity, cross-racial intimacy, and navigating multiple intersecting geographies of colonial encounter. Perhaps more important for Asian American studies, I view Spanish as itself an *indispensable* Asian Americanist methodological tool of comparative racial analysis particularly in the context of Filipinx critique. Given the movements and exchanges of Spanish colonialism, there is an alignment that potentiates this solidarity in ways that are attentive to global historical structures. This revises extant framings of Asian American studies and experience to recognize important political and epistemological linkages with Latin American and Latinx studies, which I believe should be foregrounded much more and in much more rigorous ways. And yet I have also noted the important differences among these experiences.

Queer political theorist Cathy Cohen once carefully elaborated the "radical potential" of queer politics based on shared analyses of power rather than on, as C. Riley Snorton has put it, "a fraught sense of shared identity."[8] It is my understanding of the hybrid identities of the US borderlands in queer feminist theory that radical politics imagines and renews senses of differential alignments precisely by making shared identities *more* fraught and unstable. In a similar vein, I take inspiration from queer-of-color theory, which has elaborated analyses that don't discard identity tout court and yet also uphold Cohen's intention of a radical divestment from the desire to have stable, unchanging identity referents around which we organize our political praxis. Instead, we ought to imagine "a politic and epistemic operation that attempts to bring forth 'forms of collective life that can enliven and sustain us in a future worth living.'"[9] With a radical attention to potentiating these "forms of collective life," I offer this book in order to advance a critique of mestizaje that centers the optic of racial ambivalence to imagine collective futures brought about by charting the epistemic and political intimacies forged in response to colonial violence—unexpected cross-racial alliances that exceed colonial reckoning; ones that I locate in the space of showing up meaningfully in the language in which your interlocutors learned to perceive reality at their mother's knee.

NOTES

CRIP COLONIAL CRITIQUE

1 I'm very grateful to the Asian American (sub)urban historian James Zarsadiaz
   for his help in the surprisingly mercurial task of classifying the area I grew up in.

2 I'd like to call attention to the ways in which I'll be using identity terms
   throughout my book. While I personally am in favor of the use of terms such
   as "Latinx," "Filipinx," "Filipinx American," and "Chicanx," it is also important to maintain the use of conventionally gendered terms such as "Latina/o,"
   "Filipina/o," and Chicana/o" when the self-named identity of the speaker
   or subject to which these terms pertain correlates to a particular gendered
   identity that would be overwritten in problematic ways by gender-neutral or
   gender-radical terms ending in "x." This avoids anachronistic uses of nonbi-
   nary terms. Nineteenth-century *ilustrado* Filipinos are not "Filipinx" unless
   compelling archival evidence would suggest otherwise. Additionally, mainte-
   nance of feminine endings can be particularly crucial for feminist analysts or
   figures for which the feminine-signaling "a" is important. I want to highlight
   that maintaining the use of the gender binary in some of these terms is not so
   much arguing for its merits. Instead, it demonstrates an attention to historical, social, and political contexts that would be diluted by a transhistorical
   use of "Latinx" (just as one example). However, I more often use terms like
   "Filipinx" or "Latinx" when I am referencing or prefer to endorse fields of
   critique such as "Filipinx American studies" or "Latinx studies" and the analytical maneuvers found therein. Readers will note a variety of uses of various
   gendered identity terms, which may require an attention to the details and
   contexts of passages' analyses which would be overly burdensome to explain

in every single instance. "Filipinx" and "Filipina/o" exist in parallel and with one another in my view. For instance, in this particular passage to which this endnote pertains, because it is my past childhood self that I am referencing for whom "Filipino American" would be a meaningful identity, I indeed use "Filipino American" because Filipinx did not yet exist for me empirically or personally. Nevertheless, in the majority of cases where a decision for the sake of consistency ought to be prioritized, I will use terms ending in "x" *unless* there is a compelling reason to opt for a different term ending in "o" or "a."

3   *Ulit* is a Filipino/Tagalog word meaning "to repeat."

4   Palumbo-Liu, *Asian/American*; Isaac, *American Tropics*.

5   Foucault, *The History of Sexuality*, 19.

6   Ocampo, *The Latinos of Asia*.

7   Price, "The Bodymind Problem."

8   I adapt Tobin Siebers's definition of an "ideology of ability," which many would call "ableism," to this colonial context. See Siebers, *Disability Theory*, 7–9.

9   Minich, "Mestizaje as National Prosthesis," 212–13.

10 Mitchell and Snyder, *Narrative Prosthesis*.

11 While those in disability studies will be very familiar with the term "crip" as an analytical framework, those coming across it for the first time may find it jarring. Crip, much like "queer," is a scholarly lens that analyzes the ways that power shapes our assumptions around normative embodiment and its ideal capacities. "Crip" (recuperated from the derogatory "crippled" much like queer is a recuperation) disrupts those ableist processes in ways that deemphasize the myth of pure independence seeking to build social relations that are constituted through care and our mutual interdependence. I align my use of "crip" with these moves thinking critically about how global processes of race and colonialism are fundamentally about disability.

12 For a foundational reading of modernity, the Renaissance, and the baroque from a Latin American subalternist perspective, see Mignolo, *The Darker Side of Western Modernity*. See also Blanco, "Baroque Modernity and the Colonial World."

13 Art historian Serge Gruzinski has denoted this unique mélange of "mongrel worlds" (a problematic flourish to be sure) as evocative of a "mestizo mind." Thus, it is not simply the objective existence of syncretic cultures and races but the subjective array of "hybrid conceptual frameworks from which new ways of knowing emerge"; see Gruzinski, *The Mestizo Mind*; see also Russo, *El realismo circular*, 76. Scholars of the so-called *novohispano*, like Gruzinski and Alessandra Russo, have remarked on the problematic separation of Renaissance developments in art and philosophy being confined to Europe while innovations transpiring coevally in the Americas suffer the attribution of "Columbian," thus engulfing diverse geographies, peoples, and knowledges wholly within a conquest narrative. That is, aesthetic, political, and philosophical developments in Europe during conquest are coherent on their own. Meanwhile, the colonial experience is made to seem disjointed—absent from its European referent. Their answer is to recuperate mestizo hybridity

as being a central part of the Renaissance rather than on its periphery. Other scholars with different political commitments have similarly spoken on the ways that colonialism forms the dark underside of Renaissance and Baroque modernities. Despite these developments, there is a curious way that recuperating hybridity within European frameworks might center them.

14 Byrd, *The Transit of Empire*, xviii.

15 Byrd, *The Transit of Empire*, xiii.

16 Kim, "Toward a Crip-of-Color Critique," coined the term.

17 I borrow the powerful formulation of "queercrip" from crip theorist Alison Kafer. See Kafer, *Feminist, Queer, Crip*. For the use of "racial-sexual" as an analytic, see Mendoza, *Metroimperial Intimacies*, 12–18. I find the term to be a productive frame to understand discourses of mestizaje. For an elaboration of the Marxian-informed and Asian Americanist cultural concept of "racialized gendered relations" under capitalism, see Lowe, *Immigrant Acts*, 22.

18 Quijano, "Colonialidad del poder."

19 Mojares, *Brains of the Nation*; Go, *American Empire and the Politics of Meaning*; Hau, *Elites and Ilustrados*.

20 McRuer, *Crip Theory*, 2.

21 See Stern, *Eugenic Nation*. Stern defines eugenics pithily as the desire for "better breeding" (19).

22 Siebers, *Disability Theory*.

23 Mendoza, *Metroimperial Intimacies*.

24 This particular thought was shaped by a compelling conversation with Joseph Pierce. See Pierce, "Adopted," 57–76.

25 Pierce, "Adopted," 58.

26 Simpson, *Mohawk Interruptus*, 33.

27 Simpson, *Mohawk Interruptus*, 3.

28 Simpson, *Mohawk Interruptus*, 8.

29 *Merriam-Webster.com Dictionary*, s.v. "recursion," accessed June 10, 2022, https://www.merriam-webster.com/dictionary/recursion.

30 In thinking about my own subject position as a Filipinx American, I think about the differences of Filipinos in the Philippines that have been categorized by the Philippine state as "tribal" or "Indigenous." For a stunning account of the Lumad (a conglomeration of various Philippine Indigenous groups in Mindanao) fighting against the settler violence of the Philippines and multinational extractivist corporations, see Alamon, *Wars of Extinction*.

31 Seijas, *Asian Slaves in Colonial Mexico*.

32 For a truly stunning exploration of the divergences between racial claims to Indigeneity and the political categorization under Indian, see Cotera and Saldaña-Portillo, "Indigenous But Not Indian?"

33 For a primary source that treats the topic of how white Anglo-American settler culture integrates in the Indian, see Turner, *The Significance of the Frontier*. See also Deloria, *Indians in Unexpected Places*.

34 This probably shouldn't surprise us given that administratively, as I've stated, the Philippines was technically a part of Mexico for more than two hundred years (1565–1815) and was US territory for almost fifty (1898–1946).

35 García-Abásolo, "Mestizos de un país sin mestizaje," 223–45. While García-Abásolo makes the case that the raw number of mestizos produced during the Spanish colonial period is far less when compared to New Spain, the mythic status that the mestizo has in the Philippines is quite potent in cultural production.

36 Arrizón, *Queering Mestizaje*, 119–54.

37 Schalk and Kim, "Integrating Race," 31.

38 Lowe, *The Intimacies of Four Continents*.

39 Quijano, "Coloniality of Power."

40 Anzaldúa, *Borderlands / La Frontera*, 25.

41 Anzaldúa, *Borderlands / La Frontera*, 24.

42 Schalk and Kim, "Integrating Race," 32–33. See also Bost, "Disability, Decoloniality, and Other-than-Humanist Ethics," 1562–80; Driskill, Morales, and Piepzna-Samarasinha, "Sweet Dark Places," 77–97; Kafer and Kim, "Disability and the Edges of Intersectionality," 123–38; Kim, "Toward a Crip-of-Color Critique"; Anzaldúa and Keating, *The Gloria Anzaldúa Reader*, 298–302; and McMaster, "Negotiating Paradoxical Spaces," 102.

43 Anzaldúa, "Disability and Identity."

44 McMaster, "Negotiating Paradoxical Spaces," 102.

45 Bost, "Disability, Decoloniality, and Other-than-Humanist Ethics," 1568.

46 Bost, "Disability, Decoloniality, and Other-than-Humanist Ethics," 1569.

47 Bost, "Disability, Decoloniality, and Other-than-Humanist Ethics," 1577.

48 McMaster, "Negotiating Paradoxical Spaces," 103.

49 Kafer and Kim, "Disability and the Edges of Intersectionality," 124, 126, emphasis in the original; see also Kafer, "Crip Kin, Manifesting." For the original invocation of a feminist disability studies analysis, see Garland-Thomson, "Integrating Disability."

50 In their pathbreaking article, Schalk and Kim admit that "Given our bases in US feminist-of-color scholarship, we want to emphasize that, in addition to the areas we have identified, future feminist-of-color disability studies work needs to engage transnational and postcolonial perspectives"; Schalk and Kim. "Integrating Race," 50–51.

51 Bost, "Disability, Decoloniality, and Other-than-Humanist Ethics," 1567.

52 Haraway, "A Cyborg Manifesto."

53 Bost, "Disability, Decoloniality, and Other-than-Humanist Ethics," 1567.

54 Here I am thinking through Patrick Wolfe's logic of elimination. See Wolfe, "Settler Colonialism and the Elimination of the Native."

55 Saldaña-Portillo, *The Revolutionary Imagination*, 262.

56 Saldaña-Portillo, *The Revolutionary Imagination*, 279.

57 Saldaña-Portillo, *The Revolutionary Imagination*, 286.

58 Saldaña-Portillo, *The Revolutionary Imagination*, 286.

59 Silva, *Toward a Global Idea of Race*, 25. Cotera and Saldaña-Portillo, "Indigenous But Not Indian?," 554–63, refers to this as a process of "mestizo mourning."

60 Bost, "Disability, Decoloniality, and Other-than-Humanist Ethics," 1567.

61 Cowing, "Occupied Land Is an Access Issue," 11.

62 Anzaldúa, *Borderlands / La Frontera*, 99, emphasis in the original.

63 Anzaldúa, *Borderlands / La Frontera*, 108, 25, 113.

64 Fradera, *Filipinas, la colonia más peculiar*.

65 See the very impressive online repository of Philippine literature in Spanish compiled at the web database "Humanidades digitales y literatura filipina en español," https://digiphilit.uantwerpen.be/.

66 Magellan died in the Philippines after a conflict with Indigenous peoples lead by Lapu-Lapu. He did not complete the journey that is credited to him.

67 Lifshey, *The Magellan Fallacy*.

68 For a notable critique of the "segmented" historiography of the Philippines, see Ileto, "Outlines of a Non-linear Emplotment."

69 Mojares, *Brains of the Nation*.

70 For more on this contradiction, see Velasco Shaw and Francia, *Vestiges of War*. For a more canonical treatment of "benevolent assimilation," see Miller, *"Benevolent Assimilation."*

71 Chu, "The 'Chinese' and the 'Mestizos' of the Philippines," 216. Chu's self-conscious framing with Chinese diasporic histories obliges him to define mestizos more narrowly as Chinese men and local women. Filipino mestizos, of course, included other mixtures that were not limited to Chinese as the only "foreign" element added to the autochthonous.

72 Hau, *The Chinese Question*, 5.

73 Chang, *Chino*; Paulina Lee, *Mandarin Brazil*; Lowe, *Intimacies of Four Continents*.

74 Goffe, "Chop Suey Surplus."

75 Chang, *Chino*.

76 Paulina Lee, *Mandarin Brazil*.

77 Vasconcelos, *La raza cósmica: Notas de viajes*, 17, emphasis added, my translation.

78 Chen, "The Stuff of Slow Constitution."

79 Vasconcelos, *La raza cósmica: Notas de viajes*, 9.

80 Vasconcelos, *La raza cósmica: Notas de viajes*, 9.

81 Siebers, *Disability Theory*, 7.

CHAPTER ONE

1 As I noted in the introduction, when I refer to the field of "Filipinx American studies" I elect to use the term "Filipinx" as a way of signaling my own queer political commitments and my desire for the field of which I am an embedded interlocutor. It is not meant to be prescriptive. I also mean to highlight the

ways that the use of the -*x* has, at least for the purposes of Filipinx American studies, a US-derived origin. It should be noted, however, that many varieties of Spanish across Latin America also adopt the -*x* despite inaccurate criticisms stating that it is solely a US phenomenon. Apart from the use of the term *Filipinx*, I maintain the use of "Filipino" when I am referring to texts, histories, or peoples from the Philippines. I do this so that I don't risk overwriting such histories with a blunt and inappropriate use of Filipinx, which, given those particular historical contexts, could be not only politically controversial but also anachronistic. When possible, I opt for the adjectival use of "Philippine" to lend greater clarity to these political, historical, and geographic distinctions.

2 Gopinath, *Impossible Desires*.

3 I thank scholar and artist Anthony Kim for his really assiduous and timely reminder of the multidisciplinarity of empire and how our critique of it should respond in kind.

4 Price, "The Bodymind Problem"; Schalk, *Bodyminds Reimagined*.

5 For an analysis of the differences between "rehabilitation," curing a disease or disability, and "habilitation," the acquisition or reacquisition of a skill, see Kim, *Curative Violence*, 8.

6 Rizal, *Noli me tángere*, xx.

7 Hartman, *Lose Your Mother*, 6, 45.

8 Arrizón, *Queering Mestizaje*.

9 Louis Dalrymple, "School Begins," illustration from *Puck* 44, no. 1142 (1899), centerfold, Library of Congress, LC-DIG-ppmsca-28668 (digital file from original print) and LC-USZC2-1025 (color film copy slide), https://www.loc.gov/pictures/item/2012647459/.

10 Sebring, "Civilization and Barbarism."

11 Mendoza, *Metroimperial Intimacies*, 63–94; McCoy and Roces, *Philippine Cartoons*.

12 McCoy and Roces, *Philippine Cartoons*, 15–16.

13 Kipling, "The White Man's Burden."

14 Sebring, "Civilization and Barbarism," 1–2.

15 Lowe, *The Intimacies of Four Continents*.

16 For a compelling account of the tumultuous interaction of the Mexican and US racial states, see Cotera and Saldaña-Portillo, "Indigenous but Not Indian?" Another excellent treatment of this topic is Saldaña-Portillo, *Indian Given*.

17 See Shah, *Contagious Divides*.

18 I want to personally thank Jodi Byrd for astutely pointing out this error in the image. What a great eye!

19 *Oxford English Dictionary*, online ed., s.v. "dunce," n.d., accessed December 17, 2020, http://www.oed.com/view/Entry/58445.

20 Coulthard, *Red Skin, White Masks*, 4.

21 Fear-Segal and Rose, "Introduction."

22 Silva, *Aloha Betrayed*, 178.

23 Silva, *Aloha Betrayed*, 177.

24 Silva, *Aloha Betrayed*, 178.

25 Silva, *Aloha Betrayed*, 166.

26 Lowe, *Intimacies of Four Continents*. Lowe has a remarkable discussion of liberal intimacy and the internalization of modern liberal values as part of the process of civilization.

27 Baynton, "Disability and the Justification of Inequality," 36.

28 Baynton, "Disability and the Justification of Inequality," 36.

29 Baynton, "Disability and the Justification of Inequality," 37.

30 For a detailed analysis of the political and philosophical meanings of amendments vis-à-vis racial violence, see Reddy, *Freedom with Violence*.

31 William McKinley, Executive Order, December 21, 1898, American Presidency Project, https://www.presidency.ucsb.edu/documents/executive-order-132.

32 Ferguson, *Aberrations in Black*.

33 Baynton, *Defectives in the Land*; Kudlick, "Modernity's Miss-Fits."

34 The date of the end of the Philippine-American War is contentious. The "official" end of the engagement is marked in US military history as 1902, but hostilities continued in the southern part of the archipelago until 1911.

35 See Abinales, *Making Mindanao*.

36 My use of "gift" draws from Nguyen, *The Gift of Freedom*.

37 Nguyen, *The Gift of Freedom*.

38 Miller, *"Benevolent Assimilation."*

39 For more on Filipinx American studies and US empire studies, see Anderson, *Colonial Pathologies*; Bederman, *Manliness and Civilization*; Hoganson, *Fighting for American Manhood*; Kaplan, *The Anarchy of Empire*; Kramer, *The Blood of Government*; Rafael, *White Love*; Mendoza, *Metroimperial Intimacies*; Rodríguez, *Suspended Apocalypse*; and See, *The Filipino Primitive*.

40 Kramer, *The Blood of Government*.

41 Renda, *Taking Haiti*.

42 Kaplan, *The Anarchy of Empire*.

43 Rafael, *White Love*.

44 Bederman, *Manliness and Civilization*.

45 For one of the best critical send-ups of imperialism justified as care, see Choy, *Empire of Care*.

46 Rodríguez, *Suspended Apocalypse*.

47 See, *The Filipino Primitive*.

48 See, *"An Open Wound,"* 377.

49 For a conservative estimate on the death toll of the Philippine-America War, "The Philippine-American War, 1899–1902," US Department of State, Office of the Historian, n.d., accessed June 5, 2019, https://history.state.gov/milestones/1899-1913/war.

50 Puar, *The Right to Maim*.

51 Barker and Murray, "Disabling Postcolonialism."

52 Rizal, José. *Filipinas dentro de cien años*, xx.

53 Rizal, *Filipinas dentro de cien años*.

54 For more on the legacy of mestizo enlightenment and the period of "national consciousness" in the late nineteenth-century Philippines, see Mojares, *Brains of the Nation*; Thomas, *Orientalists, Propagandists, and Ilustrados*; Anderson, *Imagined Communities*; and Anderson, *Under Three Flags*.

55 One foundational disability studies critique of Cartesian dualism can be found in Price, "The Bodymind Problem," 268–84. I am also inspired by the critical race and feminist resignification of the term in Schalk, *Bodyminds Reimagined*.

56 Pratt, *Imperial Eyes*, 7.

57 Rizal, *Filipinas dentro de Cien Años*, 18.

58 Rizal, *Filipinas dentro de Cien Años*, quoted and translated in Blanco, "Oriental Enlightenment," 60.

59 Rizal, *Filipinas dentro de cien años*, 5. This and all subsequent English translations of Rizal's text are my own.

60 Price, "The Bodymind Problem."

61 Rizal, *Filipinas dentro de cien años*, 46.

62 Rizal, *Filipinas dentro de cien años*, 11, 16, 21.

63 Rizal, *Filipinas dentro de cien años*, 46.

64 For context, the Spanish Empire abolished the sale of slaves in 1811; President Abraham Lincoln called for the freedom of US slaves through his Emancipation Proclamation in 1862, and it took official effect in 1863.

65 Lowe, *The Intimacies of Four Continents*.

66 The use of "intimate" in this paragraph is also informed by Lowe, *The Intimacies of Four Continents*.

67 Ferguson, *Aberrations in Black*.

68 Rizal, *Filipinas dentro de cien años*, 48.

69 Baldoz, *The Third Asiatic Invasion*; Lowe, *Immigrant Acts*; Ngai, *Impossible Subjects*.

70 Baldoz, *The Third Asiatic Invasion*.

71 Lowe, *Immigrant Acts*.

72 Hartman, *Lose Your Mother*, 6.

73 For more on the ways that disabled identity is a formative part of disability politics, see Oliver, "The Social Model of Disability"; and Shakespeare, "The Social Model of Disability."

74 Davis, "Constructing Normalcy," 6.

75 Reddy, *Freedom with Violence*.

CHAPTER TWO

1 Sommer, *Foundational Fictions*.

2 Blanco, "Bastards," 92.

3 For more on the ways that the nation has been historically constructed through strategic and "better breeding," see Stern, *Eugenic Nation*. While Stern speaks more specifically of histories of eugenics within the United States, her analysis articulates well with ways that the racial project of mestizaje also draws on eugenics and therefore represents a reproductive logic. For more on the eugenic genealogies of mestizaje, see Vasconcelos, *La raza cósmica: Argentina y Brasil; and Vasconcelos, La raza cósmica: Notas de viajes.*

4 Mojares, *Brains of the Nation*.

5 Reyes, *Love, Passion and Patriotism*.

6 My use of "foundational" here draws from Sommer, *Foundational Fictions*.

7 Rizal, *Noli me tángere*, 2:250. Translations are my own unless otherwise indicated.

8 Rizal, *Noli me tángere*, 2:250.

9 Sommer, *Foundational Fictions*.

10 Rizal, *Noli me tángere*, 2:251.

11 As in other chapters, my use of the disability term "bodymind" questions the hard Cartesian split between mind and body. See Price, Margaret, "The Bodymind Problem," 268–84.

12 For more on the dynamic racial meanings ascribed to the flexible corporeality of María Clara see Cruz, Denise, *Transpacific Femininities*.

13 Rizal, José, *Filipinas Dentro de Cien Años*, 15, 20.

14 Rizal, José, *Noli me tángere*, 2:251.

15 Rizal, *Noli me tángere*, 1:56. For analysis of María Clara's whiteness, see Cruz, *Transpacific Femininities*.

16 Reyes, *Love, Passion and Patriotism*, is particularly influential in arriving at this insight. Reyes makes a similar claim that the *ilustrados* managed female sexuality more particularly in terms of hygiene and respectable social behaviors. I similarly observe such sex and gender management in terms of disability.

17 Foucault, *Madness and Civilization*.

18 There are various scholars that have spoken to the extent to which a mestizo intellectual class in the Philippines—namely, the *ilustrados*—problematically duplicated colonial ideologies within the Philippines. See Kramer, *The Blood of Government*; Mendoza, *Metroimperial Intimacies*; Thomas, *Orientalists, Propagandists, and Ilustrados*; and Hartwell, "Imperial Endnotes."

19 Blanco, "Bastards," 92.

20 Blanco, "Bastards," 93.

21 Blanco, "Bastards."

22 Blanco, "Bastards."

23 Blanco, "Bastards," 92, 94.

24 Blanco, "Bastards," 98.

25 Rizal, *Noli me tángere*, 2:220–21.

26 Rizal, *Noli me tángere*, 2:222.

27 Rizal, *Noli me tángere*, 2:221–22.

28 Foucault, *Madness and Civilization*.

29 Cruz, *Transpacific Femininities*, 69, 75.

30 Work on mestizaje is prodigious. My thinking with regard to this sociohistorical force is informed by Arrizón, *Queering Mestizaje*; and Anzaldúa, *Borderlands/ La Frontera*. From a Caribbean perspective there is the inimitable Ortiz, *Cuban Counterpoint*, which brings more attention to realities of *mulataje* rather than the more privileged space of mestizaje.

31 Foucault, *The History of Sexuality*.

32 Foucault, *Madness and Civilization*.

33 Rizal, *Noli me tángere*, 1:25.

34 Anderson, *Imagined Communities*.

35 Jameson, "Third-World Literature," 65–88.

36 Rizal, *Noli me tángere*, 1:30.

37 Rizal, *Noli me tángere*, 1:31–32.

38 Blanco, "Bastards," 93.

39 Rizal, *Noli me tángere*, 2:233–35.

40 See, for example, Siebers, *Disability Theory*.

41 Kuppers, "Remembering Anarcha."

42 For a strong critique of the politics of gay marriage and queer sexuality in the context of biopolitics and imperial war, see Puar, *Terrorist Assemblages*. In the vein of the US gay rights movement and its advocacy for marriage equality, see Warner, "Normal and Normaller," 119. For ways in which the politics of "queer" have myopically focused on sexual identity at the expense of race, see Cohen, "Punks, Bulldaggers, and Welfare Queens."

43 Cohen, "Punks, Bulldaggers, and Welfare Queens."

44 For foundational work on the intersection of temporality and queerness, see Halberstam, *In a Queer Time and Place*; and Muñoz, *Cruising Utopia*.

45 Kafer, *Feminist, Queer, Crip*.

46 Sommer, *Foundational Fictions*.

47 Kafer, *Feminist, Queer, Crip*.

48 Puar, *Terrorist Assemblages*.

49 Cruz, *Transpacific Femininities*.

50 Kafer, *Feminist, Queer, Crip*; McRuer, *Crip Theory*; McRuer and Mollow, *Sex and Disability*.

51 McRuer, *Crip Theory*, 2.

52 Warner, "Fear of a Queer Planet," 3–17.

53 McRuer, *Crip Theory*.

54 Mollow, "'When Black Women Start Going on Prozac,'" 67–99.

55 Reaume, "From the Perspectives of Mad People."

56 Foucault, *Madness and Civilization*.

57 Anzaldúa, *Borderlands/La Frontera*.

58 Rizal, *Noli me tángere*, 1:24; the English translation is from Rizal, *The Social Cancer*, lvii.

59 Blanco, "Bastards," 99.

60 Rizal, *Noli me tángere*, 2:226; the English translation is from Blanco, "Bastards," 99.

61 Derbyshire, "Translator's Introduction," xxxi.

62 Lévi-Strauss, *The Savage Mind*, 129.

CHAPTER THREE

1 For more on literary theories of homosociality, see Sedgwick, *Between Men*.

2 Vasconcelos, *La Raza Cósmica*.

3 For a canonical treatment of the ways that, following the massification of travel, tourism reshaped social reality, see Urry, *The Tourist Gaze*.

4 Erevelles, *Disability and Difference*.

5 Thomas, *Orientalists, Propagandists, and Ilustrados*; Anderson, *Imagined Communities*; Mojares, *Brains of the Nation*.

6 Schalk and Kim, "Integrating Race," 32.

7 Silva, *Toward a Global Idea of Race*.

8 Erevelles, *Disability and Difference*.

9 Villaescusa Illán, *Transcultural Nationalism*.

10 Villaescusa Illán, *Transcultural Nationalism*, 20.

11 Agoncillo, "Philippine Historiography in the Age of Kalaw," 3–16.

12 Kalaw, *Hacia la tierra del zar*, 83.

13 Erevelles, *Disability and Difference*, 130.

14 Schalk and Kim, "Integrating Race, Transforming Feminist Disability Studies," 36.

15 Spivak, "Woman in Difference." I use Spivak's analysis of the figure of "Woman" not just as a literal referent in colonial relations but also as a symbolic figure evacuated of particular meaning. "Woman" is a discursive mechanism through which colonial paternalism gets enacted. This comes into play when I specify a similar symbolic referent: that of the "Chinese Woman" evacuated of interiority who simply exists as a deformed figure marking the Philippines as a successful project of racial uplift.

16 Pratt, *Imperial Eyes*, 125.

17 Pratt, *Imperial Eyes*, 125.

18 Garland-Thomson, "Integrating Disability."

19 Quayson, "Aesthetic Nervousness," 203.

20 Kalaw, *Hacia la tierra del zar*, 17. Throughout the chapter, all translations are my own.

21 Garland-Thomson, *Extraordinary Bodies*, 8–9.

22 Garland-Thomson, *Extraordinary Bodies*, 122–23.

23 Kalaw states that, while on the Japanese gunboat *Hong-Kong Maru*, "Salvador Roxas, Narciso Alegre, [Manuel] Quezon," and himself are participating in

this tour of Asia and Russia. He also acknowledges the presence of a Russian language interpreter and US diplomatic attaché Theo Rogers. Kalaw, *Hacia la tierra del zar*, 4.

24 Kalaw, *Hacia la tierra del zar*, v.

25 Spivak, *Other Asias*.

26 Spivak, *Other Asias*, 23.

27 Spivak, *Other Asias*, 23.

28 Spivak, *Other Asias*, 22.

29 Baldoz, *The Third Asiatic Invasion*.

30 Kalaw, *Hacia la tierra del zar*, 23.

31 Kalaw, *Hacia la tierra del zar*, 4.

32 Kalaw, *Hacia la tierra del zar*, 4.

33 Various scholars have commented on the nativization of the colonial bureaucracy of the Philippines under the United States. Among some of the most detailed are Kramer, *The Blood of Government*; Anderson, *Colonial Pathologies*; and Anderson, *Under Three Flags*.

34 Kalaw, *Hacia la tierra del zar*, 87.

35 Rafael, *White Love*.

36 Pratt, *Imperial Eyes*, 7.

37 Lim, *Brown Boys and Rice Queens*, 8, 10.

38 Kramer, *The Blood of Government*, 23, 73, 430, 435. Kramer calls this form of colonial nationalism "imperial indigenism" (245).

39 Here I borrow Homi Bhabha's notion of the "unhomely" as a colonial affect oscillating between the abject and the familiar; see Bhabha, "The World and the Home," 141. Here I mean that the white man / native boy dyad is an affectively familiar structuring metonymy for colonialism yet is also vigorously refused as legible knowledge. It is thus uncanny in its familiarity yet abject in its uneven uptake as a paradigm of postcolonial critique.

40 Lim, *Brown Boys and Rice Queens*, 10–11.

41 Lim, *Brown Boys and Rice Queens*, 8. I use the term *bottom* here to indicate a location in a colonial power hierarchy. But it is also a term and subject position theorized by queer Asian studies and American studies scholars to explicitly refer to the intersection of sexuality and race.

42 Mendoza, *Metroimperial Intimacies*.

43 Kalaw, *Hacia la tierra del zar*, 83.

44 Erevelles, *Disability and Difference*, 132.

45 Silva, *Toward a Global Idea of Race*.

46 Erevelles, *Disability and Difference*, 132.

47 For an elaboration of the concept of "slow death," see Berlant, *Cruel Optimism*.

48 Kalaw, *Hacia la tierra del zar*, 78, 143–44, 188. My translation: "A despotic and Slavic [nationalist] Muscovite empire" succumbing to a base "orthodox idolatry" that proves that "in Holy Russia there is more ignorance than religion."

49   Kalaw, *Hacia la tierra del zar*, 144.

50   Kalaw, *Hacia la tierra del zar*, 144.

51   Kalaw, *Hacia la tierra del zar*, 143–44.

52   Kalaw, *Hacia la tierra del zar*, 7.

53   Berlant, *Cruel Optimism*.

54   Kalaw, *Hacia la tierra del zar*, 17.

55   Ko, *Cinderella's Sisters*.

56   Ko, *Cinderella's Sisters*, 4.

57   Spivak, "Can the Subaltern Speak?," 296.

58   Cheng, *Ornamentalism*.

59   Erevelles, *Disability and Difference*.

60   Ko, *Cinderella's Sisters*.

61   Ko, *Cinderella's Sisters*, 27.

62   Tadiar, *Things Fall Away*, 13. Tadiar borrows this turn of phrase from Jonathan Beller. See Beller, *Cinematic Mode of Production*, 200.

63   Barker and Murray, "Disabling Postcolonialism."

64   Here I'm referring to Britain and the United States more specifically, as these are the sites in which the social model of disability gained traction as both a liberal political strategy to reform the state and an intellectual theoretical model.

65   Barker and Murray, "Disabling Postcolonialism," 68.

66   The ways in which I am thinking about "capacity" rather than exclusively "disability" are drawn from Puar, "Prognosis Time," and the in-depth elaboration of these concepts in Puar, *The Right to Maim*.

CHAPTER FOUR

1   Chapman to Director of Education, August 20, 1934, 851643, Aa 2, Ac, Box 30, Folder 1, Joseph Ralston Hayden Papers, Bentley Historical Library, University of Michigan, 1.

2   The Philippine Constabulary was a legion of US and US-trained Filipino police forces whose function was to maintain order in various parts of the archipelago. The significance of their appearance in this archive is the extent to which Philippine police forces were used to manage other Filipinos.

3   Kimberly A. Alidio, "Between Civilizing Mission and Ethnic Assimilation: Racial Discourse, United States Colonial Education and Filipino Ethnicity, 1901–1946," PhD diss., University of Michigan, 2001, 1–3.

4   "Moro Killings Are Reported: Two Juramentado Cases Are Sent in to Local Constabulary," *Bulletin* (Manila), October 2, 1934, 851643, Aa 2, Ac, Box 30, Folder 1, Hayden Papers.

5   Given recent events in the United States involving gun violence, the classroom might be just the place where we might see tremendous violence. What I mean to convey here is that given that in the early twentieth century the Philippines was experiencing a colonial occupation by a foreign power, mo-

ments of extreme violence would be more reminiscent of war and battle. While the colonial classroom was certainly a site of epistemic violence, it was definitely surprising to colonial officials themselves that they would be targeted by Moros run amok.

6 Carl M. Moore, *Sulu Archipelago, Philippine Islands: History, Resources and Native People*, vol. 5 (1929), quoted in Thomas R. Solomon, "Public Order among the Moros of the Philippines and the Work of the United States Army," thesis, February 13, 1937, 851643, Aa 2, Ac, Box 30, Folder 12, Hayden Papers, 127.

7 Colonial and military violence occurred here ten years after the official end of the Philippine-American War.

8 For more information on the history of what today is known as the Autonomous Region of Muslim Mindanao in the Philippines, see Abinales and Amoroso, *State and Society in the Philippines*; and Abinales, *Making Mindanao*.

9 Chapman to Director of Education, August 20, 1934, 3.

10 *Oxford English Dictionary*, online ed., s.v. "amok," n.d., accessed June 7, 2019, http://www.oed.com/view/Entry/6512. The OED gives alternate spellings of *amuck* and *amock*. Where the archival record uses a particular rendering, I maintain the original spelling. In the historical documents, I noted that when *amuck* was preceded by *run* (the most common way the term is utilized in the English language), it alternatively could be rendered "run amuck" or "run amok." But when a group of Moro or "Mohammedan" Filipinos were referred to using the term, they would be labeled *amoks*. In other words, the term *amok* was often used as a proper noun to refer to a group of frenzied Filipinos.

11 Foucault, *The History of Sexuality*.

12 See Aho, Ben-Moshe, and Hilton, "Mad Futures; Reaume, "From the Perspectives of Mad People"; and Rembis, "History of Madness."

13 The individualization of disability has been theorized in disability studies as the "social model of disability." See Shakespeare, "The Social Model of Disability."

14 Erevelles, *Disability and Difference*; Mollow, "When Black Women Start Going on Prozac," 67.

15 *Oxford English Dictionary*, online ed., s.v. "amok."

16 John Dryden, *The Hind and the Panther: A Poem in Three Parts*, part 3, n.d., Accessed June 6, 2022, https://quod.lib.umich.edu/e/eebo/A36627.0001.001/1:6?rgn=div1;view=fulltext.

17 Saint Martin, "Running Amok," 66–67.

18 Saint Martin, "Running Amok," 67.

19 Duggan, *Sapphic Slashers*; Bland, Lucy, and Doan, *Sexology in Culture*.

20 See Freud, *Dora: An Analysis of a Case of Hysteria*. It should be noted that Freud remarked that the sane and mad were barely discernible from one another. Freud didn't hold up this boundary as much as American psychiatry did when it drew from him in the mid-twentieth century. I want to thank Tiffany Ball for her insight and expertise on elaborating this point.

21 Rubin, "Thinking Sex," 150.

22 Silva, *Toward a Global Idea of Race.*

23 Bruce, "Mad Is a Place," 303, 304, emphasis in the original.

24 Bruce, "Mad Is a Place," 305; see also Pickens, *Black Madness.*

25 Foucault, *Madness and Civilization*, x–xi.

26 Foucault, *Madness and Civilization*; Quijano, "Coloniality of Power," 533; Mignolo, *The Darker Side of Western Modernity.*

27 Buck-Morss, *Hegel, Haiti, and Universal History*; Silva, *Toward a Global Idea of Race.*

28 Price, "The Bodymind Problem."

29 Silva, *Toward a Global Idea of Race.*

30 Erevelles, *Disability and Difference*; Spillers, "Mama's Baby, Papa's Maybe," 65; Bruce, "Mad Is a Place"; Pickens, *Black Madness.*

31 Bruce, "Mad Is a Place," 305.

32 Kramer, *The Blood of Government*; Rafael, *White Love*; Mendoza, *Metroimperial Intimacies.*

33 Reaume, "From the Perspectives of Mad People."

34 Stoler, *Along the Archival Grain*, 1.

35 *Oxford English Dictionary*, online ed., s.v. "amok."

36 Bruce, "Mad Is a Place."

37 Bruce, "Mad Is a Place," 305.

38 Carl M. Moore, *Sulu Archipelago, Philippine Islands: History, Resources and Native People*, vol. 5 (1929), quoted in Thomas R. Solomon, "Public Order among the Moros of the Philippines and the Work of the United States Army," thesis, February 13, 1937, 851643, Aa 2, Ac, Box 30, Folder 12, Hayden Papers, 127.

39 Foucault, *The History of Sexuality.*

40 Joaquin Espiritu, First Lieutenant of the 115th Company of the Philippine Constabulary, to the Provincial Commander, Tawi-Tawi District, August 15, 1934, 851643, Aa 2, Ac, Box 30, Folder 1, Joseph Ralston Hayden Papers.

41 This image, along with a comprehensive collection of Worcester's photography, can be found in the University of Michigan's digital collections. See "The Dean C. Worcester Photographic Collection at the University of Michigan, Museum of Anthropology," 2012, https://webapps.lsa.umich.edu/umma /exhibits/Worcester%202012/index.html.

42 Bederman, *Manliness and Civilization.*

43 Chapman to Director of Education, August 20, 1934, 3.

44 Chapman to Director of Education, August 20, 1934, 3.

45 Sgt. F. G. Roth, Deputy Governor at Large, to James Fugate, Provincial Governor of Sulu, January 24, 1935, 2011165 mf603c-615c, Box 30, Folder 1, Hayden Papers, 1, 8.

46 This is not the only instance in which "promiscuity" has been used to document and classify irregular behavior in the Philippines by scientific authorities. For instance, Warwick Anderson examines the way that US American medical officials at the turn of the twentieth century attempted through public health

measures and bacteriological science to curb the "promiscuous defecation" of Filipino natives. Anderson was even so intrepid as to theorize that US scientific imperialism established an "orificial order" in which the Filipino became a synecdoche for *anus* and the white American transfigured into the authoritative *mouth*. See Anderson, *Colonial Pathologies*, 104, 106.

47 Solomon, "Public Order among the Moros," 61.

48 Cott, *Public Vows*.

49 Baker, *From Savage to Negro*.

50 Karl Kasian "Governing the Moros," thesis, 1930, 851643, Aa 2, Ac, Box 30, Folder 12, Joseph Ralston Hayden Papers, n.p.

51 See, for instance, Worcester, *The Philippine Islands and Their People*.

52 Karsian, "Governing the Moros," n.p.

53 Wolfe, "Settler Colonialism and the Elimination of the Native," 387.

54 Foucault, *Madness and Civilization*, 69.

55 Chapman to Director of Education, August 20, 1934, 2, 3.

56 Chapman to Director of Education, August 20, 1934, 2–3.

57 I use the term *contact zone* as defined and theorized in Pratt, *Imperial Eyes*.

58 Dryden, *The Hind and the Panther*.

59 Solomon, "Public Order among the Moros," 62.

60 Stoler, *Along the Archival Grain*.

61 Quijano, "Coloniality of Power, Eurocentrism, and Latin America," 533.

EPILOGUE

1 Kim, *Curative Violence*; Reddy, *Freedom with Violence*.

2 Associated Press, "215 Bodies Found at Residential School in Canada." *Indian Country Today*, May 29, 2021. https://indiancountrytoday.com/news/more -than-200-bodies-found-at-indigenous-school-in-canada.

3 Johna Baylon and Leyland Cecco, "Attacks Make Vancouver 'Anti-Asian Hate Crime Capital of North America.'" *Guardian*, May 23, 2021. http://www .theguardian.com/world/2021/may/23/vancoucer-anti-asian-hate-crimes -increase.

4 Jessica Xiao, "AAJA Pronunciation Guide for Asian Victims of Atlanta Shootings," Asian American Journalists Association, March 19, 2021, https://www.aaja .org/2021/03/19/aaja-pronunciation-guide-for-asian-victims-of-atlanta-shootings/.

5 Spivak, *Outside in the Teaching Machine*, 191; emphasis on *is* in the original, other emphasis added.

6 Coráñez Bolton, "El español filipino-americano."

7 Isaac, *American Tropics*, x.

8 Snorton, *Black on Both Sides*, x; see also Cohen, "Punks, Bulldaggers, and Welfare Queens."

9 Snorton, *Black on Both Sides*, x.

BIBLIOGRAPHY

Abinales, Patricio N. *Making Mindanao: Cotabato and Davao in the Formation of the Philippine Nation-State*. Manila: Ateneo de Manila University Press, 2000.

Abinales, Patricio N., and Donna J. Amoroso. *State and Society in the Philippines*. 2nd ed. Lanham, MD: Rowman and Littlefield, 2017.

Agoncillo, Teodoro A. "Philippine Historiography in the Age of Kalaw." *Solidarity*, no. 5 (1984): 3–16.

Aho, Tanja, Liat Ben-Moshe, and Leon J. Hilton. "Mad Futures: Affect/Theory/Violence." *American Quarterly* 69, no. 2 (2017): 291–345.

Alamon, Arnold P. *Wars of Extinction: Discrimination and the Lumad Struggle in Mindanao*. Iligan City, Philippines: RMP-NMR, 2017.

Anderson, Benedict. *Imagined Communities: Reflections on the Origin and Spread of Nationalism*. Rev. ed. London: Verso, 2016.

Anderson, Benedict. *Under Three Flags: Anarchism and the Anti-colonial Imagination*. London: Verso, 2005.

Anderson, Warwick. *Colonial Pathologies: American Tropical Medicine, Race, and Hygiene in the Philippines*. Durham, NC: Duke University Press, 2006.

Anzaldúa, Gloria. *Borderlands / La Frontera: The New Mestiza*. 4th ed. San Francisco: Aunt Lute Books, 2012.

Anzaldúa, Gloria. "Disability and Identity: An E-mail Exchange and a Few Additional Thoughts." In *The Gloria Anzaldúa Reader*, edited by AnaLouise Keating, 298–302. Durham, NC: Duke University Press, 2009.

Arrizón, Alicia. *Queering Mestizaje: Transculturation and Performance*. Ann Arbor: University of Michigan Press, 2006.

Baker, Lee D. *From Savage to Negro: Anthropology and the Construction of Race, 1896–1954*. Berkeley: University of California Press, 1998.

Baldoz, Rick. *The Third Asiatic Invasion: Migration and Empire in Filipino America, 1898–1946*. New York: New York University Press, 2011.

Barker, Clare, and Stuart Murray. "Disabling Postcolonialism: Global Disability Cultures and Democratic Criticism." In *The Disability Studies Reader*, 4th ed., edited by Lennard J. Davis, 61–73. New York: Routledge, 2013.

Baynton, Douglas C. *Defectives in the Land: Disability and Immigration in the Age of Eugenics*. Chicago: University of Chicago Press, 2016.

Baynton, Douglas C. "Disability and the Justification of Inequality in American History." In *The Disability Studies Reader*, 4th ed., edited by Lennard J. Davis, 17–33. New York: Routledge, 2013.

Bederman, Gail. *Manliness and Civilization: A Cultural History of Gender and Race in the United States, 1880–1917*. Chicago: University of Chicago Press, 1995.

Beller, Jonathan. *The Cinematic Mode of Production: Attention Economy and the Society of the Spectacle*. Hanover, NH: Dartmouth College Press, 2006.

Berlant, Lauren. *Cruel Optimism*. Durham, NC: Duke University Press, 2011.

Bhabha, Homi. "The World and the Home." *Social Text*, no. 31/32 (1992): 141–53.

Blanco, John D. "Baroque Modernity and the Colonial World: Aesthetics and Catastrophe in Nick Joaquin's *A Portrait of the Artist as Filipino*." *Kritika Kultura*, no. 4 (2004): 5–35.

Blanco, John D. "Bastards of the Unfinished Revolution: Bolívar's Ismael and Rizal's Martí at the Turn of the Twentieth Century." *Radical History Review* 89 (2004): 92–114.

Blanco, John D. "Oriental Enlightenment and the Colonial World: A Derivative Discourse?" In *Filipino Studies: Palimpsests of Nation and Diaspora*, edited by Martin Manalansan and Augusto Espiritu, 56–83. New York: New York University Press, 2016.

Bland, Lucy, and Laura L. Doan. *Sexology in Culture: Labelling Bodies and Desires*. Chicago: University of Chicago Press, 1998.

Bost, Suzanne. "Disability, Decoloniality, and Other-than-Humanist Ethics in Anzaldúan Thought." In "Disability and the Decolonial Turn: Perspectives from the Americas," edited by Roberto Sirvent and Amy Reed-Sandoval. Special issue, *Disability and the Global South* 6, no. 1 (2019): 1562–80.

Bruce, La Marr Jurelle. "Mad Is a Place; or, the Slave Ship Tows the Ship of Fools." *American Quarterly* 69, no. 2 (2017): 303–8.

Buck-Morss, Susan. 2009. *Hegel, Haiti, and Universal History*. Pittsburgh: University of Pittsburgh Press, 2009.

Byrd, Jodi A. *The Transit of Empire: Indigenous Critiques of Colonialism*. Minneapolis: University of Minnesota Press, 2011.

Chen, Mel Y. "'The Stuff of Slow Constitution': Reading Down Syndrome for Race, Disability, and the Timing That Makes Them So." *Somatechnics* 6, no. 2 (2016): 235–48.

Cheng, Anne Anlin. *Ornamentalism*. New York: Oxford University Press, 2019.

Choy, Catherine Ceniza. *Empire of Care: Nursing and Migration in Filipino American History*. Durham, NC: Duke University Press, 2003.

Chu, Richard. "The 'Chinese' and the 'Mestizos' of the Philippines: Towards a New Interpretation." In *More Tsinoy Than We Admit: Chinese-Filipino Interactions over the Centuries*, edited by Richard Chu, 215–59. Manila: Vibal Foundation, 2015.

Cohen, Cathy J. "Punks, Bulldaggers, and Welfare Queens: The Radical Potential of Queer Politics?" In *Black Queer Studies: A Critical Anthology*, edited by E. Patrick Johnson, Mae G. Henderson, and Sharon P. Holland, 21–51. Durham, NC: Duke University Press, 2005.

Coráñez Bolton, Sony. "El español filipino-americano como ética de solidaridad." *Revista Filipina* 7, no. 1 (2020): 56–58.

Cotera, María Eugenia, and María Josefina Saldaña-Portillo. "Indigenous but Not Indian? Chicana/os and the Politics of Indigeneity." In *The World of Indigenous North America*, edited by Robert Allen Warrior, 549–68. New York: Routledge, 2015.

Cott, Nancy F. *Public Vows: A History of Marriage and the Nation*. Cambridge, MA: Harvard University Press, 2000.

Coulthard, Glen Sean. *Red Skin, White Masks: Rejecting the Colonial Politics of Recognition*. Minneapolis: University of Minnesota Press, 2014.

Cowing, Jessica. "Settler States of Ability: Assimilation, Incarceration, and Native Women's Crip Interventions." PhD diss., College of William and Mary, 2020. http://dx.doi.org/10.21220/s2-j31a-n741.

Cruz, Denise. *Transpacific Femininities: The Making of the Modern Filipina*. Durham, NC: Duke University Press, 2012.

Davis, Lennard J., ed. *The Disability Studies Reader*. 4th ed. New York: Routledge, 2013.

Deloria, Philip Joseph. *Indians in Unexpected Places*. Lawrence: University Press of Kansas, 2004.

Derbyshire, Charles. "Translator's Introduction." In *The Social Cancer: A Complete English Version of Noli me tángere from the Spanish*, by José Rizal, v–l. Translated by Charles Derbyshire. Manila: Philippine Education Company. http://hdl.handle.net/2027/nyp.33433075866735.

Duggan, Lisa. *Sapphic Slashers: Sex, Violence, and American Modernity*. Durham, NC: Duke University Press, 2000.

Erevelles, Nirmala. *Disability and Difference in Global Contexts: Enabling a Transformative Body Politic*. New York: Palgrave Macmillan, 2011.

Fear-Segal, Jacqueline, and Susan D. Rose, "Introduction." In *Carlisle Indian Industrial School: Indigenous Histories, Memories, and Reclamations*, edited by Jacqueline Fear-Segal and Susan D. Rose, 1–34. Lincoln: University of Nebraska Press, 2016.

Ferguson, Roderick A. *Aberrations in Black: Toward a Queer of Color Critique*. Minneapolis: University of Minnesota Press, 2004.

Foucault, Michel. *The History of Sexuality*. Vol. 1, *An Introduction*, translated by Robert Hurley. New York: Vintage Books, 1990.

Foucault, Michel. *Madness and Civilization: A History of Insanity in the Age of Reason*. Translated by Richard Howard. New York: Pantheon Books, 1965.

Fradera, Josep M. *Filipinas, la colonia más peculiar: La hacienda pública en la definición de la política colonial, 1762–1868*. Madrid: Consejo Superior de Investigaciones Científicas, 1999.

Freud, Sigmund. *Dora: An Analysis of a Case of Hysteria.* Edited by Philip Rieff. New York: Simon and Schuster, 1997.

García-Abásolo, Antonio. "Mestizos de un país sin mestizaje, mestizos españoles en Filipinas en la época colonial." In *Un mar de islas, un mar de gentes: Población y diversidad en las Islas Filipinas,* edited by Marta María Manchado López and Miguel Luque Talaván, 223–45. Córdoba, Spain: Universidad de Córdoba, 2014.

Garland-Thomson, Rosemarie. *Extraordinary Bodies: Figuring Physical Disability in American Culture and Literature.* New York: Columbia University Press, 1997.

Garland-Thomson, Rosemarie. "Integrating Disability, Transforming Feminist Theory." *NWSA Journal* 14, no. 3 (2002): 1–32.

Go, Julian. *American Empire and the Politics of Meaning: Elite Political Cultures in the Philippines and Puerto Rico during U.S. Colonialism.* Durham, NC: Duke University Press, 2008.

Goffe, Tao Leigh. "Chop Suey Surplus: Chinese Food, Sex, and the Political Economy of Afro-Asia." *Women and Performance: A Journal of Feminist Theory* 30, no. 1 (2020): 20–47.

Gopinath, Gayatri. *Impossible Desires: Queer Diasporas and South Asian Public Cultures.* Durham, NC: Duke University Press, 2005.

Gruzinski, Serge. *The Mestizo Mind: The Intellectual Dynamics of Colonization and Globalization.* New York: Routledge, 2002.

Halberstam, Judith. *In a Queer Time and Place: Transgender Bodies, Subcultural Lives.* New York: New York University Press, 2005.

Haraway, Donna. "A Cyborg Manifesto: Science, Technology, and Socialist-Feminism in the Late 20th Century." In *International Handbook of Virtual Learning Environments,* edited by Joel Weiss, Jason Nolan, Jeremy Hunsinger, and Peter Trifonas, 117–58. Dordrecht, Netherlands: Springer, 2006.

Hartman, Saidiya V. *Lose Your Mother: A Journey along the Atlantic Slave Route.* First paperback ed. New York: Farrar, Straus and Giroux, 2008.

Hartwell, Ernest Rafael. "Imperial Endnotes: The First Filipino and Boricua Historians." *Latin American Literary Review* 45, no. 90 (2018): 53–67.

Hau, Caroline S. *The Chinese Question: Ethnicity, Nation, and Region in and beyond the Philippines.* Singapore: NUS Press, 2014.

Hau, Caroline S. *Elites and Ilustrados in Philippine Culture.* Manila: Ateneo de Manila University Press, 2017.

Hoganson, Kristin L. *Fighting for American Manhood: How Gender Politics Provoked the Spanish-American and Philippine-American Wars.* New Haven, CT: Yale University Press, 1998.

Ileto, Reynaldo C. "Outlines of a Non-linear Emplotment of Philippine History." In *Reflections on Development in Southeast Asia,* edited by Lim Teck Ghee, 130–59. Singapore: Institute of Southeast Asian Studies, 1988.

Ileto, Reynaldo Clemeña. *Pasyon and Revolution: Popular Movements in the Philippines, 1840–1910.* Manila: Ateneo de Manila Press, 1979.

Isaac, Allan Punzalan. *American Tropics: Articulating Filipino America.* Minneapolis: University of Minnesota Press, 2006.

Jameson, Fredric. "Third-World Literature in the Era of Multinational Capitalism." *Social Text,* no. 15 (1986): 65–88.

Kafer, Alison. "Crip Kin, Manifesting." *Catalyst: Feminism, Theory, Technoscience* 5, no. 1 (2019): 1–37.

Kafer, Alison. *Feminist, Queer, Crip*. Bloomington: Indiana University Press, 2013.

Kafer, Alison, and Eunjung Kim. "Disability and the Edges of Intersectionality." In *The Cambridge Companion to Literature and Disability*, edited by Clare Barker and Stuart Murray, 123–38. Cambridge: Cambridge University Press, 2018.

Kalaw, Teodoro. *Hacia la tierra del zar*. Manila: Librería Manila Filatélica, 1908.

Kaplan, Amy. *The Anarchy of Empire in the Making of U.S. Culture*. Cambridge, MA: Harvard University Press, 2002.

Kim, Eunjung. *Curative Violence: Rehabilitating Disability, Gender, and Sexuality in Modern Korea*. Durham, NC: Duke University Press, 2017.

Kim, Jina B. "Toward a Crip-of-Color Critique: Thinking with Minich's 'Enabling Whom?'" *Lateral* 6, no. 1 (2017). http://csalateral.org/issue/6-1/forum-alt-humanities-critical-disability-studies-crip-of-color-critique-kim/.

Kipling, Rudyard. "The White Man's Burden." *The Kipling Society* (blog), April 12, 2021. https://www.kiplingsociety.co.uk/poem/poems_burden.htm.

Ko, Dorothy. *Cinderella's Sisters: A Revisionist History of Footbinding*. Berkeley: University of California Press, 2007.

Kramer, Paul A. *The Blood of Government: Race, Empire, the United States, and the Philippines*. Chapel Hill: University of North Carolina Press, 2006.

Kudlick, Catherine. "Modernity's Miss-Fits: Blind Girls and Marriage in France and America, 1820–1920." In *Women on Their Own: Interdisciplinary Perspectives on Being Single*, edited by Rudolph M. Bell and Virginia Yans, 201–18. New Brunswick, NJ: Rutgers University Press, 2008.

Kuppers, Petra. "Remembering Anarcha: Objection in the Medical Archive." *Liminalities: A Journal of Performance Studies* 42, no. 2 (2008): 1–34.

Lévi-Strauss, Claude. *The Savage Mind*. Translated by Doreen Weightman and John Weightman. Chicago: University of Chicago Press, 1966.

Lifshey, Adam. *The Magellan Fallacy: Globalization and the Emergence of Asian and African Literature in Spanish*. Ann Arbor: University of Michigan Press, 2012.

Lim, Eng Beng. *Brown Boys and Rice Queens: Spellbinding Performance in the Asias*. Durham, NC: Duke University Press, 2013.

Lowe, Lisa. *Immigrant Acts: On Asian American Cultural Politics*. Durham, NC: Duke University Press, 1996.

Lowe, Lisa. *The Intimacies of Four Continents*. Durham, NC: Duke University Press, 2015.

McCoy, Alfred W., and Alfredo R. Roces. *Philippine Cartoons: Political Caricature of the American Era, 1900-1941*. Manila: Vera-Reyes, 1985.

McMaster, Carrie. "Negotiating Paradoxical Spaces: Women, Disabilities, and the Experience of Nepantla." In *Entre Mundos / Among Worlds: New Perspectives on Gloria E. Anzaldúa*, edited by AnaLouise Keating and Chela Sandoval, 101–6. New York: Palgrave Macmillan, 2005.

McRuer, Robert. *Crip Theory: Cultural Signs of Queerness and Disability*. New York: New York University Press, 2006.

McRuer, Robert, and Anna Mollow. *Sex and Disability*. Durham, NC: Duke University Press, 2012.

Mendoza, Victor Román. *Metroimperial Intimacies: Fantasy, Racial-Sexual Governance, and the Philippines in U.S. Imperialism, 1899-1913*. Durham, NC: Duke University Press, 2015.

Mignolo, Walter. *The Darker Side of Western Modernity: Global Futures, Decolonial Options*. Durham, NC: Duke University Press, 2011.

Miller, Stuart Creighton. *"Benevolent Assimilation": The American Conquest of the Philippines, 1899-1903*. New Haven, CT: Yale University Press, 1982.

Minich, Julie Avril. "Mestizaje as National Prosthesis: Corporeal Metaphors in Héctor Tobar's *The Tattooed Soldier*." *Arizona Journal of Hispanic Cultural Studies* 17, no. 1 (2014): 211-26.

Mitchell, David T., and Sharon L. Snyder. *Narrative Prosthesis: Disability and the Dependencies of Discourse*. Ann Arbor: University of Michigan Press, 2000.

Mojares, Resil B. *Brains of the Nation: Pedro Paterno, T. H. Pardo de Tavera, Isabelo de Los Reyes, and the Production of Modern Knowledge*. Manila: Ateneo de Manila University Press, 2006.

Mollow, Anna. "'When Black Women Start Going on Prozac': Race, Gender, and Mental Illness in Meri Nana-Ama Danquah's *Willow Weep for Me*." *MELUS*, no. 3 (2006): 67-99.

Moore, Carl M. *Sulu Archipelago, Philippine Islands History, Resources and Native People*. Volume 5, Part I, by Carl M. Moore, Governor, 1929.

Morales, Aurora Levins, Qwo-Li Driskill, and Leah Lakshmi Piepzna-Samarasinha. "Sweet Dark Places: Letters to Gloria Anzaldúa on Disability, Creativity, and the Coatlicue State." In *El Mundo Zurdo II: Selected Works from the 2010 Meeting of the Society for the Study of Gloria Anzaldúa*, edited by Sonia Saldívar Hull, Norma Alarcón, and Rita Urquijo-Ruiz, 77-97. San Francisco: Aunt Lute Books, 2012.

Muñoz, José Esteban. *Cruising Utopia: The Then and There of Queer Futurity*. 10th anniversary ed. New York: New York University Press, 2019.

Ngai, Mae M. *Impossible Subjects: Illegal Aliens and the Making of Modern America*. Princeton, NJ: Princeton University Press, 2004.

Nguyen, Mimi Thi. *The Gift of Freedom: War, Debt, and Other Refugee Passages*. Durham, NC: Duke University Press, 2012.

Ocampo, Anthony Christian. *The Latinos of Asia: How Filipino Americans Break the Rules of Race*. Stanford, CA: Stanford University Press, 2016.

Oliver, Mike. "The Social Model of Disability: Thirty Years On." *Disability and Society* 28, no. 7 (2013): 1024-26.

Ortiz, Fernando. *Cuban Counterpoint: Tobacco and Sugar*. Translated by Harriet de Onis. New York: Vintage Books, 1970.

Palumbo-Liu, David. *Asian/American: Historical Crossings of a Racial Frontier*. Stanford, CA: Stanford University Press, 1999.

Pickens, Therí A. *Black Madness :: Mad Blackness*. Durham, NC: Duke University Press, 2019.

Pierce, Joseph M. "Adopted: Trace, Blood, and Native Authenticity." *Critical Ethnic Studies* 3, no. 2 (2017): 57-76.

Pratt, Mary Louise. *Imperial Eyes: Travel Writing and Transculturation*. New York: Routledge, 1992.

Price, Margaret. "The Bodymind Problem and the Possibilities of Pain." *Hypatia: A Journal of Feminist Philosophy* 30, no. 1 (2015): 268–84.

Puar, Jasbir K. "Prognosis Time: Towards a Geopolitics of Affect, Debility and Capacity." *Women and Performance* 19, no. 2 (2009): 161–72.

Puar, Jasbir K. *The Right to Maim: Debility, Capacity, Disability*. Durham, NC: Duke University Press, 2017.

Puar, Jasbir K. *Terrorist Assemblages: Homonationalism in Queer Times*. Durham, NC: Duke University Press, 2007.

Quayson, Ato. "Aesthetic Nervousness." In *The Disability Studies Reader*, 4th ed., edited by Lennard J. Davis, 202–13. New York: Routledge, 2013.

Quayson, Ato. *Aesthetic Nervousness: Disability and the Crisis of Representation*. New York: Columbia University Press, 2007.

Quijano, Aníbal. "Colonialidad del poder, eurocentrismo y América Latina." In *Cuestiones y horizontes: De la dependencia histórico-estructural a la colonialidad/descolonialidad del poder*. Buenos Aires: CLASCO, 2014.

Quijano, Anibal. "Coloniality of Power, Eurocentrism, and Latin America." Translated by Michael Ennis. *Nepantla: Views from South* 1, no. 3 (2000): 533–80.

Rafael, Vicente L. *White Love and Other Events in Filipino History*. Durham, NC: Duke University Press, 2000.

Reaume, Geoffrey. "From the Perspectives of Mad People." In *The Routledge History of Madness and Mental Health*, edited by Greg Eghigian, 277–96. Abingdon, UK: Routledge, 2017.

Reddy, Chandan. *Freedom with Violence: Race, Sexuality, and the US State*. Durham, NC: Duke University Press, 2011.

Rembis, Michael. "The Routledge History of Madness and Mental Health." *H-Net Reviews in the Humanities & Social Sciences*, February 2018, 1–3.

Renda, Mary A. *Taking Haiti: Military Occupation and the Culture of U.S. Imperialism, 1915–1940*. Chapel Hill: University of North Carolina Press, 2001.

Reyes, Raquel A. G. *Love, Passion and Patriotism: Sexuality and the Philippine Propaganda Movement, 1882–1892*. Seattle: University of Washington Press, 2008.

Rizal, José. *Filipinas dentro de cien años: Estudio político-social*. N.p. [Manila?]: n.p., 1905. http://hdl.handle.net/2027/miun.ahz9168.0001.001.

Rizal, José. *Noli me tángere (Novela tagala)*, vol. 1, 3rd ed. Barcelona: Casa Editorial Maucci, 1909. http://hdl.handle.net/2027/inu.32000004766327.

Rizal, José. *Noli me tángere (Novela tagala)*, vol. 2, 2nd ed. Barcelona: Casa Editorial Maucci, 1909. http://hdl.handle.net/2027/inu.32000004766327.

Rizal, José. *The Social Cancer: A Complete English Version of "Noli Me Tangere" from the Spanish*. Translated by Charles Derbyshire. Manila: Philippine Education Company, 1912. http://hdl.handle.net/2027/nyp.33433075866735.

Rodríguez, Dylan. *Suspended Apocalypse: White Supremacy, Genocide, and the Filipino Condition*. Minneapolis: University of Minnesota Press, 2010.

Rosario, Vernon A., ed. *Science and Homosexualities*. New York: Routledge, 1997.

Rubin, Gayle. "Thinking Sex: Notes for a Radical Theory of the Politics of Sexuality." In *Culture, Society and Sexuality: A Reader*, edited by Peter Aggleton and Richard Parker, 143–78. London: Taylor & Francis Group, 1999.

Russo, Alessandra. *El realismo circular: Tierras, espacios y paisajes de la cartografía indígena novohispana siglos XVI y XVII*. Mexico City: Universidad Nacional Autónoma de México, Instituto de Investigaciones Estéticas, 2005.

Saint Martin, Manuel L. "Running Amok: A Modern Perspective on a Culture-Bound Syndrome." *Primary Care Companion to the Journal of Clinical Psychiatry* 1, no. 3 (1999): 66–70.

Saldaña-Portillo, María Josefina. *Indian Given: Racial Geographies across Mexico and the United States*. Durham, NC: Duke University Press, 2016.

Saldaña-Portillo, María Josefina. *The Revolutionary Imagination in the Americas and the Age of Development*. Durham, NC: Duke University Press, 2003.

Schalk, Sami. *Bodyminds Reimagined: (Dis)ability, Race, and Gender in Black Women's Speculative Fiction*. Durham, NC: Duke University Press, 2018.

Schalk, Sami, and Jina B. Kim. "Integrating Race, Transforming Feminist Disability Studies." *Signs* 46, no. 1 (2020): 31–55.

Sebring, Ellen. "Civilization and Barbarism: Cartoon Commentary and 'The White Man's Burden' (1898–1902)." *Asia-Pacific Journal / Japan Focus* 13, no. 27 (2015): 1–43.

Sedgwick, Eve Kosofsky. *Between Men: English Literature and Male Homosocial Desire*. 30th anniversary ed. New York: Columbia University Press, 2016.

See, Sarita E. "*An Open Wound*: Colonial Melancholia and Contemporary Filipino/American Texts." In *Vestiges of War: The Philippine-American War and the Aftermath of an Imperial Dream, 1899–1999*, edited by Angel Velasco Shaw and Luis Francia, 376–400. New York: New York University Press, 2002.

See, Sarita Echavez. "Language Run Amok." In *Filipinx American Studies: Reckoning, Reclamation, Transformation*, edited by Rick Bonus and Antonio T. Tiongson, Jr., 271–76. New York: Fordham University Press, 2022.

See, Sarita Echavez. *The Filipino Primitive: Accumulation and Resistance in the American Museum*. New York: New York University Press, 2017.

Seijas, Tatiana. *Asian Slaves in Colonial Mexico: From Chinos to Indians*. New York: Cambridge University Press, 2014.

Shah, Nayan. *Contagious Divides: Epidemics and Race in San Francisco's Chinatown*. Berkeley: University of California Press, 2001.

Shakespeare, Tom. "The Social Model of Disability." In *The Disability Studies Reader*, 4th ed., edited by Lennard J. Davis, 214–21. New York: Routledge, 2010.

Siebers, Tobin. *Disability Theory*. Ann Arbor: University of Michigan Press, 2008.

Silva, Denise Ferreira da. *Toward a Global Idea of Race*. Minneapolis: University of Minnesota Press, 2007.

Silva, Noenoe K. *Aloha Betrayed: Native Hawaiian Resistance to American Colonialism*. Durham, NC: Duke University Press, 2004.

Simpson, Audra. *Mohawk Interruptus: Political Life across the Borders of Settler States*. Durham, NC: Duke University Press, 2014.

Snorton, C. Riley. *Black on Both Sides: A Racial History of Trans Identity*. Minneapolis: University of Minnesota Press, 2017.

Sommer, Doris. *Foundational Fictions: The National Romances of Latin America*. Berkeley: University of California Press, 1991.

Spillers, Hortense J. "Mama's Baby, Papa's Maybe: An American Grammar Book." *Diacritics* 17, no. 2 (1987): 65–81.

Spivak, Gayatri Chakravorty. "Can the Subaltern Speak?" In *Marxism and the Interpretation of Culture*, edited by Cary Nelson and Lawrence Grossberg, 271–313. Urbana: University of Illinois Press, 1988.

Spivak, Gayatri Chakravorty. *Other Asias*. New York: Blackwell, 2007.

Spivak, Gayatri Chakravorty. *Outside in the Teaching Machine*. New York: Routledge, 1993.

Spivak, Gayatri Chakravorty. "Woman in Difference: Mahasweta Devi's 'Douloti the Bountiful.'" *Culural Critique*, no. 14 (1989–90), 105–28.

Stern, Alexandra. *Eugenic Nation: Faults and Frontiers of Better Breeding in Modern America*. Berkeley: University of California Press, 2016.

Stoler, Ann Laura. *Along the Archival Grain: Epistemic Anxieties and Colonial Common Sense*. Princeton, NJ: Princeton University Press, 2009.

Tadiar, Neferti. *Things Fall Away: Philippine Historical Experience and the Making of Globalization*. Durham, NC: Duke University Press, 2009.

Thomas, Megan C. *Orientalists, Propagandists, and "Ilustrados": Filipino Scholarship and the End of Spanish Colonialism*. Minneapolis: University of Minnesota Press, 2012.

Turner, Frederick Jackson. *The Significance of the Frontier in American History (from Proceedings of the Forty-First Annual Meeting of the State Historical Society of Wisconsin)*. Madison: State Historical Society of Wisconsin, 1894.

Urry, John. *The Tourist Gaze: Leisure and Travel in Contemporary Societies*. London: Sage, 1990.

Vasconcelos, José. *La raza cosmica: Misión de la raza iberoamericana, Argentina y Brasil*. Mexico City: Espasa-Calpe Mexicana, 1948.

Vasconcelos, José. *La raza cósmica: Misión de la raza iberoamericana; Notas de viajes a la América de Sur*. Paris: Agencia Mundial de Libreria, 1925. http://hdl.handle.net/2027/pst.000008497192.

Velasco Shaw, Angel, and Luis Francia, eds. *Vestiges of War: The Philippine-American War and the Aftermath of an Imperial Dream, 1899–1999*. New York: New York University Press, 2002.

Villaescusa Illán, Irene. *Transcultural Nationalism in Hispano-Filipino Literature*. Cham, Switzerland: Springer International Publishing, 2020.

Warner, Michael. "Introduction: Fear of a Queer Planet." *Social Text*, no. 29 (1991): 3–17.

Warner, Michael. "Normal and Normaller: Beyond Gay Marriage." *GLQ: A Journal of Lesbian and Gay Studies* 5, no. 2 (1999): 119–71.

Wolfe, Patrick. "Settler Colonialism and the Elimination of the Native." *Journal of Genocide Research* 8, no. 4 (2006): 387–409.

Worcester, Dean C. *The Philippine Islands and Their People: A Record of Personal Observation and Experience, with a Short Summary of the More Important Facts in the History of the Archipelago*. New York: Macmillan, 1898.

INDEX

able-bodiedness, 7, 9, 28, 31, 57, 64–65, 93, 97, 104–7, 121, 125; compulsory, 30, 92

ableism: American, 51; anticolonial, 73, 90; capitalist, 3, 101; colonial, 7, 9–11, 15–16, 21–22, 33–35, 39, 42, 48, 63–64, 100, 128, 136, 161–62; and disability, 18, 64–65, 103–4, 172n11; of mestizaje, 9–11, 15–16, 19–22, 28, 66; Orientalization of, 100–101, 120, 127; in travel writing, 105, 107, 109, 128, 130. See also able-bodiedness; able-mindedness

able-mindedness, 7, 15, 104, 121; compulsory, 30, 84–85, 93, 98

abolitionism, 26, 29, 59–60, 158–59, 178n64

Acapulco, Mexico, 23

Africa (continent), 58–61, 142

African American people, 40, 44, 47. See also Black people

Afro-Asian people, 26–27

Age of Reason, 74, 94, 142–43, 145. See also Foucault, Michel

Agoncillo, Teodoro, 104

agricolonialism, 111–12

Aguilar, Ignacio, 132

Aguinaldo, Emilio, 42–44, 51. See also Philippine Revolution (1896)

Aho, Tanja, 137

Alameda, CA, 1

Alaska, USA, 40

Alegre, Narciso, 113

Alihasan, 150–52

Americanization, 26, 31, 99, 120

American Psychiatric Association: DSM-IV, 139–40

amoks, 31–32, 131–40, 143, 145–61, 166, 184n5, 184n10

Anderson, Warwick, 52, 185–86n46

Anglo-Saxonism, 46

Ansol of Licud, 131–34, 137, 145–47, 149, 150, 152

anthropology, 11, 47, 65, 135, 140, 142, 151, 154

anthropometry, 47

anti-Blackness, 36, 42–44, 58, 60. See also racism

antichinismo, 27

anticlericalism, 24, 66–67, 69, 84, 94, 98, 130

Anzaldúa, Gloria: Borderlands / La Frontera, 16–22, 27, 53

Aquino, Sofronio, 150–51

Arizona, USA, 39–40

Arizzón, Alicia, 36

Asian Americans, 1–5, 14–15, 26–27, 45, 63, 164–66, 168–69

García-Abásolo, Antonio, 14, 174n35
Garland-Thomson, Rosemary, 18, 107
gender: in Chinese society, 124–26, 128; and colonialism, 31, 98, 101, 104, 136, 149; and disability, 8, 101, 124–25, 141; and labor, 50, 108; and language, 171n2; in *Noli me tángere*, 67–68, 77, 83; and race, 42, 44, 68, 77, 102, 106, 108, 117–19, 146; and sexuality, 42, 77, 87, 98, 117–19. *See also* femininity; masculinity
genocide, 33, 54, 129–30, 156
Gillam, Victor, 43
Goffe, Tao Leigh, 26
Gómez, Mariano, 24
Gopinath, Gayatri, 34
Granada, Spain, 23, 134
Great Britain, 13, 38, 41, 58, 126, 131, 138, 157–58, 183n64
Gruzinski, Serge, 172n13
Guam, 49, 101

Hadjarat, 151
Haiti, 52; Haitian Revolution, 60, 129
Haraway, Donna, 19
Hartman, Saidiya, 36
Hau, Caroline, 25–26
Hawaii, 37, 40–42, 44–45, 47, 62, 101, 111
Hayden, Joseph Ralston, 151, 154
Hegel, G. W. F., 142
heteronormativity, 9, 30, 34, 45, 50, 53, 74, 82, 84, 90–93, 150, 158
heterosexuality, 9, 30, 45, 53, 68–70, 84–85, 90–95, 98, 136, 146, 149–51, 153
Hilton, Leon J., 137
Hispano-Philippine culture, 29, 66, 98, 101–3
HIV/AIDS, 93
Hobsbawm, Eric, 76
Hoganson, Kristin, 52, 62
homosociality, 99–100, 102, 107, 109–10, 115–16, 119–20, 127
Hong Kong, 99, 124
humanism: liberal, 19, 127, 129; Spanish, 5, 7–8, 15, 100, 102, 106, 120
Hume, David, 142
hybridity, 17, 22, 25–26, 80, 172–73n13
hysteria, 141, 184n20

Ibarra, Crisóstomo, 30, 67–70, 72–74, 77–82, 88–91, 96–97

"Igorot" people, 52
Illinois, USA, 1–2
ilustrados: and ableism, 31, 64, 93, 104, 120–21, 128, 130; as brains of the nation, 35, 55–58; intellectual capacities of, 68, 71–72, 74–75, 94, 97–98; and Rizal, 55, 63, 68, 71, 74, 80, 93, 97, 102, 179n16, 179n18; terms of, 24, 171n2; and travel narratives, 103–11, 113–15, 124–29; and whiteness, 115–20
India, 58
Indians: Chicanx uses of, 20–22, 27; colonial production of, 11–15, 45; and disability, 35, 39–41, 46, 66; as "industrial," 47, 66; as "lazy," 87; as queerly deviant, 7–10; and running amok, 32, 135, 138–39, 153–55, 158–61; in travel writing, 100, 103
Indigenous People. *See* Aztecs; "Bontoc Igorot" people; Cherokee people; Chickasaw people; First Nations peoples; "Igorot" people; Indians; Kahnawá:ke First Nation; Kamloops Indian Residential School; Lumad people; Malay; Mohawk people; Moros (Indigenous Muslim Filipinos)
indios, 7, 9–11, 13, 25, 41, 45, 60, 86–87, 114, 133, 155
Indonesia, 138, 145, 158
insanity. *See* madness
insurrection, 42, 50–51, 112–13, 116, 132
intellectual class (Filipino). *See ilustrados*
interstitial spaces, 6
intimacies (concept), 39, 59–60
Isaac, Allan Punzalan, 2, 168
Isabella of Castille (Queen of Spain), 134

Jameson, Frederic, 86
Japan, 31, 99, 104, 108–12, 114–15, 121
Java, 138–39, 145
Jefferson, Thomas, 142
Jewish people, 134
Jim Crow, 38, 40, 43–44, 47, 63
Jolo, Philippines, 131, 150
Judge magazine: "Our New Topsy," 42–43

Kafer, Alison, 17–18, 173n17
Kahnawá:ke First Nation, 11
Kalaw, Teodoro: *Hacia la tierra del zar*, 31, 99–100, 103–28; "La Mandchuria sangrienta," 121

Mexico, 14, 16, 22–23, 27, 29–30, 39, 44, 46, 174n34; Revolution, 27; War of Independence, 23

Middle Ages, 123, 143–44, 156

milagro japonés, 109

Miller, Stuart Miller Creighton: *Benevolent Assimilation*, 52

Mindanao, Philippines, 112, 154, 156, 158, 173n30

Minich, Julie Avril, 7

Mitchell, David, 7

model minority myth, 60, 166

Mohawk people, 11. *See also* Kahnawá:ke First Nation

Mollow, Anna, 137

"mongoloidism," 28, 47

Moore, Carl, 145–46

Morales, Aurora Levins, 17

Moro juramentado, 132–35, 139, 145–46, 152

Moros (Indigenous Muslim Filipinos), 31, 131–35, 139, 145–61, 184n5, 184n10

Morss-Buck, Susan, 143

Moscow, Russia, 99, 123

multiculturalism, 19–20, 26, 29, 36

Murray, Stuart, 130

Muslim people, 23, 31, 112, 134–35, 147–48, 150, 158, 161. *See also* Moros (Indigenous Muslim Filipinos)

national allegories, 86

nationalism: anticolonial, 76–77, 85, 93; Filipino, 26, 59–61, 63, 69, 74, 83–84, 91, 94–95, 101; in literature, 30, 80, 91; Manchurian, 110; mestizaje, 22, 24–25, 57; white, 165

neurodivergence, 93

New Mexico, USA, 39

New Spain, 23, 174n35

Nguyen, Mimi Thi, 51

normate imperial eye/I, 31, 106, 108, 111, 113, 125

novohispano, 172n13

Ocampo, Anthony Christian, 5

Orientalism: and disability, 25, 28, 100–101, 103, 120, 127; and *ilustrados*, 23, 98, 100–106, 113, 120; and Kalaw, 113–15, 120, 123–28; and Philippine mestizaje, 10, 25–26, 100–102; and Vasconcelos, 27–28, 31, 103, 127; and Worcester photographs, 147

Oxford English Dictionary, 41, 136, 138

pagan religions, 31, 151–52

Palumbo-Liu, David, 2

Papua New Guinea, 140

Paris, France, 49, 99

People Power Revolution, 163

Pershing, John J.: "Annual Report of the Governor of the Moro Province," 151–52

Persian Gulf War, 1

Philippine-American War, 25, 44, 50–54, 62, 107, 112, 116, 133, 152, 177n34

Philippine Constabulary, 31, 131, 146–49, 151, 155, 159, 183n2

Philippine Enlightenment: cripping the, 115–21; and Rizal, 24, 35, 54, 64, 66–67, 73, 84, 87, 93–94; and travel narratives, 106–9, 112–13, 122–28, 130

Philippine Revolution (1896), 24, 54, 58–59. *See also* Aguinaldo, Emilio

Philippines. *See* Jolo; Laum Tabawan; Manila; Mantabuan; Mindanao; Quezon, Manuel; Sulu; Zamboanga

pickaninny, 42–44

Pickens, Therí Alyce, 143–44

Piepzna-Samarasinha, Leah Lakshmi, 17

Pierce, Joseph, 10

Plessy v. Ferguson, 47, 63

police, 32, 132, 146–49, 151, 159, 183n2. *See also* Philippine Constabulary

political cartoons, 37–38, 42–43, 47. *See also* "School Begins" cartoon

polygamy, 31–32, 136, 151–52, 159

Pope Sixtus IV, 134

Port Said, Egypt, 100

Portuguese (language), 138, 145

postcolonialism: and disability, 90, 109, 115, 122, 128, 130; and enlightenment movements, 102, 118–20, 125, 129–30; and Filipino intellectuals, 100, 106, 109, 115; nations, 9, 12, 55, 57; and the Philippines, 35, 100, 106, 112, 156, 160; theory, 31, 102, 105, 167, 182n39; and the United States, 63

Pratt, Mary Louise, 105, 107–8, 122

primitivism, 53

progressivism, 7–8, 35, 39, 41, 45–47, 59, 65, 120, 124, 159

Propaganda Movement, 73, 103

Protestantism, 138

Puar, Jasbir K., 183n66

Printed in the USA
CPSIA information can be obtained
at www.ICGtesting.com
CBHW072025300424
7702CB00005B/14

9 781478 019565